WITHDRAWN

Folger Documents of Tudor and Stuart Civilization

OF THE RUS COMMONWEALTH

FOLGER DOCUMENTS
OF TUDOR AND STUART CIVILIZATION

THIS volume is one of a series of publications of Tudor and Stuart documents that the Folger Library proposes to bring out. These documents will consist of hitherto unprinted manuscripts as well as reprints of rare books in the Folger Library. An effort will be made to choose significant items that will throw light on the social and intellectual background of the period from 1485 to 1715. In response to almost unanimous requests of interested historians, the spelling, punctuation, and capitalization will be modernized in printed texts. In some cases, where the original printing is clear and easily read, texts may be photographically reproduced. The Folger Library is prepared to supply microfilm of original texts to scholars who require a facsimile.

THE FOLGER SHAKESPEARE LIBRARY IS ADMINISTERED
BY THE TRUSTEES OF AMHERST COLLEGE.

PERSIAN EMPIRE

Russia about the time of Fletcher's Embassy (1588–1589).

OF THE RUS COMMONWEALTH

By GILES FLETCHER

∽∽∽∽∽∽∽∽∽∽∽∽

EDITED BY

Albert J. Schmidt

PUBLISHED FOR

The Folger Shakespeare Library

BY

CORNELL UNIVERSITY PRESS

Ithaca, New York

Copyright © 1966 by the Folger Shakespeare Library

CORNELL UNIVERSITY PRESS

First published 1966

Library of Congress Catalog Card Number: 66-12250

PRINTED IN THE UNITED STATES OF AMERICA
BY VAIL-BALLOU PRESS, INC.

PREFACE

IN EDITING Giles Fletcher's *Of the Rus Commonwealth,* I have tried without making this volume one solely for the specialist to probe the authenticity of the treatise as a source for Russian history and note as well its relevance for English history. In addition, I have thought it appropriate to recount some of the ups and downs of the classic in the more than three and a half centuries of its existence. I derived most of my annotations from S. M. Seredonin's authoritative critique, which, though written nearly three-quarters of a century ago, has never been matched. The Russian edition of Fletcher (1905) proved useful as a check on Fletcher's garbled Russian words.

In order to make Fletcher's narrative readable, I have modernized punctuation and spelling but retained all archaic words in the text. Apparent printer's errors have been silently corrected in a few places. This same spelling practice applies to Russian words used by Fletcher, even though his peculiar spelling reflected his limited fluency in that language. I have sought to compensate for my highhandedness here by including all of Fletcher's spellings in brackets beside the corrected Russian form in the index and in a separate glossary. For the sake of simplicity, I have used the nominative plural form of Fletcher's Russian nouns when the plural is called for. Proper names used

Preface

by Fletcher proved to be one of the most nagging dilemmas. Such names of towns and provinces as Plesko (or Vobsko), Ghaletsa, Twerra, Youghoria (Ioughoria), Permia, Vadska, Boulghoria, Oudoria, Obdoria, and Condora (Condensa), I have read Pskov, Galich, Tver, Iugorsk, Perm, Viatka, Bulgaria, Udorsk, Obdorsk, and Kondiinsk. The map, based on an examination of both sixteenth-century and Soviet maps of Muscovy, is unavoidably imprecise in the location of these ancient provinces. Towns bearing the same names as provinces denote the general area. I have rendered names of individuals in their proper Russian form rather than as they appeared in the original text.

In all cases I have followed the Library of Congress system of transliteration, except for the omission of diacritical marks, ligatures, and apostrophes for "soft" and "hard" marks. In the "Folger Documents of Tudor and Stuart Civilization" series there has been a conscious effort to reduce documentation to a minimum. Unfortunately, in *Of the Rus Commonwealth,* where so many of the terms are alien and where the author committed numerous errors, I have felt compelled to depart from this established pattern; moreover, since literature on sixteenth-century Anglo-Russian relations has shown a marked increase over the past few years, I have cited a number of these secondary works for further reference. Fletcher's marginal notes serving as pointers have been omitted. One citation, however, has been inserted in the text (p. 2), and one has been incorporated into footnote 3 of Chapter I.

I am indebted to my student assistants, Miss Linda Eichmeier, Miss Carole Farmer, Miss Karen McMurray, Miss Barbara North, and Mr. Alexander Almasov; to Mrs. Betty Fisher for her interlibrary loan acquisitions; and to my colleagues at Coe College, Professors Charles K. Cannon and Alexei A. Almasov, and Professor Samuel Baron of Grinnell College for their valuable suggestions. Special thanks must go to Mrs. Dorothy Dukes and Mrs. Janet Nisely for typing the manuscript, to Miss

Preface

Virginia LaMar for final scrutiny, and to my wife, Kathryn, for her many hours of proofreading.

Although the present work was completed before the appearance of Professor Lloyd Berry's impressive *The English Works of Giles Fletcher, the Elder*, I did have the opportunity to refer to it in time to make several factual changes in my own commentary on Fletcher.

A. J. SCHMIDT

Cedar Rapids, Iowa
January 11, 1965

CONTENTS

Preface	v
Introduction	xi
Of the Rus Commonwealth	xlv
The Epistle Dedicatory	1
Chapter I: The Description of the Country of Russia, with the Breadth, Length, and Names of the Shires	3
Chapter II: Of the Soil and Climate	7
Chapter III: The Native Commodities of the Country	11
Chapter IV: The Chief Cities of Russia	19
Chapter V: Of the House or Stock of the Rus Emperors	23
Chapter VI: Of the Manner of Crowning or Inauguration of the Rus Emperors	27
Chapter VII: The State or Form of Their Government	30
Chapter VIII: The Manner of Holding Their Parliaments	33
Chapter IX: Of the Nobility, and by What Means It Is Kept in an Underproportion Agreeable to That State	36
Chapter X: Of the Government of Their Provinces and Shires	43
Chapter XI: Of the Emperor's Council	50
Chapter XII: Of the Emperor's Customs and Other Revenues	52

Contents

Chapter XIII: Of the State of the Commonalty, or Vulgar Sort of People, in the Country of Russia ... 64

Chapter XIV: Of Their Public Justice and Manner of Proceeding in Civil and Criminal Matters ... 70

Chapter XV: Their Forces for the Wars, with the Chief Officers and Their Salaries ... 75

Chapter XVI: Of Their Mustering and Levying of Forces, Manner of Armor, and Provision of Victual for the Wars ... 80

Chapter XVII: Of Their Marching, Charging, and Other Martial Discipline ... 83

Chapter XVIII: Of Their Colonies and Maintaining of Their Conquests, or Purchases by Force ... 85

Chapter XIX: Of the Tartars and Other Borderers to the Country of Russia with Whom They Have Most to Do in War and Peace ... 90

Chapter XX: Of the Permians, Samoyeds, and Lapps ... 103

Chapter XXI: Of Their Ecclesiastical State, with Their Church Offices ... 107

Chapter XXII: Of Their Liturgy, or Form of Church Service, and Their Manner of Administering the Sacraments ... 124

Chapter XXIII: Of the Doctrine of the Rus Church and What Errors It Holdeth ... 130

Chapter XXIV: Of the Manner of Solemnizing Their Marriages ... 135

Chapter XXV: Of the Other Ceremonies of the Rus Church ... 138

Chapter XXVI: Of the Emperor's Domestic or Private Behavior ... 144

Chapter XXVII: Of the Emperor's Private or Household Officers ... 148

Chapter XXVIII: Of the Private Behavior or Quality of the Rus People ... 150

Glossary of Russian Words ... 159

Index ... 165

INTRODUCTION

Giles Fletcher's *Of the Rus Commonwealth* (1591), one of the most important works of Elizabethan travel literature, testifies to that adventuresome spirit and breadth of interest possessed by Englishmen during the era of Drake and Hakluyt. Like many later visitors to Russia, Fletcher wrote an exposé of that enigmatic polity and its people, but his success in arousing readers was greater than most. He not only delighted a generation whose appetite had already been whetted by Hakluyt but produced a controversial work which evoked a broad range of reaction from the time of its first printing.

Fletcher wrote about Muscovy during a crucial moment in her history. Even though the Renaissance failed to penetrate those lands, which until the late fifteenth century were under the Tartar yoke, the sixteenth century became for Russia as transitional as it was for most parts of Western Europe. During this formative period of the Moscow state, internal tensions were only too obvious to any close observer; moreover, Muscovy initiated her dramatic expansion eastward into Siberia and to Europe's discomfort was emerging as a factor in both the politics and the economy of Europe. It was a time propitious for an analysis of Moscow, and no doubt the lasting popularity of Fletcher's treatise is in part the result of its timeliness.

Introduction

It is easy, of course, to overrate the early intercourse between Europe and Muscovy; nevertheless, the West was jogged to an awareness of Russia's presence by the Tsar's quest for Italian architects and engineers to work on his kremlin, Muscovy's aggrandizement in Livonia, and the entrepreneurial activity of the English Muscovy Company. Certainly by 1600 there had emerged in England especially a rather definite if not particularly attractive image of Muscovy which had resulted largely from the contacts of the previous half century.[1]

English contacts with Moscow began with the arrival of the "Edward Bonaventure" of Richard Chancellor in the Dvina estuary via the White Sea one August day in 1553. Chancellor's quest for new markets in China did not deter him from exploiting his advantage of the moment. Making his way to Moscow, he procured from Tsar Ivan IV unusually favorable commercial privileges: almost by chance sprang up the famous Muscovy Company of England.

Patriotic English and dogmatic Soviet scholars have been tempted to exaggerate, for different reasons, the economic importance of the trade between Tudor England and Muscovite Russia.[2] In reality, the volume of the traffic neither enriched

[1] This subject is best covered in Karl H. Ruffmann, *Das Russlandbild im England Shakespeares* (Göttingen, 1952). The best analysis of what foreigners had to say about the various facets of sixteenth-century Muscovy is Vasilii Kliuchevskii, *Skazaniia Inostrantsev o Moskovskom Gosudarstve* (*Foreign Accounts about the Moscow State*) (Petrograd, 1918), which, incidentally, has not been included in the recent Soviet edition of the author's complete works. There is also an unpublished doctoral dissertation: John Q. Cook, "The Image of Russia in Western European Thought in the Sixteenth Century," University of Minnesota, 1960.

[2] The bibliography on Anglo-Russian relations in the sixteenth century is extensive and covered well in Ruffmann above. The numerous works of Inna Liubimenko should be noted, especially her major work, *Les relations commerciales et politiques de L'Angleterre avec la Russie avant Pierre le Grand* (Paris, 1933). Also of major importance are the works of T. S. Willan, especially his *The Early History of the Russia Company, 1553–1603* (Manchester, 1956). Edward A. Bond, *Russia at the Close of*

Introduction

England nor resulted in undue exploitation of Muscovy, but the trade did offer Englishmen some psychological compensation for their failure to equal the mid-century feats of the Spaniards and Portuguese. Viewed from hindsight, it was also symptomatic of England's later commercial and colonial dynamism.

Moscow, engaged in a contest with Poland-Lithuania for a Baltic outlet, viewed the ties with England as more than a mere commercial matter. In need of technological instruction, armaments, munitions, and political support in contending with a Baltic coalition bent on keeping Muscovy isolated and out of Europe, Tsar Ivan could not but look with satisfaction at the English circumvention of the traditional Baltic route by approaching Rus via the White Sea. Small wonder the Muscovites called it "God's great ocean way"! Also Ivan, often at odds with his subjects, expected to control foreign merchants more easily than his own.

Both the low volume of trade and numerous external and internal troubles experienced by the company deprived the Moscow commercial venture of some of its epic quality. English merchants had constantly to defend their monopoly against the Dutch, against interlopers who traded at Kola and Narva, and against corrupt members of their own house. Then, too, when the political wishes of the Tsar went unfulfilled, his wrath could be expected to fall upon the vulnerable merchants. Added to

---

the *Sixteenth Century*, Hakluyt Society, no. XX (London, 1856 and recently reissued), contains a lengthy comment on Anglo-Russian relations and Fletcher's treatise. Briefer accounts are M. S. Anderson, *Britain's Discovery of Russia, 1553–1815* (New York, 1958); M. Wretts-Smith, "The English in Russia during the Second Half of the Sixteenth Century," in *Transactions of the Royal Historical Society*, 4th series, III (London, 1920), 72–102; Sergei Yakobson, "Early Anglo-Russian Relations (1553–1613)," *Slavonic Review*, XIII (1934–35), 597–610; Ian Grey, "Ivan the Terrible and Elizabeth of England," *History Today*, XII (1962), 648–651. I have not seen Iu. V. Gote, *Angliiskie Puteshestvenniki v Moskovskom Gosudarstve v XVI Veke* (*English Travellers in the Moscow State in the Sixteenth Century*) (Leningrad, 1937).

xiii

Introduction

these problems were the natural risks involved in the enterprise. The tiny ships of perhaps 120 tons usually left England in early May in order to ensure arrival at the mouth of the Dvina in July. Despite every precaution, storms and ice made the trip extremely hazardous.

According to the charter granted by Ivan, the English enjoyed the right of internal trade and of free transit to Persia. Rose Island, at the mouth of the Dvina, was the starting point for the long trek into Muscovy's interior. There the English commodities—dyed and dressed cloth, pewter, lead and tin, armaments and munitions, wine and spices—were unloaded from the English ships, which in turn took on Russian cables and cordage, wax, tallow, flax, train oil, furs, and hides. By barge English commodities were shipped to markets farther south. Up the Dvina the barges moved to the English house at Kholmogory—a market center for Lapps, Samoyeds, and Karelians—and thence seven hundred miles farther to Vologda, and from there either by water to Iaroslavl or overland directly to Moscow. In these towns of wooden buildings the English stored their merchandise and housed their factors, who lived under the almost absolute authority of the agent of the company. The largest house was, of course, in Moscow, located after 1567 near the Tsar's palace.

This proximity to the Tsar was necessary to facilitate negotiation and to obtain his protection in case of xenophobic outbursts by boiars or the populace, but it had its disadvantages too. Merchants in Moscow found prices higher than in the provinces; moreover, pressures exerted on them by the nobility and royalty to extend "credit" for goods purchased made trade there extremely hazardous.

The commercial road did not always end in Moscow; the more enterprising pushed on to the Caspian and Persia beyond in quest of silks, spices, and turquoises. The heartiest of this breed of adventurers to Persia was the heroic Anthony Jenkin-

Introduction

son.[3] Tsar Ivan sanctioned the English commercial monopoly in Muscovy only so long as it suited his political interests. Incessantly he pressed Elizabeth for greater support in his Livonian imbroglio: in 1567 he made to Jenkinson a formal offer of alliance. He sought as well a place of asylum should his boiars overwhelm him, and lastly he negotiated almost to his dying day for an English wife. Elizabeth, not to be taken in by Ivan, followed a conservative Baltic policy: she continued to ship munitions and arms to the Tsar, but dependence on the Baltic nations for naval stores and grain made her reluctant to antagonize them by a formal alliance with Muscovy. Elizabeth's procrastination so enraged Ivan that for a time he even suspended the English monopoly; but when it proved advantageous for him to restore it, he did. Despite this conflict between economics and politics Anglo-Russian relations were relatively harmonious during the reign of Ivan IV, whose unhappy boiars even labeled him the "English tsar."

After Ivan's death in 1584 the English increasingly encountered obstacles; they were expelled that very year by the Anglophobe Secretary Shchelkalov. The increasing number of "incidents" suggested that Ivan's successor regarded that state's welfare as better served by extending rather than limiting the scope of trade. The Dutch, in particular, profited from this new commercial orientation by Moscow. In England, Elizabeth, eager to work out a *modus vivendi* in order that trade might continue, sent to the court of Tsar Fedor a special ambassador and specialist in commercial matters, the humanist and civilian Giles Fletcher.

Like other Tudor humanists who served the Crown, this man tapped to aid the cause of the Muscovy merchants possessed

[3] See E. D. Morgan and C. H. Coote, *Early Voyages and Travels to Russia and Persia, by Anthony Jenkinson and Other Englishmen*, Hakluyt Society, nos. LXXII and LXXIII (London, 1886 and recently reissued). There is a recent biography of Jenkinson: Graham Morton, *The Jenkinson Story* (Glasgow, 1962).

Introduction

great versatility.[4] A hard-headed diplomat, ruthless examiner of subversives, and writer of sonnets, he had forsaken the cloistered life of the university to attain that fame and preferment which came only through service at court or in assignments abroad.

Fletcher's public life was articulated by his ardent Protestantism, which identified him with the Puritan faction in Elizabeth's Privy Council. He came by these religious convictions and his adventuresome spirit naturally enough. His Yorkshireman father, ordained in the presence of Nicholas Ridley and mentioned by Foxe in his account of Marian martyrs, had once served as ambassador to the Sophy of Persia. The elder Fletcher, surviving the rigors of Mary's reign, lived out his days in his charge in Cranbrook, Kent. There the father's spiritual fire kindled an ample response in his sons. Richard, succeeding Aylmer as the Bishop of London in 1594, became one of Elizabeth's most famous Puritan bishops. The second son, Giles, born about 1546, furthermore, was nurtured in those strongholds of the new faith, Eton (1561) and King's (1565), the latter the most Protestant of Cambridge colleges.

Giles's scholarly inclination initially promised a fruitful career at the university, but difficulties with the authorities possibly contributed to his decision to leave in 1581. From then until his death some thirty years later Fletcher continually sought patronage to extricate himself from debt. Turning naturally to men of influence and similar religious persuasion, Fletcher counted as patrons Sir Thomas Randolph, his brother Richard, Sir Francis Walsingham, and the ill-fated Earl of Essex. Although

---

[4] For biographical information on Giles Fletcher the best account is in Lloyd Berry, *The English Works of Giles Fletcher, the Elder* (Madison, 1964). The *Dictionary of National Biography* and chapters II and III in A. B. Langdale, *Phineas Fletcher, Man of Letters, Science and Divinity* (New York, 1937) should be consulted. Extremely useful is Lloyd E. Berry, "Phineas Fletcher's Account of His Father," *Journal of English and Germanic Philology*, LX (1961), 258–267.

Introduction

Fletcher's enemies occasionally denied him the rewards that he probably deserved, his own choice of patrons proved nearly disastrous to him. He narrowly escaped prison when he assumed responsibility for Richard's debts after the worldly bishop's death and just missed the scaffold for his devotion to the seditious Essex.[5]

Fletcher projected the image of a hard-working, intelligent, ambitious, though usually impoverished, public servant. He was a member of Parliament in 1585, both an extraordinary and ordinary master in the Court of Requests, Remembrancer of London from 1586/87 to 1605, occasional interrogator of papists, besides being an indefatigable writer.[6] He served on missions to Scotland, the Netherlands, and to Hamburg to negotiate with the Hanse. His broad knowledge of commercial affairs stemmed from training in the civil law and duties as Remembrancer as well as from his experience abroad. Although the Earl of Essex apparently expected the Remembrancer's assistance in rallying Londoners to rebellion, Fletcher managed to avoid the block only because he had not been made privy to the conspiracy. His alignment with the radicals at court lost him all favor with William Cecil, Lord Burghley, who denied every request Fletcher ever made to him and who, of course, ordered *Of the Rus Commonwealth* suppressed.

In his private life, the elder Giles Fletcher conformed to the social pattern of his age. He married, in Cranbrook, Joan Sheaffe, daughter of a well-to-do clothier, whose family had

[5] Cf. Lloyd Berry, "Biographical Notes on Richard Fletcher," and "Giles Fletcher, the Elder, and the Earl of Essex," in *Notes and Queries*, new ser. VII, 377–378 and 42–46 respectively. Some evidence of Fletcher's disillusionment during the early 1590's may be discerned in his dedication of *Licia* in Sidney Lee, ed., *Elizabethan Sonnets* (London, 1904), II, 26–29.

[6] Fletcher's English poetical writings included *Licia, or Poems of Love* and *The Rising to the Crown of Richard the Third*. A projected Latin history of Elizabeth's reign was never completed, but sixty-six years after the author's death his brief treatise, *The Tartars or Ten Tribes*, was published (in 1677). A number of Fletcher's letters also survive.

Introduction

married with the gentry Knatchbulls and Robarts. By Joan, who so often bore alone family responsibilities, Giles had three sons and two daughters. The most famous of this brood were his two poet sons, Giles the Younger and Phineas. They, with their cousin John, the Bishop's son, were to bring to the next generation of Fletchers a splendid literary reputation. Their patrons became the Molyneux, Willoughby, and Neville families, into which North Country Fletchers had married.

Giles Fletcher was appointed ambassador to Muscovy on June 6, 1588. He arrived at Kholmogory three months later and returned to England again in July or August of the following year. His detailed record of this embassy, besides including reflections on mercantile and political problems, revealed his bitterness about the treatment accorded him by his hosts.[7] Fletcher observed that "from my first arrival till toward the very end was such as if they had devised means of every purpose to show their utter disliking both of the trade of the merchants and of the whole English nation." He received neither official welcome nor any indication as to when he could see either the Emperor or the real power, Boris Godunov, who was the Russian equivalent of Lord Protector. When at last an interview was arranged, he was vehemently censured for not enumerating all the Tsar's titles and for the meanness of his queen's gifts to Fedor: "The presents . . . were the day following returned to me and very contemptuously cast down before me." Fletcher further charged that his petition to the Tsar had been "altered and falsified" by Chancellor Shchelkalov and that he was kept virtually a prisoner in a "house very unhandsome, unwholesome" and "not suffered to send any letter into England . . . to signify of my proceeding, not so much as of my health, though I desired it

---

[7] See "Papers Relating to the Embassy of Dr. Giles Fletcher to the Russian Court" (from Lansdowne MS LX, art. 59) printed in Bond, *Russia*, pp. 342–351, and also in Henry Ellis, ed., *Original Letters of Eminent Literary Men* (London, 1843), pp. 80–85.

Introduction

earnestly." He further complained that his allowance for victual was "bare and base." Even after departing from Moscow for the North, Fletcher experienced discourtesies, or at least frustrations. At Vologda he learned of an order, reputedly by Shchelkalov, that no one might "hire out horse or boat to any Englishman, which bred an opinion in the people there that there was great matter of disliking from the Emperor toward the English nation, which was a cause of great danger toward me and my company."

On this occasion the impecunious Elizabeth underestimated the Muscovite. The skimpiness of her gifts to the Tsar and Boris, coupled with her blunder in sending letters carried by Fletcher to Boris from the Privy Council rather than from herself, left the proud Muscovite smarting. Boris wrote to his confidant, the Englishman Jerome Horsey: "It is no small disparagement unto my princely dignity that the Queen and noblemen have written letters unto me most unseemly and very undecent joining the chancellory with me therein." [8] England's great friend was perturbed for other reasons: he failed to receive certain commodities requested; he suffered embarrassment when the company too clearly distinguished between his and Tsar Fedor's gifts to Elizabeth; and he resented the company's treatment of Jerome Horsey. The reception accorded Fletcher therefore was hardly surprising in the light of this English ineptitude and thin-skinned Muscovite pride and the traditional Muscovite practice of isolating foreign emissaries. Even Jenkinson had once awaited the Tsar's pleasure for five months in Kholmogory and for another six weeks in Pereiaslavl before being invited to proceed to Moscow. As it turned out, the affront to Boris proved most costly to Fletcher, because the Lord Protector left negotiations to Shchelkalov.

The principal issue confronting Fletcher was the location of

[8] George Tolstoi, ed., *The First Forty Years of Intercourse between England and Russia (1553–1593)* (St. Petersburg, 1875), p. xlvii.

Introduction

the English trade. After recent military setbacks in the Baltic, the Russians wished to remove all trade from Narva and Riga to the more secure White Sea port of St. Nicholas. Vexed that the English forbade other nations from trading there, the Dutch and Russians responded by opening in 1584 the port of Archangel. Fletcher asserted that the English would abandon neither the Baltic nor White Sea trade. They, after all, deserved the White Sea monopoly for their initiative and had used it to provide the Tsar with materials of war when going by way of Narva proved impossible. He warned of Muscovy's plight were Sweden to close the Baltic and England to bar all trade from the White Sea. Muscovites would then "have no way to vent their own commodities nor to receive in foreign, especially powder, saltpeter, brimstone, lead, etc., necessary for the Emperor's wars."

Fletcher, reflecting on these same issues once he had returned to England, concluded that an increase in trade at the White Sea port of St. Nicholas would have been the most feasible solution to the problems dividing the English and Muscovites.[9] He proposed, therefore, removing the staple from Moscow, Iaroslavl, Vologda, and Kholmogory to that port. Besides reducing expenses and improving relations with the Muscovites, this move would have lessened the possibility of seizures and would have forced Russian merchants to seek out the English at St. Nicholas.

Departure from Moscow and elimination thereby of mer-

[9] Fletcher's observations were contained in "Means of Decay of the Rus Trade," printed in Morgan and Coote, *Early Voyages and Travels*, I, cviii–cxiii. Although these editors assumed that the document was the work of Christopher Borough, E. S. Vilenskaia in "K istorii russko-angliiskikh otnoshenii v XVI v." ("A contribution to the history of Russo-English relations in the sixteenth century"), *Istoricheskie Zapiski*, XXIX (1949), 123–134, has convincingly argued for the authorship of Fletcher. She did assume, however, that the document had never been published. Cf. Willan, *Russia Company*, pp. 205–206 n.

Introduction

chants engaged in private trade would also have reduced the personal dealing or embezzlement by the low-paid underlings of the company itself. Even men in high places, like Jerome Horsey, took part in "inland trade, buying at one part of the country and selling at the other, as if they were Rus merchants, to the great dislike of the Rus." These people were even so bold as to ship their goods in Flemish bottoms to St. Nicholas, Riga, and Narva. Fletcher recommended coercion if Muscovy refused to comply with Elizabeth's wishes to move the staple: England could have blocked trade to St. Nicholas and urged Poland, Sweden, and the Turks to belligerency. If the Muscovites had seized English goods, then the English in turn could have raided Pechora, where furs worth £100,000 were stored. Although Fletcher's proposal for gunboat diplomacy never materialized, his remarks clearly revealed his attitude toward Muscovy after his return to England.

In Moscow, Fletcher had been taunted that the English company "was utterly disliked by your Highness, by your council, by all the merchants of England, . . . being now more notable monopoliers than they were before" and that Elizabeth would like the company dissolved in order that trade could be open for all subjects. He had not only denied this accusation but refuted the insinuations that the Queen's letters on the company's behalf "were got by importunity, that your Highness set your hand to many things which you never read over" and that Fletcher himself had been sent out "but as a messenger, not as an ambassador" and had never even spoken with the Queen.[10]

Fletcher flatly told his tormentors that he was very much an ambassador with instructions and that Elizabeth had great concern for her merchants, whom she regarded "not as *muzhiks* or base people . . . but as very special and necessary members of your commonwealth." His queen, he added, cared more for her

[10] Bond, *Russia*, pp. 345–346; the following commentary on Fletcher's embassy is derived from Bond, pp. 345–351.

Introduction

honor than for revenue, and in any case the earnings of her merchants in Muscovy were a pittance compared with that gained elsewhere. Fletcher countered Boris Godunov's peeve by convincing him that he still rated highly with Elizabeth, who desired nothing more than his favor for her merchants. The latter promised to make just amends if they in turn offended Boris.

Aside from such particulars as individual debts, customs, and rent, the ambassador reported at the conclusion of negotiations that trading privileges, which prompted his coming in the first place, had been completely affirmed: "They promise a continuance of the privilege forever without any revocation." Fletcher also won approval on such additions to the former privileges as the right of English trade down the Volga "into Media, Persia, Bukhara, etc., and no stranger shall be permitted trade that way but they." The Muscovite merchants were to compensate the English immediately for goods taken for the Emperor's use; moreover, guarantees were given against extortion by Moscow officials. Care was taken to register all who were of the company, and only they were to enjoy the prerogatives of the same. The Muscovites assured Fletcher that no Englishman suspected of crime would be subjected to harsh treatment but all would be kept safely until thorough investigation could be made. The ambassador won an especially important point when the company of merchants was removed from authority of the despised Shchelkalov and placed under Godunov's office of treasury.

On the debit side, Fletcher failed to secure reimbursement for goods and money previously extracted from the company: in effect, Fletcher, hoping that the future would bring better relations between the two countries, settled by wiping the past slate clean. He reported to his queen that during negotiations he maintained a stoic attitude which he believed better to serve his purpose: the Muscovites, not wishing that he should tell Elizabeth of his privations, "yielded divers points and in a manner all that I entreated of them."

Introduction

The worthy Fuller reported that Fletcher, "returning home and being safely arrived in London, . . . sent for his intimate friend Mr. Wayland, prebendary of St. Paul's and senior fellow of Trinity College in Cambridge, . . . with whom he heartily expressed his thankfulness to God for his safe return from so great danger." [11] This embassy's conclusion marked the beginning of the romance of Fletcher's classic treatise about Muscovy. The ambassador conceived writing *Of the Rus Commonwealth* while still sojourning in Russia. He noted in his Epistle Dedicatory: "I observed the state and manners of that country and . . . reduced the same into some order by the way as I returned." Although Fletcher spent less than a year in Moscow and returned by the summer of 1589, he gave his work its final form by the end of that year and completed it during the next.[12]

Published by the printer Thomas Charde in 1591, the book focused on the usual attractions for a traveler: topography and climate, cities, commodities, government, social classes, dress and customs, justice, the Emperor and his routine, finances, military affairs, the church and religion, and other aspects of Moscow life. The author's strong opinions, however, gave the book its distinctive quality. The book's tone was clearly articulated in the dedication to Queen Elizabeth: "In their manner of government your Highness may see both a true and strange face of a tyrannical state most unlike to your own, without true knowledge of God, without written law, without common justice save that which proceedeth from their speaking law—to wit, the

---

[11] Thomas Fuller, *The Worthies of England*, ed. John Freeman (New York, 1952), p. 279.

[12] Professor Lloyd Berry has discovered in Queen's College, Cambridge, University College, Oxford, and the James Ford Bell Collection, University of Minnesota, manuscript copies of *Of the Rus Commonwealth* which substantiate Fletcher's statement in the Epistle Dedicatory. These manuscripts also indicate that the sections on the Tartars and references to such historians as Kromer and Bonfinius were inserted after his return from Russia, when presumably Fletcher had access to these authors' works.

Introduction

magistrate, who hath most need of a law to restrain his own injustice."

Hakluyt alluded to Fletcher's forthcoming book in his late 1589 edition of *Principal Navigations*.[13] He included, in fact, a two-page brief of "The late embassage of Master Giles Fletcher, Doctor of Civil Law, sent from Her Majesty to the Emperor of Russia, anno 1588." Besides describing the mission and tabulating the commercial privileges obtained, Hakluyt observed that "the said ambassador Giles Fletcher, as I understand, hath drawn a book entitled *Of the Rus Commonwealth*." This aggressive publicist, sensing the interests of his anxious readers, recorded a partial, generally accurate, listing of the chapters of the forthcoming book, but concluded prophetically that "the book itself he thought not good, for divers considerations, to make public at this time." Presumably Hakluyt had read Fletcher's book in manuscript and decided that its improprieties warranted postponing publication.

If these indeed were Hakluyt's thoughts, they were vindicated once the first edition of *Of the Rus Commonwealth* had appeared in print. The English Muscovy merchants, distressed by Fletcher's deprecation of the Russians, appealed to Lord Burghley to suppress the book. In their petition the merchants emphasized that "trading to Moscovia having been many ways prejudiced by the errors which have been committed by Her Majesty's subjects employed by the company in those parts, in giving offense or some color of offense to the government of the state of the country of Russia, [we] do greatly fear that a book lately set out by Mr. Doctor Fletcher . . . will turn the company to some great displeasure with the Rus emperor and endanger both their people and goods now remaining there."

---

[13] Hakluyt's involvement with *Of the Rus Commonwealth* has been analyzed by Robert O. Lindsay, "Richard Hakluyt and *Of the Rus Commonwealth*," *Papers of the Bibliographical Society of America*, LVII (1963), 312–327; my comments are largely drawn from this source.

Introduction

Burghley was urged to call in all books already printed and to issue some statement indicating the Queen's "dislike of the publishing of the same." The petition specified those passages in the book especially offensive to the Muscovites: the author's remarks about the military, the government, the Emperor's revenue, the nature of the people, and the persons of Ivan IV, Fedor, and Boris Godunov.[14] These topics were "couched in so hard terms as that the company doubt the revenge thereof will light on their people and goods remaining in Russia and utterly overthrow the trade forever." Particularly offensive passages were cited at the end of the document. Burghley, never a friend of Fletcher, heeded without delay the plea of the merchants and ordered *Of the Rus Commonwealth* suppressed. This act of censorship prompted Thomas Nashe to quip: "Out steps me an infant squib of the Inns of Court that hath not half greased his dining cap or scarce warmed his lawyer's cushion. And he, to approve himself an extravagant statesman, catcheth hold of a rush and absolutely concludeth it is meant of the Emperor of Russia and that it will utterly mar the traffic into that country if all the pamphlets be not called in, and suppressed wherein that libeling word is mentioned." [15]

Fletcher's treatise did not disappear entirely from the public view. An edition of Hakluyt between 1598 and 1600 contained an abbreviated and thoroughly expurgated version of the original of 1591. Hakluyt's handling of Fletcher sheds light on both the editorial ability and integrity of this great Tudor publicist. Although Hakluyt inserted in his table of contents twenty-four of the twenty-eight chapters of the suppressed edition, he incorporated in his narrative only ten, while adding three descriptive ones of his own. A scrutiny of this abridgment reveals that its

---

[14] The petition is printed in its entirety in both Ellis, *Original Letters*, pp. 77–79, and Bond, *Russia*, pp. 352–355.

[15] Edwin H. Miller, *The Professional Writer in Elizabethan England* (Cambridge, Mass., 1959), pp. 199–200.

Introduction

editor went far beyond the demand made by the merchants to Burghley. Their concern had centered on the Epistle Dedicatory and ten specified chapters. While Hakluyt did indeed delete the Epistle, eight of the chapters in question, and the objectionable parts of the other two, he also omitted seven chapters not queried by the merchants and slashed lesser parts of six more. In the end, only five of the original twenty-eight escaped unscathed. Hakluyt's censorship is especially curious in that he failed both to eliminate all Fletcher's offensive passages and to apply the same rigorous standards to the equally uncomplimentary remarks about Moscow by Chancellor, Randolph, Jenkinson, and Turberville.

During the seventeenth century, *Of the Rus Commonwealth* remained before the English reading public in one form or another. It was reprinted in expurgated form and with certain verbal changes in Samuel Purchas, *Purchas His Pilgrims* (1625).[16] That editor admitted that he had "in some places contracted, in others mollified, the biting or more bitter style which the author useth of the Russian government, that I might do good at home without harm abroad."

Sometime during the 1630's Milton composed *A Brief History of Moscovia*, which drew heavily upon Fletcher.[17] Milton, who described Fletcher as "judicious and exact," made no pretense at writing an original work. He presumably synthesized the best of available secondary works on Muscovy; however, analysis of *Moscovia* has shown that the author "presents the material common to *Moscovia* and *Of the Rus Commonwealth* from the same point of view as does Fletcher." Alongside Milton's pride in England ran a corresponding disdain for all things Russian. He

---

[16] XII (Glasgow, 1906), 499–633.

[17] Milton's dependence on Fletcher is thoroughly explored in Lloyd E. Berry, "Giles Fletcher, the Elder, and Milton's *Brief History of Moscovia*," in *Review of English Studies*, new ser., XI, no. 42 (1960), 150–156. I have relied on this article for my comment. Cf. also R. R. Cawley, *Milton and the Literature of Travel* (Princeton, 1951).

Introduction

would have agreed with Fletcher that "Russia symbolized tyranny, oppression, and ignorance."

Unabridged versions of Fletcher appeared again in 1643, 1656, and 1657, under the title *The History of Russia, or, The Government of the Emperor of Muscovia with the Manners and Fashion of the People of That Country*.[18] In the following century, selections from Fletcher appeared in John Harris, *Navigantium atque itinerantium bibliotheca, or, A Complete Collection of Voyages and Travels*.[19] In 1856 Edward A. Bond edited for the Hakluyt Society the works of both Fletcher and Jerome Horsey in *Russia at the Close of the Sixteenth Century*. This uncritical re-issue of the 1591 edition was followed within the decade by an only slightly annotated French version edited by Charles du Bouzet.[20]

Even before Fletcher's original experienced this renaissance in Western Europe, members of the Imperial Society of History and Russian Antiquities, affiliated with Moscow University, undertook in the 1840's to publish Fletcher, with other originals and translations of sixteenth-century foreign commentaries on Muscovy.[21] Then, as two and a half centuries earlier, the book provoked a storm; for these university men, not reckoning with official reaction to those same passages purged by Burghley,

[18] A description of these later editions, the one of 1591, the latter's manuscript antecedents, and a bibliography of Fletcher's poems and letters are given in Lloyd E. Berry, "Giles Fletcher, the Elder: A Bibliography," in *Transactions of the Cambridge Bibliographical Society*, III, 3 (1961), 200–215.

[19] I (1705). The 1744–1748 edition did not contain selections from Fletcher.

[20] *La Russie* (Paris, 1864).

[21] For this account I have relied on S. A. Velokurov, "Delo Fletchera ("The Fletcher Affair"), 1848–1864," in *Chteniia v Imperatorskom Obshchestve Istorii i Drevnostei Rossiiskikh pri Moskovskom Universitete* (*Readings* in the Imperial Society of History and Russian Antiquities), bk. 3 (1910), pp. 3–39. See also the introduction (v–xiii) of the first published Russian edition of Fletcher, *O Gosudarstve Russkom Sochinenie Fletchera* (St. Petersburg, 1905).

xxvii

Introduction

collided head-on with the censor of Nicholas I and thus precipitated the "Fletcher affair."

A prime mover in this Moscow University publication venture was one Prince M. A. Obolenskii, former director of the Moscow Main Archive of the Ministry of Foreign Affairs and an active member of the Society since 1834. At a meeting in September, 1847, he announced that *Of the Rus Commonwealth*, both the original and translation, had been sent to the printer. While the assumption has persisted that Obolenskii himself was the translator, that task apparently had been performed only through his initiative but actually by an obscure scholar in the Archive named D. I. Gippius (Hippius). The latter's translation was completed and subjected to severe editing by one N. V. Kalachev, who had joined the Moscow Archive in 1846. The entire project, therefore, had been completed for some time before the September, 1847, meeting.

A year later the distribution of the *Chteniia*, the Society's periodical, to its members initiated the *cause célèbre*. In the background but certainly relevant to the whole affair was the bitter hostility existing between S. G. Stroganov, prominent figure in both Society and University circles, and Sergei S. Uvarov, Nicholas I's Minister of Public Instruction and the incarnation of the spirit of reaction during this period. The two had clashed on other university matters prior to Stroganov's joining with Obolenskii in advocating publication of the Fletcher essay. When Uvarov saw the *Chteniia*, he immediately ordered its suppression. A comedy of errors ensued. The principals somehow were ignored: Gippius had already been dismissed from his post in 1846; while Kalachev, nominated an extraordinary professor at Moscow University in 1848, continued in the Archives. Obolenskii obtained leave of absence and departed for Petersburg, perhaps to offer an explanation for his role in this venture. The main punishment fell on the heads of two individuals who apparently had little to do with the conception of the scheme.

Introduction

Stroganov fell into disgrace and so remained during the few remaining years of Nicholas' reign. A severer treatment befell O. M. Bodianskii, the secretary of the Society and sometimes identified as the translator of the "1848 edition" of *Of the Rus Commonwealth*. Bodianskii, also a professor at Moscow University, was summarily transferred to Kazan University, while a professor there was nominated to replace him in Moscow. As it turned out, Bodianskii did not report to Kazan; as for Grigorovich, his replacement, he felt so ostracized in Moscow that he happily returned to Kazan the next year.

This episode in Russian censorship was virtually repeated after Nicholas I's death in 1855, when the Moscow professors once again tried their luck at rehabilitating Fletcher. No Uvarov interfered this time, as he had been dismissed within a year after his success in suppressing Fletcher's work. Bodianskii rightly observed that selections from the controversial tract had since 1848 appeared elsewhere; he therefore saw no logical reason for prohibiting publication of the entire book. Although Stroganov's support again was obtained, Golovnin, the Minister of Public Instruction, and Tsar Alexander II proceeded cautiously. Ultimately the Emperor decreed that a committee of ministers should study Fletcher's work and decide its fate. Although a majority of this committee passed favorably on the treatise, the minority voiced reservations about sections critical of the Orthodox Church. Once again a tsar was persuaded to prohibit publication. With this failure in 1864, the bizarre Fletcher affair had run its course. Standing as a superb case study of Imperial Russian censorship, it paralleled in a fascinating manner English censorship under the Tudors.

It was apparently this same Russian version, *O Gosudarstve Russkom*, which appeared in 1867, printed in either London, Basel, or Geneva. In 1891 the Russian scholar Sergei Mikhailovich Seredonin published an extensive critique of Fletcher based on Bond's 1856 reprint of the original 1591 edition. This

Introduction

sweeping commentary, discussed in some detail below, probably stimulated anew efforts to publish in Russia the old Gippius-Obolenskii version.[22] Success finally came in 1905, when it appeared with a lengthy though incomplete discussion of the "affair" by A. A. Titov.

Current Western interest in Russian and Soviet affairs has sparked a renewed interest in Giles Fletcher. Besides the recent reprint of Bond's edition, two new versions of *Of the Rus Commonwealth* in addition to the present one are forthcoming.[23]

Fletcher's treatise has evoked widely varying comment from scholars over the centuries. Milton thought it scholarly and accurate, while Bond offered no negative criticism in his lengthy introduction. Charles du Bouzet believed that the work faithfully mirrored sixteenth-century Russia by focusing on the naïve barbarism bereft of foreign elements. This portrait of Muscovy, he added, had its value not only as a historical source but as a clear guide to the understanding of mid-nineteenth-century Russia, "because of all the evil that still remains in the country." [24] At the beginning of the present century that prodigious student of Russian history K. Waliszewski observed that Fletcher's book, despite its numerous errors and the deliberate malevolence so often attributed to it, "remains the most precious document for the ordering of political, social, and economic history of Muscovy during the late sixteenth century." [25] More re-

---

[22] It has generally been assumed that Bodianskii translated the edition of 1848 and that Obolenskii was responsible for that of 1867; however, there was only one Russian version of Fletcher, that by Gippius-Obolenskii.

[23] One is Professor Lloyd E. Berry's work already alluded to. Professor Richard Pipes, a Russian specialist, and John H. Fine, of Harvard, expect to publish in the near future an annotated facsimile edition of the 1591 version.

[24] *La Russie,* Introduction, xv.

[25] K. Waliszewski, *La Crise révolutionnaire, 1584–1614* (Paris, 1906), p. 22.

Introduction

cently, M. S. Anderson observed that Fletcher had "provided Englishmen with a description of the country which was not surpassed in many essentials till the eighteenth century," Michael Florinsky has remarked on the "uncanny accuracy" with which Fletcher foresaw the Time of Troubles, and Jerome Blum in his important work unhesitatingly cited Fletcher as an authority.[26]

The great Russian Romantic historian Nikolai M. Karamzin first called Fletcher's writing to the attention of his countrymen and thereby possibly inspired the ill-fated effort of 1848.[27] No less a scholar than Inna Liubimenko, authority on sixteenth-century Anglo-Russian relations, termed Fletcher "very judicious," possessed of a "calm character, prudent and level-headed," while his book she described as "remarkable."[28] The great Kliuchevskii asserted that Fletcher's work "represented a systematical description of the different sides of the state establishment, social and private life."[29]

Sergei Platonov, Russian authority on the period, referred to "the cautious Fletcher, that learned Englishman," but noted that even he "did not escape the general tendency toward general bias." Platonov felt that Fletcher "was not entirely objective in his attitude toward the memory of the Muscovite tyrant, making Ivan personally responsible for all the disorganization of contemporary Muscovite life."[30]

The most careful of all Fletcher's pre-Revolutionary Russian critics was Sergei Mikhailovich Seredonin.[31] Writing late in the

[26] Anderson, *Britain's Discovery of Russia*, p. 12; Michael Florinsky, *Russia: A History and Interpretation*, I (New York, 1953), 219; and Jerome Blum, *Lord and Peasant in Russia from the Ninth to the Nineteenth Century* (Princeton, 1961), *passim*.

[27] *Histoire de l'Empire de Russie* (Paris, 1926), X, 412.

[28] *Les relations commerciales*, p. 282.

[29] *Skazaniia Inostrantsev*, pp. 20–21.

[30] "Ivan the Terrible in Russian Historiography," in S. Harcave, ed., *Readings in Russian History*, I (New York, 1962), 189–190.

[31] *Sochinenie Dzhilsa Fletchera "Of the Russe Common Wealth" kak Istoricheskii Istochnik* (*The Treatise of Giles Fletcher as a Historical Source*) (St. Petersburg, 1891). Hereafter cited as "Seredonin, *Sochinenie*."

Introduction

nineteenth century, he observed the "high place" occupied by Fletcher's treatise and expressed admiration for its first-hand account of the mode of Moscow life and the manner in which it echoed the popular political attitudes of the day. Most of all he praised Fletcher for an orderly mind which made it possible to render such a coherent essay; nonetheless, Seredonin ultimately cast a cloud of doubt over the value of Fletcher's work as a historical source. His scrupulous analysis indicated that Fletcher, who was not sufficiently fluent in Russian to engage in fruitful discussion with the Russians, composed his work carelessly and in great haste. His numerous errors resulted from a failure to check the authenticity of his data and to use obvious Russian historical sources. Fletcher permitted his preconceptions and biases to color whatever he did perceive: he viewed Muscovite political life exclusively from the vantage point of an English patriot and Russian Orthodoxy from that of an ardent Protestant. Seredonin charged that the author generalized on the basis of his very limited experiences or on hearsay evidence of unique happenings, especially when these conformed to his preconceptions. By highly prejudicial remarks he vented his hostility on Russian officialdom for their harsh dealing with him at the time of his arrival. According to Seredonin, "not one foreigner writing on Russia constructed so clearly a view of the state structure of Russia so one-sided and basically untrue as Fletcher." [32]

Aside from puncturing the inflated authority of Fletcher's treatise, Seredonin lamented that visitors to Muscovy should view Russians as a barbarous people akin to Persians, Tartars, or Turks and therefore easy prey for both political and economic exploitation.[33] That Russians indeed were Europeans, as signified by their religion, was an ignored fact; they were hindered rather than aided in catching up with their more fortunate Western brethren. While foreigners could not possibly have

---

[32] This quotation from *ibid.*, p. 70.
[33] See Seredonin's conclusion, *ibid.*, pp. 370–376.

Introduction

fathomed the spirit of the Russian people, they should have tried to understand the Russian past. Fletcher, like the others, had "comprehended neither the character of the Russian people nor their future role in the affairs of Europe." Although he had sympathized with the burdened Russian people and wished that they could have been tutored by the enlightened West, he had urged restricting Russia to the farthest reaches of Europe; or better still that the Muscovite might make war on the Tartars and clear the way to Persia, China, and Bukhara for the English. Fletcher, Seredonin charged, had assumed that the Muscovite wars with the West stemmed from the greediness of Russian statesmen, whose refusal to grant commercial monopolies to the English resulted from fears that contacts between peoples would undermine the Moscow autocracy. It was disappointing to Seredonin that writers who had sought to correct misconceptions had not used a "more attentive attitude toward the society under study." Fletcher, he noted, "did not see that Russian people were prepared to make very many material sacrifices in order to get back everything lost during a period of grinding poverty and secure for themselves a beneficial and honorable position in the midst of the Christian people of Europe."

The main thrust of Soviet historical studies has been a denial both of past foreign influences on Russia and the validity of foreign appraisals; there has not been, therefore, any concerted effort to resurrect Fletcher. Whatever stature he may have possessed with pre-Soviet historians has now diminished in the U.S.S.R. *The Great Soviet Encyclopedia (Bolshaia Sovetskaia Entsiklopediia)*, while calling Fletcher "one of the most important historians of Russia in the second half of the sixteenth century," concludes its significantly brief comment with the assertion that his work is "possessed of many mistakes and distortions" and that "its statistical information is not worthy of special confidence." [34]

[34] Second ed., XLV, 242.

Introduction

The Soviet historian Sadukov in his recent work on the *oprichnina* included much information on Ivan IV's administrative machinery but recognized no debt to Fletcher, whom he curtly dismissed for his mistakes.[35] The standard Soviet histories focusing on sixteenth-century Moscow have cited Fletcher only casually, thereby accentuating the impression of his irrelevance to Soviet historiography.[36]

A notably harsh judgment of Fletcher came from the late Professor Robert Wipper (Vipper) who produced a highly favorable historical portrait of Ivan IV.[37] Dealing sternly with detractors of his hero, Wipper charged that the "limited judgment of Ivan Groznyi that is characteristic of the historians of the nineteenth century" was traceable partly to "their ignorance of numerous extremely important sources which have been discovered during the past two decades and partly to the fact that most of them belong to the liberal bourgeois school." The latter, he added, had "easily succumbed to the influence of Fletcher, one of the brilliant writers of the heroic period of liberalism." Wipper, asserting that Fletcher's embassy had resulted from nefarious dealings by the Muscovy Company's own agents and from attempts by the company to extend its monopoly in Muscovy, suggested that the ambassador was himself responsible for his hardships in Moscow because he had violated Muscovite standards of etiquette. Ignoring the fact that Fletcher ultimately ended his mission with some degree of success, Ivan's biographer suggested that

Fletcher had to explain his failure to Queen Elizabeth, for he had counted on occupying the place of Elizabeth's court historiographer.

[35] *Ocherki po Istorii Oprichniny* (*Study of the History of the Oprichnina*) (Leningrad and Moscow, 1950), p. 400.

[36] Cf. especially *Ocherki Istorii S.S.S.R.: Period Feodalizma, konets XV v.–nachalo XVII v.* (Moscow, 1955) and *Istoriia Moskvy* (Moscow, 1952), II.

[37] *Ivan Grozny* (Moscow, 1947). The following quotes are to be found pp. 241–243.

Introduction

He decided that he could achieve both objects by writing a description of the kingdom of Muscovy and depicting its methods of government which were "quite unlike your [Majesty's] own," as he wrote in his preface, i.e., if he depicted Moscow as a barbarous country governed by cruel, Asiatic methods, ignorant and decaying as a consequence of its being unfamiliar with enlightened Europe. Against this gloomy background the lawful and constitutional government of the English Queen would stand but all the brighter.

Wipper praised Seredonin for revealing the superficial and distorted character of Fletcher's work and observed that the English ambassador

wrote in the period of nascent political liberalism, represented in the sixteenth century by the talented school of "Monarchomachus," French publicists who condemned unlimited monarchy. Their eloquent, sonorous and audacious phrases about the harmfulness of unlimited monarchy, about the rights of the people being protected by representatives of public opinion, and about the wisdom of parliamentarianism often served to cover up the barrenness of their own program, the aristocratic narrowmindedness and selfishness of the class to which the orators and writers who sang the praises of liberty belonged. Enchanted by all forms of opposition to autocracy, the historians of the nineteenth century easily slipped into the rut of the early naïve denunciation of despotism and for that reason willingly accepted the judgment of the fathers of liberalism, the sixteenth century publicists.

Wipper concluded that Fletcher won approval in the last century because "his political verdict and his denunciation of the Russian people suited the book of those historians who failed to understand the profound gifts, the great mental, social and technical talent of the Russian people." Wipper's severe criticism of Fletcher was simply a corollary of his highly favorable portrait of Ivan IV, which had great vogue in Stalin's day.

Although Giles Fletcher was undoubtedly the best educated Englishman to visit Muscovy in the sixteenth century, his cri-

Introduction

tique did indeed contain many of the shortcomings of which he has been accused. He must, first of all, be scored for his use of historical sources. Although he cited a number of them, he used none extensively. Through Martin Kromer's Polish history, he made references to Strabo, Moses, and Josephus and drew almost uncritically from Herberstein for descriptions of Moscow and the countryside.[38] Fletcher used only incidentally those cited authorities Pachymeres, Nicephorus Gregoras, Laonikos Chalcondyles, Bonfinius, and Berossus—all of whom wrote primarily on subjects peripheral to Russian history. The author's reliance on classical and biblical lore and non-Russian sources for early Russian history betrayed his very meager understanding of the Russian past.

Probably most of all Fletcher depended on the unsophisticated but garrulous Jerome Horsey, whom the ambassador brought back a prisoner to England.[39] Horsey himself recorded that of his written materials, "some passages . . . are set down long since by Mr. Hakluyt in his book of voyages, some by Mr. Camden, and most by Doctor Fletcher, more scholastically by reason of some inference out of other histories." Horsey claimed that he had furnished Fletcher with a treatise on "the original nature and disposition of the Rus people, the laws, languages, government, discipline for their church and commonwealth, revenues, commodities, and climate."[40] Defects in Horsey's character prevent blanket acceptance of his word here, for there is no trace of such a document. Unquestionably Horsey's acquaintance with Muscovy was both broader and deeper than Fletcher's and his range of personal contacts more impressive. Seredonin has shown conclusively that Fletcher drew heavily on Horsey, even if he did not merely rewrite the latter's notes. The author possibly gleaned information about the Lapps from An-

---

[38] Martin Kromer was author of *De origine et rebus gestis Polonorum*, ed. Basel (1568).
[39] Bond, *Russia*, pp. 336–337. [40] *Ibid.*, p. 256.

Introduction

thony Marsh, who had visited the northern reaches of the Muscovite empire.

Fletcher must be cited for his bias. Conditioned by Puritanism and Elizabethan patriotism, he permitted, as Seredonin noted, these attributes to color his vision of Muscovy. During these critical years of the 1580's it probably seemed to an Englishman that a Jesuit or Spaniard lurked behind every throne in Europe. Even in Eastern Europe there were signs of papal and Habsburg intrigue. Rumors of a joint crusade against the Turk to be launched by Muscovy, Spain, and the Papacy savored of another Catholic League.[41] The succession question in Poland after Stephen Bathory's sudden death in 1586 left that country, too, vulnerable to Habsburg probing. The anti-Habsburg faction in Poland won when Sigismund Vasa of Sweden accepted the throne; nevertheless, Habsburg interest continued for some time afterward. Doubtless, too, Fletcher's uncomplimentary remarks about Orthodoxy were inspired not only by his Puritanical dislike of its forms but by a deep-seated distrust of its patriarch, who was a visitor in both Rome and Moscow at this time.

In his haste in composing, Fletcher committed errors of fact and judgment. Although carelessness and a tendency to oversimplify cost the author dearly, his greatest handicap—through no fault of his own—was an inability to appraise correctly those aspects of Moscow life which he witnessed. Fletcher, with only

[41] That more than trade concerned Fletcher was evidenced in his account (Bond, *Russia*, pp. 346–347) of the mission. Reporting that he found in Moscow "a league in hand betwixt the Emperor and the King of Spain about an opposition against the Turk," he suspected collusion between the banished Patriarch and the Pope as well. When Fletcher heard from Sir Francis Drake of the debacle of the Armada, he had these and other documents translated into Russian and thus "all this concept of a Spanish League vanished away." In vain did the Imperial ambassador inveigh against England and minimize the Spanish disaster. Fletcher, assuming that Russo-Spanish accord contributed toward his "hard entertainment" at the outset of his mission, also noted this foreign intrigue in Moscow in his book.

Introduction

a shallow knowledge of Russian history, had no way of comprehending the profound changes which had taken place in Muscovy during the century before his arrival and in certain instances were still in process.

Since the late fifteenth century, Moscow had successfully absorbed rival appanage principalities that had existed in Mongol Russia.[42] This success had led to the subordination of such princes as those of Tver, Iaroslavl, Suzdal, and Riazan to the authority of the grand prince of Moscow. These princes, Fletcher observed, composed the highest strata of society in the sixteenth-century Rus commonwealth. Formerly their greatness had rested on the military support which they had received from their boiars, nobles who derived their independence from unrestricted ownership of their land (*votchina*). The fate of the boiars under Muscovite hegemony is discernible in the evolutionary change which beset landholding tenure. Although during the fourteenth and fifteenth centuries the unrestricted *votchina* had been sharply distinguished from land granted in service tenure (*pomeste*) to a noble by a prince, by the sixteenth century the distinction had blurred. Some form of government service became compulsory for all landowners; moreover, these new circumstances deprived the once fiercely independent boiar of his ancient right to choose his prince—save the one of Moscow. Desertion to Lithuania, held to be treason by the Tsar, led to the boiar's forfeiture of those very lands which had hitherto been the source of his independence. As landholders increasingly held their land in *pomeste* tenure, they became identified as a serving nobility. Some, the *deti boiarskie*, or the lesser gentry, as Fletcher noted, even drew salary for their services to the Tsar.

Fletcher had precious little to say about the *oprichnina*, probably because he, like most foreign visitors to Muscovy at this

---

[42] Appanage, or *udelnye*, was a term used to describe these independent or semi-independent principalities or princes during the Mongol period.

Introduction

time, was able to procure little information about it and so knew only in a general way about the persecution connected with it. In the end the *oprichnina* merely hastened what was already taking place—the reduction of the political influence of the landholding boiars and a significant transfer of landownership. Ivan IV's scheme called for the division of his realm into two parts, the *oprichnina* and the *zemshchina*.[43] From the strategically more important *oprichnina* boiar landowners who had resided there were ruthlessly expelled and thereby experienced a loss of political influence or worse. Although the old landholders most often suffered in this scheme, there were unpredictable developments: some of the most ardent *oprichniki* were of the great princely families; moreover, *oprichniki* were notable among Ivan's victims.

Even though "new men"—serving nobles, clerks, or secretaries (*diaki*)—came to play an increasingly prominent role in political affairs, Ivan did not completely divest himself of the services of the old nobility. The boiar *duma*, or council, had not become, as Fletcher asserted, completely *pro forma*. The great pre-Revolutionary historian Kliuchevskii put it better when he stated that

> although the tsar conceived schemes of carrying out a wholesale extermination of the boiar class (which constituted his right hand in the administration), he never removed that class from participation in the working of the State, for the reason that it represented a body with which he could not afford to dispense. Meanwhile the class in question suffered and petitioned, though its pusillanimous ideas never seem to have strayed beyond schemes of flight to Lithuania; while, for his part, the tsar grew ever more callous in his shedding of non-boiar blood, and his flock of *oprichniki* . . . kept settling in ever-increasing numbers over the land. . . . Yet of open

[43] The *oprichnina* was the special royal domain created by Ivan IV and exclusive of the jurisdiction of the general administration. The *zemshchina* was that part of the realm, excepting the *oprichnina*, under the general administration.

Introduction

protest never a spark appeared. . . . It was as though one party in the feud had lost all feeling of fear and sense of responsibility for the over-exercise of its powers, while the other party—the million-headed people—forgot the measure of its pain. . . . Yet over the community, and over the petty concerns and calculation of the two contending social forces, there seems always to have hovered some supreme interest—an interest which periodically compelled those forces, willy-nilly, to act in harmony. That supreme interest was the defense of the Empire against external foes.[44]

    The boiars' contest with the Tsar was but the most important of that group's political problems during the sixteenth century. Every appanage prince had had boiar followers; subservience of these princes to Moscow had led, of course, to their boiars' doing the same. It meant that the old Moscow boiars, whose political independence had already been sapped by their own prince, now had to safeguard their ancient status and privileges against these interloper boiars and their princes from outside. There thus ensued a strenuous competition for status and influence manifested in an incredible order of precedence (*mestnichestvo*), mentioned but not well understood by Fletcher. Although the Tsar departed from it in official appointments as early as the mid-sixteenth century, the *mestnichestvo* endured and contributed to the sluggishness of Moscow political life for another century and a half.

    Fletcher obviously did not have the perspective to evaluate the evolution of serfdom, which made dramatic progress between 1550 and 1650, but he did perceive the increasing deprivations of the common folk in Muscovy. The peasant, like the boiar above him, had once been free to serve whom he pleased. By the sixteenth century, peasants no longer easily exercised this old right; their mobility was greatly restricted, to the advantage of the autocracy. The accrual of absolute power to the Tsar of Muscovy was quite in keeping with the character of the cen-

[44] *A History of Russia*, II (New York, 1960), 318–319.

Introduction

tralized bureaucratic state of the Renaissance, but the Muscovite autocracy differed significantly from the New Monarchy in the West. Long under the domination of the Tartars, the princes of Moscow inherited methods alien to Western sovereigns. The Tsar's sop to his serving nobility was serfdom, and it became more deeply entrenched as the autocracy consolidated its authority.

Fletcher's critique of the administrative apparatus of Moscow was extensive but again demonstrated his lack of perspective, and it contained numerous errors. Although the tradition persisted in Moscow that the state was but the private domain of the prince, in reality the sixteenth-century polity had grown too large and complex to be governed in such an archaic manner. Just as a new military organization had risen on the wreckage of the old land tenure, so a new bureaucracy evolved from the old household offices of the prince. These *prikazy,* proto-ministries, which Fletcher noted in great detail, numbered about thirty by 1600. They included the *Bolshoi Prikhod* (revenue), *Posolskii Prikaz* (foreign affairs), and others mentioned in the text. The Tsar continued to retain the counsel of the boiar *duma,* whose members generally followed the *mestnichestvo.* An overhaul of local government officially took place about the middle of the century. Despotic governors (*kormlentshiki*), whose income derived from their exploitation of the populace, were supposedly replaced by elected elders (*gubnye starosty*) responsible directly to the central government. This reform did not prevent the persistence of many evils in local administration. Fletcher's discourses on finance and military organization were once considered the most important sections of the book; however, his errors nullify to a large extent his perception and detailed analysis of these facets of the Moscow administration.

Fletcher's Moscow was as energetic from without as from within. The ambassador sensed the tension and anxiety caused in Russia by Crimean Tartar raids from the South. The Tartar's

Introduction

quest for booty and especially prisoners for the Near Eastern slave markets, compounded by the terror and destruction of their raids, proved Moscow's greatest external problem of the period. Fletcher also perceived Ivan's unsuccessful bid for a foothold on the Baltic and Moscow's push to the East after the conquest of Kazan and Astrakhan about mid-century. It was within the decade prior to Fletcher's arrival that the conquest of Siberia was initiated.

Like most foreign commentators, Fletcher depicted Muscovites as debased, given to violence and drunkenness. Arriving in Moscow in the aftermath of Ivan's *oprichnina*, he could only foresee civil strife igniting from the smoldering hatreds which had been created. Although Fletcher was given to generalizing from fragmentary experiences, in this instance he correctly ascertained the hatred that existed between Ivan IV and his boiars, the suspicion which centered on Boris Godunov, the impending fate of young Dimitrii, and the general instability of Moscow on the eve of the Time of Troubles. Seredonin's suggestion that foreigners contributed to Moscow's social failure and that "Russian vices were of the body but not of the soul" does not convincingly refute some of the assertions made by Fletcher.

As a civil lawyer Fletcher was understandably contemptuous of a society whose procedures for litigation were so primitive as Russia's. Curiously, his comments on punishment for crime fell far short of the precision of other foreign observers. Like so many visitors to Muscovy, Fletcher expounded on topography, climate, resources, cities, and provinces; but only rarely did he add significantly to the observations of others. Errors and superficiality featured this part of his commentary. His remarks on soil were particularly thin compared with those of Herberstein. His interest in natural resources, which closely related to his general concern for commerce between Muscovy and England, added nothing new. Only in touching upon minerals did Fletcher make a unique contribution. His concern for Muscovy's colonies and

Introduction

the Tartars, though valuable, contained errors. He also displayed a notable failing in his notions of the political geography of Muscovy, for many of the provincial names mentioned were part of the royal title but had little relevance beyond that.

This ambassador unquestionably excelled when he portrayed various aspects of Russian daily life. His descriptions of the coronation and a day in the life of the Tsar and his detailed listing of Russian apparel remain classics.

An evaluation of Fletcher must rest on three criteria: the validity of his work as a guide to the understanding of Russian history, the degree to which it molded contemporary and subsequent opinion about Muscovy, and the manner in which it mirrored the Tudor mind. On the first point Seredonin's critique cannot be ignored. His depiction of Fletcher—careless, mercenary, prejudiced, and blinded by erroneous preconceptions—has effaced Fletcher's image as a careful scholar, despite some perceptive observations and the truly valuable bits of information which he imparted.

Seredonin's indictment, however, is not the final word. Fletcher's treatise displays a genius for combining personal observation, strong bias, gossip, and moralizing with data casually lifted from varied written sources. So vividly did Fletcher flash before his Elizabethan audience an image of Muscovy that it was immediately accepted and remained for more than a century the best book in English on Russia.[45]

Finally, Fletcher's catering to the taste and mood of Elizabethan England resulted in a book which reflected the senti-

[45] Berry, *The English Works of Giles Fletcher, the Elder*, pp. 149–150, notes Fletcher's influence on Dekker, Webster, Raleigh, Beaumont, John and Phineas Fletcher, Jonson, Milton, Sidney, and possibly others. R. R. Cawley, *The Voyagers and Elizabethan Drama* (Boston, 1938), has noted (p. 253) that Fletcher's work was the principal model for those interested in Muscovy. Ruffmann, *Russlandbild*, is important for the impact of Muscovy on English culture. Willan, *Russia Company*, pp. 282–284, touches briefly on this theme. See also Leslie Hotson, *The First Night of "Twelfth Night"* (New York, 1954), pp. 185–195.

Introduction

ments of the age. For the student of English history this work is a splendid commentary on the Tudor mind, with its insatiable curiosity for the exotic and foreign, especially when by contrast the exotic and foreign heightened the Englishman's pride in his own country's achievement. Xenophobic Elizabethans, keyed to a high emotional pitch by the political and religious tensions of their age, delighted in the kind of invective and raw humor used by Fletcher when he enumerated Moscow's shortcomings. The treatise had a favorable response because it gave its readers precisely what they wanted; that is, a view of Russia that, for all its bizarre features, reinforced more than it called into question the narrow Tudor preconceptions of the semibarbaric East.

In short, Fletcher's *Of the Rus Commonwealth,* with all its faults, is significant. It is intended that the present volume, edited with both the Russian and English viewpoint in mind, will result in a reasonably balanced appraisal—a formidable task considering the treatise's stormy history!

OF THE RUS COMMONWEALTH

By Giles Fletcher

THE EPISTLE DEDICATORY

To the Queen's Most Excellent Majesty

MOST gracious sovereign, being employed in your Majesty's service to the Emperor of Russia, I observed the state and manners of that country. And having reduced the same into some order by the way as I returned, I have presumed to offer it in this small book to your Most Excellent Majesty. My meaning was to note things for mine own experience, of more importance than delight and rather true than strange. In their manner of government your Highness may see both a true and strange face of a tyrannical state (most unlike to your own) without true knowledge of God, without written law, without common justice save that which proceedeth from their speaking law—to wit, the magistrate, who hath most need of a law to restrain his own injustice. The practice hereof, as it is heavy and grievous to the poor oppressed people that live within those countries, so it may give just cause to myself and other your Majesty's faithful subjects to acknowledge our happiness on this behalf and to give God thanks for your Majesty's most prince-like and gracious government; as also to your Highness more joy and contentment in your royal estate, in that you are a prince of subjects, not of slaves, that are kept within duty by love, not by fear. The Almighty still bless your Highness with a most long and happy reign in this life and with Christ Jesus in the life to come.

Your Majesty's most humble
subject and servant,
G. FLETCHER

CHAPTER I

The Description of the Country of Russia, with the Breadth, Length, and Names of the Shires

THE country of Russia was sometimes called Sarmatia. It changed the name (as some do suppose) for that it was parted into divers small and yet absolute governments, not depending nor being subject the one to the other. For Rus in that tongue doth signify as much as to part or divide. The Rus reporteth that four brethren—Truvor, Rurik, Sineus, and Varivus—divided among them the north parts of the country.[1] Likewise that the south parts were possessed by four other—Kiy, Shchok, Khoriv, and their sister Lybed—each calling his territory after his own name.[2] Of this partition it was called Russia about the year from Christ 860. As for the conjecture which I find in some cosmographers that the Rus nation borrowed the name of the

---

[1] According to *The Primary Chronicle,* Rurik came with two brothers, Sineus and Truvor, to Russia. See ed. S. H. Cross and O. P. Sherbowitz-Wetzor (Cambridge, Mass., 1953), pp. 59–60. These brothers' names do not appear in Western accounts and may be merely epithets for Rurik. In Norse *Signjotr* and *Thruwar* mean "victorious" and "trustworthy" respectively. Cf. George Vernadsky, *Ancient Russia* (New Haven, 1943), pp. 339–340.

[2] These three brothers and the sister traditionally receive credit for the founding of Kiev, which took its name from the eldest brother, Kiy. See Cross, *Primary Chronicle,* pp. 54–55, and Vernadsky, *Ancient Russia,* pp. 332–333.

people called Roxellani and were the very same nation with them, it is without all good probability, both in respect of the etymology of the word (which is very far fet), and especially for the seat and dwelling of that people, which was betwixt the two rivers of Tanais and Boristhenes, as Strabo reporteth, quite another way from the country of Russia.[3]

When it bare the name of Sarmatia, it was divided into two chief parts, the White and the Black. The White Sarmatia was all that part that lieth toward the north and on the side of Liefland; [4] as the provinces now called Dvina, Vaga, Ustiug, Vologda, Kargopol, Novgorod, etc.; whereof Novgorod Velikii was the metropolite or chief city. Black Sarmatia was all that country that lieth southward toward the Euxine, or Black Sea, as the dukedom of Vladimir, of Moscow, Riazan, etc. Some have thought that the name of Sarmatia was first taken from one Sarmates, whom Moses and Josephus call Asarmathes, son to Joctan and nephew to Heber, of the posterity of Shem (Gen. 10; Joseph. *lib.* 1, *cap.* 14). But this seemeth to be nothing but a conjecture taken out of the likeness of the name Asarmathes. For the dwelling of all Joctan's posterity is described by Moses to have been betwixt Mash, or Masius, an hill of the Ammonites, and Sephar, near to the river Euphrates. Which maketh it very unlikely that Asarmathes should plant any colonies so far off in the north and northwest countries. It is bounded northward by the Lapps and the North Ocean, on the south side by the Tartars called Crims.[5] Eastward they have the Nogai Tartar, that possesseth all the country on the east side of Volga toward the Caspian Sea. On the west and southwest border lie Lithuania, Livonia, and Polonia.

The whole country, being now reduced under the government

[3] Tanais and Boristhenes refer to the Don and Dnieper rivers respectively. In the margin Fletcher cites Strabo "in his 7. Booke of Geog." Strabo's reference actually appears in bk. 3 of his *Geography*.
[4] Livonia, or a part of what is today the Latvian S.S.R.
[5] Crims, or Crimean Tartars.

Names of the Shires

of one, containeth these chief provinces or shires: Vladimir (which beareth the first place in the emperor's style, because their house came of the dukes of that country), Moscow, Nizhnii Novgorod, Pskov, Smolensk, Novgorod Velikii (or Novgorod of the low country), Rostov, Iaroslavl, Beloozero, Bezan, Dvina, Kargopol, Meshchera, Vaga, Ustiug, Galich.[6] These are the natural shires pertaining to Russia but far greater and larger than the shires of England, though not so well peopled. The other countries or provinces which the Rus emperors have gotten perforce added of late to their other dominion are these which follow: Tver, Iugorsk, Perm, Viatka, Bulgaria, Chernigov, Udorsk, Obdorsk, Kondiinsk, with a great part of Siberia, where the people though they be not natural Rus yet obey the Emperor of Russia and are ruled by the laws of his country, paying customs and taxes as his own people do.[7] Besides these, he hath under him the kingdoms of Kazan and Astrakhan, gotten by conquest not long since.[8] As for all his possession in Lithuania—to the number of thirty great towns and more—with Narva and Dorpat in Livonia, they are quite gone, being sur-

[6] Fletcher wrote Pskov variously as Plesko and Vobsko. He confused Novgorod the Great (Velikii) with Nizhnii (Lower) Novgorod and by Bezan meant Riazan. Fletcher probably relied on Jenkinson's map of Muscovy published by Ortelius.

[7] Iugorsk (Iugoriia, Iugra), Udorsk (Udoriia), Obdorsk (Obdoriia), and Kondiinsk (Kondoriia) were names of regions lying in the northern reaches of Russia. Since their relevance for political geography was limited, Fletcher presumably lifted them from the royal title. Cf. below, p. 29. The locations given these provinces on the map in this volume are derived mainly from "Karta Rossii, 1613" in A. V. Efimov, ed., *Atlas Geograficheskikh Otkrytii v Sibiri i v Severo-Zapadnoi Amerike*, XVII–XVIII vv. (Moscow, 1964), nos. 26 and 27, and from R. H. Fisher, *The Russian Fur Trade, 1550–1700* (Berkeley, Calif., 1943). Fisher locates Iugra as "embracing the territory along both sides of the northern Urals, extending eastward to the Ob River" (p. 6). Obdoriia was "the territory between the lower Ob River and the Urals" (p. 19), and Kondoriia was "the region of the middle Ob" (p. 19). Bulgaria signified the land of the Volga Bulgars.

[8] Muscovy annexed Kazan in 1552 and Astrakhan approximately four years later.

Of the Rus Commonwealth

prised of late years by the kings of Poland and Sweden. These shires and provinces are reduced all into four jurisdictions, which they call *chetverti*, that is, tetrarchies or fourth parts.[9] Whereof we are to speak in the title or chapter concerning the provinces and their manner of government.

The whole country is of great length and breadth. From the north to the south (if you measure from Kola to Astrakhan, which bendeth somewhat eastward) it reacheth in length about 4,260 versts or miles.[10] Notwithstanding, the Emperor of Russia hath more territory northward, far beyond Kola unto the river of Tromschua,[11] that runneth 1,000 versts wellnigh beyond Pechenga, near to Wardhouse [Vardguz], but not entire nor clearly limited by reason of the kings of Sweden and Denmark, that have divers towns there as well as the Rus, plotted together the one with the other: every one of them claiming the whole of those north parts as his own right. The breadth (if you go from that part of his territory that lieth farthest westward on the Narva side to the parts of Siberia eastward, where the Emperor hath his garrisons) is 4,400 versts or thereabouts. A verst by their reckoning is 1,000 paces yet less by one quarter than an English mile. If the whole dominion of the Rus emperor were all

---

[9] Fletcher's use of the word *Chetvert* is most perplexing. He was probably right in observing that Muscovy was divided into four jurisdictions (administered by *diaki*, or secretaries), but he erred when he assumed that he witnessed a rigidly established order. These *Chetverti* varied in number from time to time. Seredonin believed that either three or four existed while Fletcher was there. Fletcher's confusion also stemmed from the fact that *chetvert* does mean literally "fourth." The relationship of these jurisdictions to the ministries, or *prikazy*, is discussed below on p. 43 and the *Chetvert* as an office of receipt for taxes on p. 52. To compound confusion, the *chetvert* was also a measure for grain. Cf. below, p. 11. Seredonin, *Sochinenie*, pp. 245–270, discusses the *Chetvert* in considerable detail.

[10] Verst or *versta*. A measure of length equal to .66 miles or 1.067 kilometers. The distance between Kola and Astrakhan is about 2,300 rather than 4,260 versts.

[11] Fletcher's intent is not clear. Even the Russian version of this book failed to provide a Russian equivalent.

Of the Soil and Climate

habitable and peopled in all places as it is in some, he would either hardly hold it all within one regiment or be overmighty for all his neighbor princes.

CHAPTER II

Of the Soil and Climate

THE soil of the country for the most part is of a slight sandy mold, yet very much different one place from another for the yield of such things as grow out of the earth. The country northward toward the parts of St. Nicholas and Kola and northeast toward Siberia is all very barren and full of desert woods, by reason of the climate and extremity of the cold in wintertime. So likewise along the river Volga, betwixt the countries of Kazan and Astrakhan, where (notwithstanding the soil is very fruitful) it is all unhabited saving that upon the river Volga on the west side the Emperor hath some few castles with garrisons in them. This happeneth by means of the Crim Tartar, that will neither himself plant towns to dwell there (living a wild and vagrant life) nor suffer the Rus (that is far off with the strength of his country) to people those parts. From Vologda, which lieth almost 1,700 versts from the port of St. Nicholas, down toward Moscow and so toward the south part that bordereth upon the Crim, which containeth the like space of 1,700 versts or thereabouts,[1] is a very fruitful and pleasant country, yielding pasture and corn, with woods and waters in very great plenty. The like is betwixt Riazan, that lieth southeast from Moscow, to Novgorod and Pskov, that reach farthest toward the northwest. So betwixt Moscow and Smolensk, that lieth southwest toward Lithuania, is a very fruitful and pleasant soil.

The whole country differeth very much from itself by reason

[1] This figure of 1,700 versts is a gross exaggeration.

Of the Rus Commonwealth

of the year, so that a man would marvel to see the great alteration and difference betwixt the winter and summer Russia. The whole country in the winter lieth under snow, which falleth continually and is sometime of a yard or two thick, but greater toward the North. The rivers and other waters are all frozen up a yard or more thick, how swift or broad soever they be; and this continueth commonly five months, viz., from the beginning of November till toward the end of March, what time the snow beginneth to melt. So that it would breed a frost in a man to look abroad at that time and see the winter face of that country. The sharpness of the air you may judge of by this, for that water dropped down or cast up into the air congealeth into ice before it come to the ground. In the extremity of winter, if you hold a pewter dish or pot in your hand, or any other metal—except in some chamber where their warm stoves be—your fingers will freeze fast unto it and draw off the skin at the parting. When you pass out of a warm room into a cold, you shall sensibly feel your breath to wax stark and even stifling with the cold as you draw it in and out. Divers, not only that travel abroad but in the very markets and streets of their towns, are mortally pinched and killed withal, so that you shall see many drop down in the streets, many travelers brought into the town sitting dead and stiff in their sleds. Divers lose their noses, the tips of their ears, and the balls of their cheeks, their toes, feet, etc. Many times, when the winter is very hard and extreme, the bears and wolves issue by troops out of the woods, driven by hunger, and enter the villages, tearing and ravening all they can find, so that the inhabitants are fain to fly for safeguard of their lives.[2] And yet in the summertime you shall see such a new hue and face of a country, the woods—for the most part which are all of fir and birch—so fresh and so sweet, the pastures and meadows so

---

[2] This passage closely follows Herberstein. Cf. R. H. Major, ed., *Sigismund von Herberstein's Notes upon Russia*, Hakluyt Society, nos. XI and XII (New York, n.d.), II, 2–3.

Of the Soil and Climate

green and well grown—and that upon the sudden—such variety of flowers, such noise of birds—especially of nightingales, that seem to be more loud and of a more variable note than in other countries—that a man shall not lightly [3] travel in a more pleasant country.

And this fresh and speedy growth of the spring there seemeth to proceed from the benefit of the snow, which, all the wintertime being spread over the whole country as a white robe and keeping it warm from the rigor of the frost, in the springtime, when the sun waxeth warm and dissolveth it into water, doth so thoroughly drench and soak the ground, that is somewhat of a slight and sandy mold, and then shineth so hotly upon it again, that it draweth the herbs and plants forth in great plenty and variety in a very short time. As the winter exceedeth in cold, so the summer inclineth to overmuch heat—especially in the months of June, July, and August, being much warmer than the summer air in England.

The country throughout is very well watered with springs, rivers, and *ozera* or lakes. Wherein the providence of God is to be noted: for that, much of the country being so far inland as that some part lieth 1,000 miles and more every way from any sea, yet it is served with fair rivers, and that in very great number, that, emptying themselves one into another, run all into the sea. Their lakes are many and large, some of 60, 80, 100, and 200 miles long, with breadth proportionate.

The chief rivers are these: 1) Volga, that hath his head or spring at the root of an alder tree about 200 versts above Iaroslavl and groweth so big by the increase of other rivers by that time it cometh thither that it is broad an English mile and more and so runneth into the Caspian Sea about 2,800 versts or miles of length.

The next is Boristhenes (now called Dnieper), that divideth the country from Lithuania and falleth into the Euxine Sea.

[3] Ordinarily; often.

Of the Rus Commonwealth

The third, Tanais or Don (the ancient border betwixt Europe and Asia), that taketh his head out of Riazan Ozero and so, running through the country of the Crim Tartar, falleth into the great sea lake or mere called Maeotis, by the city of Azov. By this river (as the Rus reporteth) you may pass from their city Moscow to Constantinople and so into all those parts of the world by water, drawing your boat, as their manner is, over a little isthmus or narrow slip of land a few versts overthwart. Which was proved not long since by an ambassador sent to Constantinople, who passed the river of Moskva and so into another called Oka, whence he drew his boat over into Tanais and thence passed the whole way by water.

The fourth is called Dvina, many hundred miles long, that falleth northward into the Bay of St. Nicholas and hath great alabaster rocks on the banks toward the seaside.

The fifth, Dvina, that emptieth into the Baltic Sea by the town Riga.

The sixth, Onega, that falleth into the bay at Solovetskii, 90 versts from the port of St. Nicholas. This river, below the town Kargopol, meeteth with the river Volok, that falleth into the Finland Sea by the town Iam. So that from the port of St. Nicholas into the Finland Sea and so into the sound you may pass all by water, as hath been tried by the Rus.[4]

The seventh, Sukhona, that floweth into Dvina and so into the North Sea.

The eighth, Oka, that fetcheth his head from the borders of the Crim and streameth into Volga.

The ninth, Moskva, that runneth through the city Moscow and giveth it the name.

[4] Fletcher erred when he construed the Russian word for "portage" (*volok*) to be the name for the river. That Fletcher, a specialist on commercial matters in the North, was unaware of the failure to procure a water road from St. Nicholas to the Finland gulf is curious. Fletcher also erred when he said that the Don rose out of Riazan Ozero instead of Ivan Ozero. Solovki is the proper designation for the islands on one of which is located the Solovetskii monastery. Solovetskii may also refer to the bay (*zaliv*). North Sea is a reference to White Sea.

The Native Commodities

There is Vychegda also, a very large and long river, that riseth out of Perm and falleth into Volga.[5] All these are rivers of very large streams, the least to be compared to the Thames in bigness and in length far more, besides divers other. The pole at Moscow is 55 degrees 10 minutes. At the port of St. Nicholas toward the North, 63 degrees and 50 minutes.[6]

CHAPTER III

The Native Commodities of the Country

FOR kinds of fruits they have apples, pears, plums, cherries red and black—but the black wild—a *dynia* like a muskmelon but more sweet and pleasant, cucumbers and gourds, which they call *arbuz,* rasps, strawberries, and hurtleberries, with many other berries in great quantity in every wood and hedge. Their kinds of grain are wheat, rye, barley, oats, peas, buckway, psnytha, that in taste is somewhat like to rice.[1] Of all these grains the country yieldeth very sufficient, with an overplus quantity, so that wheat is sold sometime for two *altyny*[2] or tenpence sterling the *chetvert,*[3] which maketh almost three English bushels.

Their rye is sowed before the winter; all their other grain in the springtime, and for the most part in May. The Permians and

---

[5] Fletcher here mistook the Vychegda for the Kama, a tributary of the Volga.

[6] The exact latitude of Moscow is 55° 45′ 45″; that of St. Nicholas, 64° 31′.

[1] *Arbuz* means literally "watermelon" in Russian. The "hurtleberry" is simply the whortleberry; "buckway" refers to buckwheat. "Psnytha" may be a garbled version of Russian *proso,* or millet.

[2] An old monetary unit equal to six *dengi,* or three kopecks. Wheat may have been more expensive than indicated by Fletcher. Cf. Seredonin, *Sochinenie,* pp. 118–120.

[3] This use of *chetvert* by Fletcher should be distinguished from his previous usage as a jurisdiction within the realm or a ministry.

Of the Rus Commonwealth

some other that dwell far north and in desert places are served from the parts that lie more southward and are forced to make bread sometimes of a kind of root called *vaghnoy* [4] and of the middle rind of the fir tree. If there be any dearth (as they accounted this last year, anno 1588, wheat and rye being at thirteen *altyny* or five shillings fivepence sterling the *chetvert*), the fault is rather in the practice of their nobility, that use to engross it, than in the country itself.

The native commodities of the country, wherewith they serve both their own turns and send much abroad, to the great enriching of the Emperor and his people, are many and substantial. First, furs of all sorts—wherein the providence of God is to be noted—that provideth a natural remedy for them to help the natural inconvenience of their country by the cold of the climate. Their chief furs are these: black fox; sables; lucerns; dun fox; martens; *gornostai,* or ermines; lassets, or miniver; beaver; wolverines; the skin of a great water rat that smelleth naturally like musk; calaber, or gray squirrel; red squirrel; red and white fox.[5] Besides the great quantity spent within the country—the people being clad all in furs the whole winter—there are transported out of the country some years by the merchants of Turkey, Persia, Bukhara, Georgia, Armenia, and some other of Christendom to the value of four or five hundred thousand rubles, as I have heard of the merchants. The best sable fur groweth in the country of Pechora, Mangazeia,[6] and Obdorsk; the worser sort in Siberia, Perm, and other places. The black fox and red come out of Siberia; white and dun from Pechora, whence also come the white wolf and white bearskin. The best wolverine also thence and from Perm. The best martens are from Siberia, Kadom, Murom, Perm, and Kazan. Lucerns,

---

[4] The correct Russian for *vaghnoy* is not evident.
[5] A lucern is a lynx; a dun fox, one of a dull or dingy brown color; and the calaber may be a reference to the Siberian gray squirrel.
[6] Apparently in or around Iugorsk.

The Native Commodities

miniver, and ermine—the best are out of Galich and Uglich, many from Novgorod and Perm. The beaver of the best sort breedeth in Murmansk by Kola. Other common furs and most of these kinds grow in many and some in all parts of the country.

The second commodity is of wax, whereof hath been shipped into foreign countries (as I have heard it reported by those that best know it) the sum of 50,000 *pudy* yearly, every *pud* containing forty pounds, but now about 10,000 *pudy* a year.[7]

The third is their honey, whereof, besides an exceeding great quantity spent in their ordinary drinks (which is mead of all sorts) and their other uses, some good quantity is carried out of the country. The chief increase of honey is in Mordva and Kadom near to the Cheremisian Tartar, much out of Seversk, Riazan, Murom, Kazan, Dorogobuzh, and Viazma.

Fourthly, of tallow they afford a great weight for transportation, not only for that their country hath very much good ground apt for pasturage of cattle, but also by reason of their many Lents and other fasts, and partly because their greater men use much wax for their lights—the poorer and meaner sort, birch dried in their stoves and cut into long shivers which they call *luchiny*. Of tallow there hath been shipped out of the realm a few years since about 100,000 *pudy* yearly, now not past 30,000 or thereabouts. The best yield of tallow is in the parts and territories of Smolensk, Iaroslavl, Uglich, Novgorod, and Vologda, Tver, and Gorodets.

Another principal commodity is their *los*[8] and cowhide. Their *los* or buff hide is very fair and large. Their bull and cowhide (for oxen they make none, neither yet wether) is of a small size. There hath been transported by merchants strangers some years 100,000 hides; now it is decreased to 30,000 or thereabouts[9]—

---

[7] A *pud* equals thirty-six pounds in weight.   [8] An elk.

[9] Fletcher obviously compared exports before the Livonian wars with those at the time of his embassy. Although he spoke authoritatively about the sea trade, he apparently knew little of Muscovy's overland trade.

Of the Rus Commonwealth

besides great store of goatskins, whereof great numbers are shipped out of the country. The largest kind of *los* or buff breedeth about Rostov, Vychegda, Novgorod, Murom, and Perm; the lesser sort, within the kingdom of Kazan.

Another very great and principal commodity is their train oil,[10] drawn out of the seal fish. Where it will not be impertinent to show the manner of their hunting the seal which they make this oil of, which is in this sort. Toward the end of summer, before the frost begins, they go down with their boats into the Bay of St. Nicholas to a cape called Kukonos or Foxnose, where they leave their boats till the next spring tide.[11] When the sun waxeth warm toward the spring and yet the ice not melted within the bay, they return thither again. Then, drawing their boats over the sea ice, they use them for houses to rest and lodge in. There are commonly about seventeen or eighteen fleet of them of great large boats, which divide themselves into divers companies, five or six boats in a consort.

They that first find the haunt fire a beacon, which they carry with them for the nonce.[12] Which being espied by the other companies, by such among them as are appointed of purpose, they come all together and compass the seals round about in a ring, that lie sunning themselves together upon the ice, commonly four or five thousand in a shoal, and so they invade them, every man with his club in his hand. If they hit them on the nose, they are soon killed. If on the sides or back, they bear out the blow and many times so catch and hold down the club with their teeth by main force that the party is forced to call for help to his fellows.

The manner of the seals is, when they see themselves beset, to gather all close together in a throng or plump [13] to sway down

---

[10] Seal oil or blubber.
[11] Kukonos (Cusconess) and Foxnose were not one and the same; the former was a promontory a short distance to the south.
[12] For that particular purpose; for the occasion.
[13] Of animals that go in flocks.

The Native Commodities

the ice and to break it (if they can), which so bendeth the ice that many times it taketh the sea water upon it and maketh the hunters to wade a foot or more deep. After the slaughter, when they have killed what they can, they fall to sharing, every boat his part in equal portions; and so they flay them, taking from the body the skin and the lard or fat withal that cleaveth to the skin. This they take with them, leaving the bodies behind, and so go to shore, where they dig pits in the ground of a fathom and an half deep or thereabouts. And so, taking the fat or lard off from the skin, they throw it into the pit and cast in among it hot burning stones to melt it withal. The uppermost and purest is sold and used to oil wool for cloth; the grosser, that is of a red color, they sell to make soap.

Likewise of *ikra*, or caviar, a great quantity is made upon the river of Volga out of the fish called *beluga*, the sturgeon, the *sevriuga*, and the *sterliad*.[14] Whereof the most part is shipped by French and Netherlandish merchants for Italy and Spain; some, by English merchants.

The next is of flax and hemp, whereof there hath been shipped (as I have heard merchants say) at the port of Narva a great part of 100 ships, small and great, yearly; now, not past five.[15] The reason of this abating and decrease of this and other commodities that were wont to be transported in a greater quantity is the shutting up of the port of the Narva toward the Finland Sea, which now is in the hands and possession of the Sweden. Likewise the stopping of the passage overland by the way of Smolensk and Polotsk by reason of their wars with the Polonian, which causeth the people to be less provident in maintaining and gathering these and like commodities, for that

[14] *Ikra* means caviar in Russian. *Beluga* is literally a white sturgeon. *Sevriuga* is another kind of sturgeon. The *sterliad*, or sterlet, a small sturgeon, provides the finest caviar.

[15] Cf. note 9. Narva was in Russian hands from 1558 to 1581; therefore, English merchants had access to the Russian market via the Baltic as well as the White Sea for more than twenty years.

Of the Rus Commonwealth

they lack sales. Partly also for that the merchants and *muzhiki*, for so they call the common sort of people, are very much discouraged by many heavy and intolerable exactions that of late time have been imposed upon them, no man accounting that which he hath to be sure his own, and therefore regard not to lay up anything or to have it beforehand, for that it causeth them many times to be fleeced and spoiled not only of their goods but also of their lives. For the growth of flax, the province of Pskov and the country about is the chief and only place; for hemp, Smolensk, Dorogobuzh, and Viazma.[16]

The country besides maketh great store of salt. Their best salt is made at Staraia Rusa in very great quantity, where they have great store of salt wells about 250 versts from the sea. At Astrakhan salt is made naturally by the sea water, that casteth it up into great hills, and so it is digged down and carried away by the merchants and other that will fetch it from thence. They pay to the Emperor for acknowledgment or custom 3*d*. Rus upon every hundredweight. Besides these two, they make salt in many other places of the realm, as in Perm, Vychegda, Totma, Kineshma, Solovetskii, Una, Umba, and Nenoksa—all out of salt pits save at Solovetskii, which lieth near to the sea.[17]

Likewise of tar they make a great quantity out of their fir trees in the country of Dvina and Smolensk, whereof much is sent abroad. Besides these, which are all good and substantial commodities, they have divers other of smaller account that are natural and proper to that country: as the fish tooth, which they call *rybii zub*,[18] which is used both among themselves and the

[16] Other foreign accounts state that flax was grown in Novgorod, Vologda, and Iaroslavl too.

[17] Fletcher recorded the last three as "Ocona, Bombasey, and Nonocks." They are rivers as well as towns. The Stroganovs owned the saltworks in Perm and along the Vychegda, but Fletcher erred when he asserted that the latter was a source for rock salt. Cf. Seredonin, *Sochinenie*, p. 126. Here Solovetskii apparently refers to the monastery.

[18] By *rybii zub* Fletcher meant walrus tusk. He undoubtedly heard this expression, which was used in the North.

The Native Commodities

Persians and Bukharians, that fetched it from thence for beads, knives, and sword hafts of noblemen and gentlemen, and for divers other uses. Some use the powder of it against poison, as the unicorn's horn. The fish that weareth it is called a *morzh* and is caught about Pechora. These fish teeth, some of them, are almost two foot of length and weigh eleven or twelve pound apiece.

In the province of Karelia [Korela] and about the river Dvina toward the North Sea there groweth a soft rock which they call *sliuda*.[19] This they cut into pieces and so tear it into thin flakes, which naturally it is apt for, and so use it for glass lanthorns [20] and suchlike. It giveth both inwards and outwards a clearer light than glass and for this respect is better than either glass or horn, for that it neither breaketh like glass nor yet will burn like the lanthorn. Saltpeter they make in many places, as at Uglich, Iaroslavl, and Ustiug, and some small store of brimstone upon the river Volga, but want skill to refine it.

Their iron is somewhat brittle, but a great weight of it is made in Karelia, Kargopol, and Ustiug Zhelezna. Other mine they have none growing within the realm.

Their beasts of strange kinds are the *los*, the *olen*,[21] the wild horse, the bear, the wolverine or wood dog, the lucern, the beaver, the sable, the marten, the black and dun fox, the white bear, toward the seacoast of Pechora the *gornostai*, the lasset or miniver. They have a kind of squirrel that hath growing on the pinion of the shoulderbone a long tuft of hair much like unto feathers, with a far broader tail than have any other squirrels, which they move and shake as they leap from tree to tree much like unto a wing. They skise [22] a large space and seem for to fly withal, and therefore they call them *letuchie vekshy*, that is, the

---

[19] Russian mica in thin transparent plates. [20] Lanterns.
[21] Deer.
[22] The derivation of this word was discussed by Bond, *Russia*, p. 14: the word is found in Halliwell's *Dictionary of Archaic and Provincial Words* as in use in the Isle of Wight.

flying squirrels. Their hares and squirrels in summer are of the same color with ours; in winter the hare changeth her coat into milk white, the squirrel into gray, whereof cometh the calaber.

They have fallow deer, the roebuck, and goats very great store. Their horses are but small but very swift and hard; they travel them unshod both winter and summer without all regard of pace. Their sheep are but small and bear coarse and harsh wool. Of fowl they have divers of the principal kinds: first, great store of hawks, the eagle, the gerfalcon, the slightfalcon, the goshawk, the tassel, the sparhawk, etc.;[23] but the principal hawk that breedeth in the country is counted the gerfalcon.

Of other fowls, their principal kinds are the swan, tame and wild—whereof they have great store—the stork, the crane, the tedder[24]—the color of a pheasant but far bigger and liveth in the fir woods. Of pheasant and partridge they have very great plenty. An owl there is of a very great bigness—more ugly to behold than the owls of this country—with a broad face and ears much like unto a man.

For fresh water fish besides the common sorts, as carp, pikes, perch, tench, roach,[25] etc., they have divers kinds very good and delicate, as the *beluga*, or *beluzhina*, of four or five ells long, the *osetrina*, or sturgeon, the *sevriuga* and *sterliad*, somewhat in fashion and taste like to the sturgeon but not so thick nor long. These four kinds of fish breed in the Volga and are catched in great plenty and served thence into the whole realm for a great food. Of the roes of these four kinds they make very great store of *ikra*, or caviar, as was said before.

They have besides these that breed in the Volga a fish called the *belorybitsa*, or white salmon, which they account more delicate than they do the red salmon, whereof also they have ex-

[23] A gerfalcon is a large falcon. The goshawk is a large short-winged hawk. By tassel, Fletcher may have meant tercel, the male of any kind of hawk. Sparhawk refers to sparrowhawk.

[24] Fletcher probably meant the *teterev*, Russian for black grouse.

[25] Tench and roach: both fresh water fish allied to the carp.

The Chief Cities of Russia

ceeding great plenty in the rivers northward, as in Dvina, the river of Kola, etc. In the *ozero*, or lake, near a town called Pereiaslavl, not far from the Moscow, they have a small fish which they call the fresh herring, of the fashion and somewhat of the taste of a sea herring. Their chief towns for fish are Iaroslavl, Beloozero, Novgorod, Astrakhan, and Kazan, which all yield a large custom to the Emperor every year for their trades of fishing, which they practice in summer but send it frozen in the wintertime into all parts of the realm.

CHAPTER IV

The Chief Cities of Russia

THE chief cities of Russia are Moscow, Novgorod, Rostov, Vladimir, Pskov, Smolensk, Iaroslavl, Pereiaslavl, Nizhnii Novgorod, Vologda, Ustiug, Kholmogory, Kazan, Astrakhan, Kargopol, Kolomna.

The city of Moscow is supposed to be of great antiquity, though the first founder be unknown to the Rus.[1] It seemeth to have taken the name from the river that runneth on the one side of the town. Berossus the Chaldean in his fifth book telleth that Nimrod, whom other profane stories call Saturn, sent Assyrius, Medus, Moscus, and Magog into Asia to plant colonies there, and that Moscus planted both in Asia and Europe—which may make some probability that the city, or rather the river whereon it is built, took the denomination from this Moscus: the rather because of the climate and situation, which is in the very farthest part and list of Europe, bordering upon Asia.[2] The city

[1] Moscow was first mentioned in the chronicles in 1147.
[2] Seredonin, *Sochinenie*, p. 53, has suggested that Fletcher used here as his source an anthology of Berossus published in 1510. Significantly, Kromer, upon whom Fletcher often relied, rejected this interpretation of the origin of Moscow.

Of the Rus Commonwealth

was much enlarged by one Ivan or John, son to Daniel, that first changed his title of duke into king, though that honor continued not to his posterity—the rather because he was invested into it by the Pope's legate, who at that time was Innocentius the Fourth, about the year 1246, which was very much misliked by the Rus people, being then a part of the Eastern or Greek Church.[3] Since that time the name of this city hath grown more famous and better known to the world, insomuch that not only the province but the whole country of Russia is termed by some by the name of Moscovia, the metropolite city. The form of this city is in a manner round, with three strong walls circling the one within the other and streets lying between, whereof the inmost wall and the buildings closed within it—lying safest, as the heart within the body, fenced and watered with the river Moskva, that runneth close by it—is all accounted the Emperor's castle.[4] The number of houses (as I have heard) through the whole city, being reckoned by the Emperor a little before it was fired by the Crim, was 41,500 in all.[5] Since the Tartar besieged and fired the town, which was in the year 1571, there lieth waste of it a great breadth of ground which before was well set and planted with buildings—especially that part on the south side of Moskva, built not long before by Vasilii the Emperor for his

---

[3] Ivan or John refers to Ivan I, Kalita, or "Moneybags" (1328–1341), the first Grand Prince of Muscovy. Fletcher obviously confused Ivan's father, Daniel Aleksandrovich, with the King of Galich, Daniel Romanovich. Innocent IV (1243–1254) was instrumental in achieving a union with Rome of the Orthodox peoples of Daniel Romanovich's realm by 1253, although the investiture mentioned may be a fiction.

[4] The expanding city center with its walled kremlin and walled merchants' section (Kitai Gorod) was enclosed 1586–1593 by a stone wall (Belyi Gorod). Beyond the Belyi Gorod there was still another belt—until 1591 a wooden wall but afterward an earthen rampart with wooden fortifications (Zemlianoi Gorod).

[5] The author took the number of houses in Moscow before the fire directly from Herberstein, *Notes*, II, 5.

The Chief Cities of Russia

garrison of soldiers. To whom he gave privilege to drink mead and beer at the dry or prohibited times when other Rus may drink nothing but water, and for that cause called this new city by the name of *Naleika,* that is, "skink" or "pour in," [6] so that now the city of Moscow is not much bigger than the city of London.

The next in greatness, and in a manner as large, is the city Novgorod, where was committed (as the Rus saith) the memorable war, so much spoke of in stories, of the Scythian servants that took arms against their masters, which they report in this sort: viz., that the boiars or gentlemen of Novgorod and the territory about (which only are soldiers after the discipline of those countries) had war with the Tartars, which being well performed and ended by them, they returned homewards, where they understood by the way that their *khlopy,* or bondslaves, whom they left at home had in their absence possessed their towns, lands, houses, wives, and all. At which news, being somewhat amazed and yet disdaining the villeiny of their servants, they made the more speed home and so not far from Novgorod met them in warlike manner marching against them. Whereupon, advising what was best to be done, they agreed all to set upon them with no other show of weapon but with their horsewhips, which as their manner is every man rideth withal, to put them in remembrance of their servile condition, thereby to terrify them and abate their courage. And so, marching on and lashing altogether with their whips in their hands, they gave the onset, which seemed so terrible in the ears of their villeins and struck such a sense into them of the smart of the whip which they had felt before that they fled altogether like sheep before the drivers. In memory of this victory the Novgorodians ever since have stamped their coin, which they call a *denga Novgo-*

---

[6] *Naleika* is derived from the Russian *naliv,* or "pouring in." As Fletcher noted, "skink" has the same meaning. Cf. again Herberstein, *Notes,* II, 4.

Of the Rus Commonwealth

rodskaia, current through all Russia, with the figure of a horseman shaking a whip aloft in his hand.[7] These two cities exceed the rest in greatness. For strength their chief towns are Pskov, Smolensk, Kazan, and Astrakhan, as lying upon the borders.

But for situation Iaroslavl far exceedeth the rest. For besides the commodities that the soil yieldeth of pasture and corn, it lieth upon the famous river Volga and looketh over it from a high bank very fair and stately to behold, whereof the town taketh the name. For Iaroslavl in that tongue signifieth as much as a fair or famous bank. In this town, as may be guessed by the name, dwelt the Rus King Vladimir, surnamed Iaroslav, that married the daughter of Harold, King of England, by mediation of Sveno the Dane, as is noted in the Danish story about the year 1067.[8]

The other towns have nothing that is greatly memorable, save many ruins within their walls, which showeth the decrease of the Rus people under this government. The streets of their cities and towns instead of paving are planked with fir trees planed and laid even close the one to the other. Their houses are of wood without any lime or stone, built very close and warm with fir trees planed and piled one upon another. They are fastened together with dents or notches at every corner and so clasped fast together. Betwixt the trees or timber they thrust in moss, whereof they gather plenty in their woods, to keep out the air. Every house hath a pair of stairs that lead up into the chambers out of the yard or street, after the Scottish manner. This building seemeth far better for their country than that of stone and

[7] The original story is found in Herodotus, bk. IV, chs. 1–4. Fletcher presumably followed Herberstein in relating this tale to Novgorod. Cf. Seredonin, *Sochinenie,* p. 52. No such coin as that mentioned by Fletcher was ever struck in Novgorod. A *denga* was a silver coin equal to half a kopeck; in modern Russian *dengi* means money.

[8] Fletcher was confused here: Gyda, daughter of Harold of England (d. 1066), married Vladimir Monomakh (1113–1125), son of Vsevolod (1078–1093), not Iaroslav the Wise (1019–1054). The "Danish story" was the *Historia Danica* of Saxo Grammaticus.

The House or Stock of the Rus Emperors

brick, as being colder and more dampish than their wooden houses—especially of fir, that is a dry and warm wood, whereof the providence of God hath given them such store as that you may build a fair house for twenty or thirty rubles or little more where wood is most scant. The greatest inconvenience of their wooden building is the aptness for firing, which happeneth very oft and in very fearful sort by reason of the dryness and fatness of the fir that, being once fired, burneth like a torch and is hardly quenched till all be burnt up.

CHAPTER V

Of the House or Stock of the Rus Emperors

THE surname of the imperial house of Russia is called Bela.[1] It took the original, as is supposed, from the kings of Hungary, which may seem the more probable for that the Hungarian kings many years ago have borne that name, as appeareth by Bonfinius and other stories written of that country.[2] For about the year 1059 mention is made of one Bela, that succeeded his brother Andreas, who reduced the Hungarians to the Christian faith, from whence they were fallen by atheism and Turkish persuasion before. The second of that name was called Bela the Blind, after whom succeeded divers of the same name.[3]

---

[1] Fletcher's assumption that the Russian imperial house was derived from the Hungarian was fallacious. Apparently he assumed that reference to the Tsar as *Belyi*, or White Tsar, implied connection with the Hungarian house of Bela. When Herberstein spoke of the "white king," he supposed that it referred to the latter's white garments. Cf. Herberstein, *Notes*, I, 34.

[2] Bonfinius, or Antonio Bonfini, was an Italian humanist at the court of the Hungarian King Matthias Corvinus. His *Ungaricarum rerum decades IV et dimidia* in forty-five books recorded Hungarian history to 1496.

[3] Andrew I (1047–1060) was succeeded by Bela I (1060–1063). Bela the Blind reigned 1131–1141. Although the conversion of Hungary is

23

Of the Rus Commonwealth

That their ancestry came not of the Rus nation Ivan Vasilevich, father to this Emperor, would many times boast, disdaining, as should seem, to have his progeny derived from the Rus blood. As namely, to an Englishman, his goldsmith, that had received bullion of him to make certain plate, whom the Emperor commanded to look well to his weight, "for my Rus," said he, "are thieves all." Whereat, the workman, looking upon the Emperor, began to smile. The Emperor, being of quick conceit, charged him to tell him what he smiled at. "If your Majesty will pardon me," quoth the goldsmith, "I will tell you. Your Highness said that the Rus were all thieves and forgot in the meanwhile that yourself was a Rus." "I thought so," quoth the Emperor, "but thou art deceived. For I am no Rus. My ancestors were Germans." For so they account of the Hungarians to be part of the German nation, though indeed they come of the Huns that invaded those countries and rested in those parts of Pannonia now called Hungary.[4]

How they aspired to the dukedom of Vladimir, which was their first degree and ingrafting into Russia, and whether it were by conquest or by marriage or by what other means, I could not learn any certainty among them. That from these beginnings of a small dukedom, that bare notwithstanding an absolute government with it, as at that time did also the other shires or provinces of Russia, this house of Bela spread itself forth and aspired by degrees to the monarchy of the whole country is a thing well known and of very late memory. The chiefs of that house that advanced the stock and enlarged their dominions were the three last that reigned before this Emperor, to wit, Ivan, Vasilii and Ivan, father to the other that reigneth at this time. Whereof the first that took unto him the name and title of emperor was

---

generally attributed to St. Stephen I (1000–1038), a pagan reaction accompanied by civil dissension did occur after his death.

[4] Pannonia was the Roman province now generally comprising Hungary. This anecdote again betrays Fletcher's weak grasp of Russian history.

The House or Stock of the Rus Emperors

Vasilii, father to Ivan and grandfather to this man;[5] for before that time they were contented to be called great dukes of Moscow. What hath been done by either of these three and how much they have added to their first estate by conquest or otherwise may be seen in the chapter of their colonies or purchases perforce. For the continuance of the race this house of Bela at this present is in like case as are many of the greatest houses of Christendom, viz., the whole stock and race concluded in one, two, or some few of the blood.[6] For besides the Emperor that now is, who hath no child neither is like ever to have for aught that may be conjectured by the constitution of his body and the barrenness of his wife after so many years' marriage, there is but one more, viz., a child of six or seven years old, in whom resteth all the hope of the succession and the posterity of that house.[7] As for the other brother, that was eldest of the three and of the best towardness, he died of a blow given him by his father upon the head in his fury with his walking staff or, as some say, of a thrust with the prong of it driven deep into his head. That he meant him no such mortal harm when he gave him the blow may appear by his mourning and passion after his son's death, which never left him till it brought him to the grave. Wherein may be marked the justice of God, that punished his delight in shedding of blood with this murder of his son by his own hand, and so ended his days and tyranny together with the murdering of himself by extreme grief for this his unhappy and unnatural fact.

The Emperor's younger brother, of six or seven years old, as was said before, is kept in a remote place from the Moscow under the tuition of his mother and her kindred of the house of

---

[5] Tsar Fedor Ivanovich's three predecessors were Ivan III (1462–1505), Vasilii III (1505–1533), and Ivan IV, Groznyi (1533–1584).

[6] The succession problem plagued the dynasties of France, Poland, and England when Fletcher wrote his treatise.

[7] Irene ultimately did give birth to a daughter who died in infancy. The boy mentioned was Dimitrii (b. 1582), youngest son of Ivan IV.

Of the Rus Commonwealth

the Nagoi, yet not safe, as I have heard, from attempts of making away by practice of some that aspire to the succession if this Emperor die without any issue.[8] The nurse that tasted before him of certain meat, as I have heard, died presently. That he is natural son to Ivan Vasilevich the Rus people warrant it by the father's quality, that beginneth to appear already in his tender years. He is delighted, they say, to see sheep and other cattle killed and to look on their throats while they are bleeding, which commonly children are afraid to behold, and to beat geese and hens with a staff till he see them lie dead. Besides these of the male kind there is a widow that hath right in the succession—sister to the old Emperor and aunt to this man, sometime wife to Magnus, Duke of Holst, brother to the King of Denmark, by whom she had one daughter.[9] This woman since the death of her husband hath been allured again into Russia by some that love the succession better than herself, which appeareth by the sequel. For herself with her daughter, so soon as they were returned into Russia, were thrust into a nunnery, where her daughter died this last year while I was in the country, of no natural disease, as was supposed. The mother remaineth still in the nunnery, where, as I have heard, she bewaileth herself and curseth the time when she returned into Russia, enticed with the hope of marriage and other fair promises in the Emperor's name. Thus it standeth with the imperial stock of Russia of the house of Bela, which is like to determine in those that now are and to make a conversion of the Rus estate. If it be into a government of some better temper and

---

[8] Dimitrii, son of Ivan by his seventh wife Maria Nagoi, died at Uglich in 1591. Popular opinion placed the guilt on Boris Godunov, whose path was cleared to succeed Fedor as Tsar.

[9] The reference here is to Maria, a niece of Ivan IV and widow of Magnus, Duke of Holstein and brother of Frederick II of Denmark. Magnus had died in 1583. Godunov apparently had commissioned Jerome Horsey to entice Maria and her daughter back to Russia. Maria lived until 1609.

milder constitution, it will be happy for the poor people, that are now oppressed with intolerable servitude.

CHAPTER VI

Of the Manner of Crowning or Inauguration of the Rus Emperors

THE solemnities used at the Rus emperor's coronation are on this manner. In the great church of Prechistaia,[1] or Our Lady, within the Emperor's castle, is erected a stage, whereon standeth a screen that beareth upon it the imperial cap and robe of very rich stuff. When the day of the inauguration is come, there resort thither, first, the Patriarch with the metropolitans, archbishops, bishops, abbots, and priors, all richly clad in their *pontificalibus*. Then enter the deacons with the choir of singers, who, so soon as the Emperor setteth foot into the church, begin to sing, "Many years may live noble Fedor Ivanovich, etc." Whereunto the Patriarch and metropolite with the rest of the clergy answer with a certain hymn in form of a prayer, singing it all together with a great noise. The hymn being ended, the Patriarch with the Emperor mount up the stage, where standeth a seat ready for the Emperor. Whereupon the Patriarch willeth him to sit down and then, placing himself by him upon another seat provided for that purpose, boweth down his head toward the ground and sayeth this prayer, "O Lord God, King of kings, Lord of lords, which by Thy prophet Samuel didst choose Thy servant David and anoint him for king over Thy people Israel, hear now our prayers and look from Thy sanctuary upon this Thy servant Fedor, whom Thou hast chosen and exalted for

[1] Probably the Uspenskii (Cathedral of the Assumption) in the Moscow kremlin.

Of the Rus Commonwealth

king over these Thy holy nations; anoint him with the oil of gladness; protect him by Thy power; put upon his head a crown of gold and precious stones; give him length of days; place him in the seat of justice; strengthen his arm; make subject unto him all the barbarous nations. Let Thy fear be in his whole heart; turn him from an evil faith and from all error; and show him the salvation of Thy holy and universal Church, that he may judge the people with justice and protect the children of the poor and finally attain everlasting life." This prayer he speaketh with a low voice and then pronounceth aloud: "All praise and power to God the Father, the Son, and the Holy Ghost." The prayer being ended, he commandeth certain abbots to reach the imperial robe and cap, which is done very decently and with great solemnity, the Patriarch withal pronouncing aloud: "Peace be unto all." And so he beginneth another prayer to this effect: "Bow yourselves together with us and pray to Him that reigneth over all. Preserve him, O Lord, under Thy holy protection; keep him that he may do good and holy things; let justice shine forth in his days, that we may live quietly without strife and malice." This is pronounced somewhat softly by the Patriarch, whereto he addeth again aloud: "Thou art the King of the whole world, and the savior of our souls, to Thee, the Father, Son, and Holy Ghost, be all praise forever and ever. Amen." Then, putting on the robe and cap, he blesseth the Emperor with the sign of the cross, saying withal, "In the name of the Father, the Son, and the Holy Ghost." The like is done by the metropolites, archbishops, and bishops, who all in their order come to the chair and one after another bless the Emperor with their two forefingers. Then is said by the Patriarch another prayer that beginneth, "O most Holy Virgin, Mother of God, etc." After which a deacon pronounceth with an high loud voice, "Many years to noble Fedor, good, honorable, beloved of God, great duke of Vladimir, of Moscow, emperor and monarch of all Russia, etc." Whereto the other priests and deacons, that stand

The Manner of Inauguration of the Rus Emperors

somewhat far off by the altar or table, answer singing, "Many years, many years to the noble Fedor." The same note is taken up by the priests and deacons that are placed at the right and left side of the church, and then all together they chant and thunder out singing, "Many years to the noble Fedor, good, honorable, beloved of God, great duke of Vladimir, Moscow, emperor of all Russia, etc." These solemnities being ended, first cometh the Patriarch with the metropolites, archbishops, and bishops, then the nobility and the whole company in their order, to do homage to the Emperor, bending down their heads and knocking them at his feet to the very ground.

The style wherewith he is invested at his coronation runneth after this manner:

Fedor Ivanovich, by the grace of God great lord and emperor of all Russia; great duke of Vladimir, Moscow, and Novgorod; king of Kazan; king of Astrakhan; lord of Pskov; and great duke of Smolensk, of Tver, Iugorsk, Perm, Viatka, Bulgaria, and others; lord and great duke of Novgorod of the Low Country, of Chernigov, Riazan, Polotsk, Rostov, Iaroslavl, Beloozero, Liefland, Udorsk, Obdorsk, and Kondiinsk; commander of all Siberia and of the north parts; and lord of many other countries, etc.

This style containeth in it all the Emperor's provinces and setteth forth his greatness, and therefore they have a great delight and pride in it, forcing not only their own people but also strangers that have any matter to deliver to the Emperor by speech or writing to repeat the whole form from the beginning to the end, which breedeth much cavil and sometimes quarrel betwixt them and the Tartar and Poland ambassadors, who refuse to call him tsar, that is, emperor, and to repeat the other parts of his long style.

Myself when I had audience of the Emperor thought good to salute him only with thus much, viz., "Emperor of all Russia; great duke of Vladimir, Moscow, and Novgorod; king of Kazan;

Of the Rus Commonwealth

king of Astrakhan." The rest I omitted of purpose because I knew they gloried to have their style appear to be of a larger volume than the queen's of England. But this was taken in so ill part that the chancellor, who then attended the Emperor with the rest of the nobility, with a loud chafing voice called still upon me to say out the rest. Whereto I answered that the Emperor's style was very long and could not so well be remembered by strangers, that I had repeated so much of it as might show that I gave honor to the rest, etc. But all would not serve till I commanded my interpreter to say it all out.

CHAPTER VII

The State or Form of Their Government

THE manner of their government is much after the Turkish fashion, which they seem to imitate as near as the country and reach of their capacities in political affairs will give them leave to do.

The state and form of their government is plain tyrannical, as applying all to the behoof of the prince and that after a most open and barbarous manner, as may appear by the *sophismata* or secrets of their government afterward set down, as well for the keeping of the nobility and commons in an underproportion and far uneven balance in their several degrees, as also in their impositions and exactions, wherein they exceed all just measure without any regard of nobility or people—farther than it giveth the nobility a kind of injust and unmeasured liberty to command and exact upon the commons and baser sort of people in all parts of the realm wheresoever they come, especially in the place where their lands lie or where they are appointed by the Emperor to govern under him, also to the commons some small contentment in that they pass over their lands by descent of in-

Their State and Form of Government

heritance to whether[1] son they will, which commonly they do after our gavelkind [2] and dispose of their goods by gift or testament without any controlment. Wherein, notwithstanding, both nobility and commons are but storers for the prince, all running in the end into the Emperor's coffers, as may appear by the practice of enriching his treasury and the manner of exactions set down in the title of his customs and revenues.

Concerning the principal points and matters of state wherein the sovereignty consisteth—as the making and annulling of public laws, the making of magistrates, power to make war or league with any foreign state, to execute or to pardon life with the right of appeal in all matters both civil and criminal—they do so wholly and absolutely pertain to the Emperor and his council under him, as that he may be said to be both the sovereign commander and the executioner of all these. For as touching any law or public order of the realm, it is ever determined of before any public assembly or parliament be summoned. Where, besides his council, he hath none other to consult with him of such matters as are concluded beforehand but only a few bishops, abbots, and friars, to no other end than to make advantage of the peoples' superstitions even against themselves, which think all to be holy and just that passeth with consent of their bishops and clergymen, whatsoever it be. For which purpose the emperors are content to make much of the corrupt state of the Church as now it is among them and to nourish the same by extraordinary favors and immunities to the bishops' sees, abbeys and friaries, as knowing superstition and false religion best to agree with a tyrannical state and to be a special means to uphold and maintain the same.

Secondly, as touching the public offices and magistracies of the realm, there is none hereditary, neither any so great nor so

---

[1] Whichever.

[2] The custom of dividing an intestate's estate equally among the sons or other heirs.

Of the Rus Commonwealth

little in that country but the bestowing of it is done immediately by the Emperor himself. Insomuch that the very *diaki*, or clerks, in every head town are for the most part assigned by himself. Notwithstanding, the Emperor that now is, the better to intend his devotions, referreth all such matters pertaining to the state wholly to the ordering of his wife's brother, the Lord Boris Fedorovich Godunov.[3]

Thirdly, the like is to be said of the jurisdiction concerning matters judicial, especially such as concern life and death. Wherein there is none that hath any authority or public jurisdiction that goeth by descent or is held by charter but all at the appointment and pleasure of the Emperor. And the same practiced by the judges with such awe and restraint as they dare not determine upon any special matter but must refer the same wholly up to the Moscow to the Emperor's council. To show his sovereignty over the lives of his subjects, the late Emperor Ivan Vasilevich, in his walks or progresses, if he had misliked the face or person of any man whom he met by the way or that looked upon him, would command his head to be struck off, which was presently done and the head cast before him.

Fourthly, for the sovereign appeal and giving of pardons in criminal matters to such as are convicted, it is wholly at the pleasure and grace of the Emperor. Wherein also the Empress that now is, being a woman of great clemency and withal delighting to deal in public affairs of the realm—the rather to supply the defect of her husband—doth behave herself after an absolute manner, giving out pardon—especially on her birthday and other solemn times—in her own name by open proclamation, without any mention at all of the Emperor. Some there have been of late of the ancient nobility that have held divers provinces by right of inheritance, with an absolute authority and jurisdiction over them to order and determine all matters within

[3] Boris Godunov was brother to Irene, wife of Fedor.

The Manner of Holding Their Parliaments

their own precinct without all appeal or controlment of the Emperor; but this was all annulled and wrung clean from them by Ivan Vasilevich, father to this Emperor.[4]

CHAPTER VIII

The Manner of Holding Their Parliaments

THEIR highest court of public consultation for matter of state is called the *Sobor*, that is, the public assembly.[1] The states and degrees of persons that are present at their parliaments are these in order: 1) the Emperor himself; 2) some of his nobility, about the number of twenty, being all of his council; 3) certain of the clergymen, etc., about the same number. As for burghers or other to represent the commonalty, they have no place there, the people being of no better account with them than as servants or bondslaves, that are to obey, not to make laws nor to know anything of public matters before they are concluded.

The court of parliament called *Sobor* is held in this manner. The Emperor causeth to be summoned such of his nobility as himself thinketh meet, being, as was said, all of his council together with the Patriarch, who calleth his clergy—to wit, the two metropolites, the two archbishops, with such bishops, abbots, and friars as are of best account and reputation among them. When they are all assembled at the Emperor's court, the

[4] See below, pp. 36–38 *passim*.

[1] Critics (e.g., Ruffmann, *Russlandbild*, pp. 88–89) of Fletcher, frequently assuming that this *sobor* was the *zemskii sobor*, have censured the author for his inaccuracies. Seredonin has convincingly shown that Fletcher really described a joint session of the boiar *duma* and sacred *sobor*. Not knowing of the existence of the *zemskii sobor*, Fletcher assumed that the extended *duma*, herein noted, was the highest parliamentary body in the government. Cf. lengthy discussion in Seredonin, *Sochinenie*, pp. 228–234.

33

Of the Rus Commonwealth

day is intimated when the session shall begin, which commonly is upon some Friday, for the religion of that day.

When the day is come, the clergymen assemble before at the time and place appointed, which is called the *Stoly*.[2] And when the Emperor cometh attended by his nobility, they arise all and meet him in an outroom, following their patriarch, who blesseth the Emperor with his two forefingers, laying them on his forehead and the sides of his face, and then kisseth him on the right side of his breast. So they pass on into their parliament house, where they sit in this order. The Emperor is enthronized on the one side of the chamber. In the next place not far from him at a small square table, that giveth room to twelve persons or thereabouts, sitteth the Patriarch with the metropolites and bishops and certain of the principal nobility of the Emperor's council, together with two *diaki,* or secretaries (called *dumnye diaki*), that enact that which passeth. The rest place themselves on benches round about the room, every man in his rank after his degree. Then is there propounded by one of the secretaries, who representeth the speaker, the cause of their assembly and the principal matters that they are to consider of. For to propound bills what every man thinketh good for the public benefit, as the manner is in England, the Rus Parliament alloweth no such custom nor liberty to subjects.

The points being opened, the Patriarch with his clergymen have the prerogative to be first asked their vote or opinion what they think of the points propounded by the secretary. Whereto they answer in order according to their degrees, but all in one form, without any discourses, as having learned their lesson before, that serveth their turns at all parliaments alike, whatsoever is propounded. Commonly it is to this effect: That the Emperor and his council are of great wisdom and experience, touching

[2] *Stol* literally means table in Russian. Fletcher probably used this term instead of *Stolovaia palata,* or palace, which originally housed such a gathering.

The Manner of Holding Their Parliaments

the policies and public affairs of the realm, and far better able to judge what is profitable for the commonwealth than they are, which attend upon the service of God only and matters of religion; and therefore it may please them to proceed. That instead of their advice they will aid them with their prayers, as their duties and vocations do require, etc. To this or like effect having made their answers, every man in his course, up standeth some abbot or friar more bold than the rest, yet appointed beforehand as a matter of form, and desireth the Emperor it would please His Majesty to command to be delivered unto them what His Majesty's own judgment and determinate pleasure is as touching those matters propounded by his *diak*.

Whereto is replied by the said secretary in the Emperor's name that His Highness with those of his noble council upon good and sound advice have found the matters proposed to be very good and necessary for the commonwealth of his realm. Notwithstanding, forasmuch as they are religious men and know what is right, His Majesty requireth their godly opinions, yea, and their censures, too, for the approving or correcting of the said propositions. And therefore desireth them again to speak their minds freely, and, if they shall like to give their consents, that then the matters may pass to a full conclusion. Hereunto, when the clergymen have given their consents, which they use to do without any great pausing, they take their leaves with blessing of the Emperor, who bringeth the Patriarch on his way so far as the next room and so returneth to his seat till all be made ready for his return homeward. The acts that thus are passed by the *Sobor*, or parliament, the *diaki*, or secretaries, draw into a form of proclamation, which they send abroad into every province and head town of the realm to be published there by the dukes and *diaki*, or secretaries, of those places. The session of parliament being fully ended, the Emperor inviteth the clergymen to a solemn dinner. And so they depart every man to his home.

Of the Rus Commonwealth

CHAPTER IX

Of the Nobility, and by What Means It Is Kept in an Underproportion Agreeable to That State

THE degrees of persons or estates of Russia besides the sovereign state or Emperor himself are these in their order: 1) The nobility, which is of four sorts, whereof the chief for birth, authority, and revenue are called the *udelnye kniazia*, that is, the exempted or privileged dukes. These held sometime a several jurisdiction and absolute authority within their precincts, much like unto the states or nobles of Germany; [1] but afterward, reserving their rights upon composition, they yielded themselves to this house of Bela, when it began to wax mighty and to enlarge itself by overmatching their neighbors. Only they were bound to serve the Emperor in his wars with a certain number of horse. But the late Emperor Ivan Vasilevich, father to this prince, being a man of high spirit and subtle in his kind, meaning to reduce his government into a more strict form, began by degrees to clip off their greatness and to bring it down to a lesser proportion, till in the end he made them not only his vassals but his *khlopy*, that is, his very villeins or bondslaves.[2] For so they term and write themselves in any public instrument or private petition which they make to the Emperor, so that now they hold their authorities, lands, lives, and all at the Emperor's pleasure as the rest do.

The means and practice whereby he wrought this to effect against those and other of the nobility, so well as I could note out of the report of his doings, were these and suchlike. First, he

[1] That is, within the Holy Roman Empire.

[2] Distinguished nobles were indeed mentioned in charters of the reign of Ivan as *khlopy*, but Fletcher took this word's meaning much too literally.

Of the Nobility

cast private emulations among them about prerogative of their titles and dignities. Wherein he used to set on the inferiors to prefer or equal themselves to those that were accounted to be of the nobler houses, where he made his advantage of their malice and contentions the one against the other by receiving devised matter and accusations of secret practice and conspiracies to be intended against his person and state. And so, having singled out the greatest of them and cut them off with the good liking of the rest, he fell at last to open practice by forcing of the other to yield their rights unto him.[3]

2) He divided his subjects into two parts or factions by a general schism. The one part he called the *oprichnina,* or select men. These were such of the nobility and gentry as he took to his own part to protect and maintain them as his faithful subjects. The other he called *zemskie,* or the commons. The *zemskie* contained the base and vulgar sort, with such noblemen and gentlemen as he meant to cut off as suspected to mislike his government and to have a meaning to practice against him. Wherein he provided that the *oprichnina* for number and quality of valor,[4] money, armor, etc., far exceeded the other of the *zemskie* side, whom he put (as it were) from under his protection so that if any of them were spoiled or killed by those of the *oprichnina,* which he accounted of his own part, there was no amends to be sought for by way of public justice or by complaint to the Emperor.[5]

The whole number of both parts was orderly registered and kept in a book, so that every man knew who was a *zemskii* man and who of the *oprichnina.* And this liberty of the one part to

---

[3] Fletcher, not understanding the order of precedence (*mestnichestvo*), distorted its true nature when he suggested it was merely a political device of Ivan IV.

[4] Value in money.

[5] The *zemskii,* or *zemshchina,* contained not just the "base and vulgar sort" but many of the boiar families. Fletcher incorrectly observed that the *oprichniki* were more numerous than the *zemshchiny.*

Of the Rus Commonwealth

spoil and kill the other without any help of magistrate or law—that continued seven years—enriched that side and the Emperor's treasury and wrought that withal which he intended by this practice, viz., to take out of the way such of the nobility as himself misliked; whereof were slain within one week to the number of three hundred within the city of Moscow.[6] This tyrannical practice of making a general schism and public division among the subjects of his whole realm proceeded, as should seem, from an extreme doubt and desperate fear which he had conceived of most of his nobility and gentlemen of his realm in his wars with the Polonian and Crim Tartar. What time he grew into a vehement suspicion, conceived of the ill success of his affairs, that they practiced treason with the Polonian and Crim; whereupon he executed some and devised his way to be rid of the rest.

And this wicked policy and tyrannous practice, though now it be ceased, hath so troubled that country and filled it so full of grudge and mortal hatred ever since that it will not be quenched, as it seemeth now, till it burn again into a civil flame.[7]

3) Having thus pulled them and seized all their inheritance, lands, privileges, etc., save some very small part which he left to their name, he gave them other lands of the tenure of *pomeste* (as they call it) that are held at the Emperor's pleasure, lying far off in another country, and so removed them into other of his provinces, where they might have neither favor nor authority, not being native nor well known there.

So that now these of the chief nobility, called *udelnye kniazia*, are equaled with the rest, save that in the opinion and favor of

---

[6] The probable duration of the *oprichnina* was 1565–1572.

[7] This prophecy of the Time of Troubles is perhaps the classic passage in this work, although Horsey made a similar prediction. Cf. Bond, *Russia*, p. 173.

Of the Nobility

the people they are of more account and keep still the prerogative of their place in all their public meetings.

Their practice to keep down these houses from rising again and recovering their dignities are these and suchlike. First, many of their heirs are kept unmarried perforce, that the stock may die with them. Some are sent into Siberia, Kazan, and Astrakhan under pretense of service and there either made away or else fast clapped up. Some are put into abbeys and shear themselves friars by pretense of a vow to be made voluntary and of their own accord but, indeed, forced unto it by fear upon some pretensed crime objected against them. Where they are so guarded by some of special trust and the convent itself—upon whose head it standeth that they make no escape—as that they have no hope but to end their lives there. Of this kind there are many of very great nobility. These and suchlike ways begun by the Emperor Ivan Vasilevich are still practiced by the Godunovs, who, being advanced by the marriage of the Empress, their kinswoman, rule both the Emperor and his realm—especially Boris Fedorovich Godunov, brother to the Empress—and endeavor by all means to cut off or keep down all of the best and ancientest nobility. Whereof divers already they have taken away whom they thought likeliest to make head against them and to hinder their purpose, as Kniaz Andrei Kurakin-Bulgakov, a man of great birth and authority in the country.[8] The like they have done with Petr Golovin, whom they put into a dungeon where he ended his life, with Kniaz Vasilii Iurevich Golitsyn, with Andrei Ivanovich Shuiskii, accounted among them for a man of a great wisdom. So this last year was killed in a monastery whither they had thrust him one Kniaz Ivan Petrovich Shuiskii, a man of great valor and service in that country, who about five or six years since bare out the siege of the city

---

[8] Fletcher erred, for he really meant Prince Andrei Petrovich Kurakin, who survived his disgrace and lived until 1615. It is not clear why Fletcher added Bulgakov to Kurakin's name.

Of the Rus Commonwealth

Pskov made by Stephen Bathory, King of Polonia, with 100,000 men and repulsed him very valiantly, with great honor to himself and his country and disgrace to the Polonian.[9] Also Nikita Romanovich, uncle to the Emperor by the mother's side, was supposed to have died of poison or some like practice.[10]

The names of these families of greatest nobility are these in their order. The first is of Kniaz Vladimir, which resteth at this time in one daughter—a widow and without children, mentioned before, sometime wife to Herzog [11] Magnus, brother to the King of Denmark—now closed within a nunnery. The second, Kniaz Mstislavskii, thrust into a friary, and his only son kept from marriage to decay the house.[12] The third, Glinskii, but one left of his house and he without children save one daughter. The fourth, Shuiskii, whereof there are four brethren, young men and unmarried all. The fifth, Trubetskoi, of this house are four living. The sixth, Bulgakov, now called Golitsyn house, whereof are five living, but youths all. The seventh, Vorotynskii, two left of that stock. The eighth, Odoevskii, two. The ninth, Teliatevskii, one. The tenth, Tatev, three. These are the names of the chief families called *udelnye kniazia*, that in effect have lost all now save the very name itself and favor of the people, which is like one day to restore them again, if any be left.

The second degree of nobility is of the boiars. These are such as the Emperor honoreth, besides their nobility, with the title of councilors. The revenue of these two sorts of their nobles, that riseth out of their lands assigned them by the Emperor and held

---

[9] The Polish failure to capture Pskov (1581–1582) resulted in peace between Poland and Muscovy, but for Ivan IV this Livonian venture had proved disastrous. Cf. below, p. 86.

[10] Nikita Romanovich Iurev, uncle to Tsar Fedor, died April 23, 1586. Fletcher's allegation here has not been substantiated. The name "Nikita" appeared here as "Michita" (Micheta), which is now archaic.

[11] Fletcher wrote "Herzog" as "Hartock." Cf. Chapter V, n. 9, above.

[12] Prince Ivan Mstislavskii, famed military figure, suffered incarceration in a friary for conspiracy against Godunov.

Of the Nobility

at his pleasure (for of their own inheritance there is little left them, as was said before), is about a thousand marks a year, besides pension which they receive of the Emperor for their service in his wars to the sum of seven hundred rubles a year and none above that sum.

But in this number the Lord Boris Fedorovich Godunov is not to be reckoned, that is like a transcendent and in no such predicament with the rest, being the Emperor's brother-in-law, his protector for direction, for command and authority Emperor of Russia. His yearly revenue in land and pension amounteth to the sum of 93,700 rubles and more, as appeareth by the particulars. He hath of inheritance, which himself hath augmented in Viazma and Dorogobuzh, 6,000 rubles a year. For his office of *Koniushii,* or Master of the Horse, 12,000 rubles or marks, raised out of the *Koniushennaia Sloboda,* or the liberties pertaining to that office, which are certain lands and towns near about the Moscow, besides all the meadow and pasture ground on both sides the bank of the river Moscow, thirty versts up the stream and forty versts downward. For his pension of the Emperor, besides the other for his office, 15,000 rubles. Out of the province or shire of Vaga there is given him for a peculiar exempted out of the *Posolskaia Chetvert* 32,000 rubles, besides a rent of furs. Out of Riazan and Seversk, another peculiar, 30,000 rubles. Out of Tver and Torzhok, another exempt place, 8,000 rubles. For rent of bathstoves and bathing houses without the walls of Moscow, 1,500 rubles, besides his *pomeste,* or lands, which he holdeth at the Emperor's pleasure, which far exceedeth the proportion of land allotted to the rest of the nobility.[13]

One other there is of the house of Glinskii that dispendeth [14] in land and pension about 40,000 rubles yearly, which he is

---

[13] Seredonin, *Sochinenie,* pp. 190–191, concluded that Fletcher procured these figures from either Horsey and/or Anthony Marsh, both of whom were close to Godunov. Boris may have wished to impress Englishmen by these sums, significantly exaggerated.

[14] Has an income.

Of the Rus Commonwealth

suffered to enjoy because he hath married Boris his wife's sister, being himself very simple and almost a natural. The ordering of him and his lands are committed to Boris.

In the third rank are the *voevody,* or such nobles as are or have been generals in the Emperor's wars, which deliver the honor of their title to their posterities also, who take their place above the other dukes and nobles that are not of the two former sorts, viz., of the *udelnye kniazia* nor of the boiars.[15]

These three degrees of their nobility, to wit, the *udelnye kniazia,* the boiars, and the *voevody,* have the addition of *vich* put unto their surname, as Boris Fedorovich, etc., which is a note of honor that the rest may not usurp. And in case it be not added in the naming of them, they may sue the *bescheste,*[16] or penalty of dishonor, upon them that otherwise shall term them.

The fourth and lowest degree of nobility with them is of such as bear the name of *kniazia,* or dukes, but come of the younger brothers of those chief houses through many descents and have no inheritance of their own save the bare name or title of duke only. For their order is to deliver their names and titles of their dignities over to all their children alike, whatsoever else they leave them, so that the sons of a *voevoda,* or general in the field, are called *voevody,* though they never saw the field, and the sons of a *kniaz,* or duke, are called *kniazia,* though they have not one groat of inheritance or livelihood to maintain themselves withal. Of this sort there are so many that the plenty maketh them cheap, so that you shall see dukes glad to serve a mean man for five or six rubles or marks a year, and yet they will stand highly upon their *bescheste,* or reputation of their honors. And these are their several degrees of nobility.

The second degree of persons is of *synovia boiarskie,* or the

[15] While Fletcher correctly noted that the *voevody* had begun to assume a higher station in society, there is no evidence that their title had become hereditary.

[16] Fletcher was not clear in his use of this term, which means "dishonor" or "ignominy." Below he used it for precisely its opposite meaning.

The Government of Their Provinces

sons of gentlemen, which all are preferred and hold that name by their service in the Emperor's wars, being soldiers by their very stock and birth.[17] To which order are referred their *diaki*, or secretaries, that serve the Emperor in every head town, being joined in commission with the dukes of that place.[18]

The last are their commons, whom they call *muzhiki*. In which number they reckon their merchants and their common artificers. The very lowest and basest sort of this kind, which are held in no degree, are their country people, whom they call *krestiane*. Of the *synovia boiarskie*, which are all soldiers, we are to see in the description of their forces and military provisions; concerning their *muzhiki*, what their condition and behavior is, in the title, or chapter, "Of the Common People."

CHAPTER X

Of the Government of Their Provinces and Shires

THE whole country of Russia (as was said before) is divided into four parts, which they call *chetverti*, or tetrarchies. Every *chetvert* containeth divers shires and is annexed to a several office whereof it takes the name. The first *chetvert*, or tetrarchy, beareth the name of *Posolskaia Chetvert*, or the jurisdiction of the office of the embassages, and at this time is under the chief secretary and officer of the embassages, called Andrei Shchelkalov.[1] The standing fee or stipend that he receiveth yearly

[17] Fletcher used the term *synovia boiarskie* rather than the more acceptable *deti boiarskie*. Cf. below, pp. 75–76.

[18] While the majority of the *diaki* were undoubtedly of the servitor class, some traced their origins to the *votchina* nobility.

[1] While Fletcher was quite right in noting the relationship between the *Chetvert* and *prikazy*, he erred when he contended that the *prikazy* carried the name *Chetvert*. Fletcher's confusion derived from his construing *chet*, meaning "ministry," as *Chetvert*. As noted previously, the *diaki*, who administered the *Chetverti*, also had responsibility for the *prikazy*. Thus,

43

Of the Rus Commonwealth

of the Emperor for this service is 100 rubles or marks.

The second is called the *Rozriadnaia Chetvert,* because it is proper to the *Rozriadnyi,* or high constable. At this time it pertaineth by virtue of office to Vasilii Shchelkalov, brother to the chancellor; but it is executed by one Sapun Abramov. His pension is an hundred rubles yearly.

The third is the *Pomestnaia Chetvert,* as pertaining to that office. This keepeth a register of all lands given by the Emperor for service to his noblemen, gentlemen, and others; giveth out and taketh in all assurances for them. The officer at this time is called Elizar Vyluzgin. His stipend is 500 rubles a year.

The fourth is called *Kazanskii Dvorets,* as being appropriate to the office that hath the jurisdiction of the kingdoms of Kazan and Astrakhan, with the other towns lying upon the Volga, now ordered by one Druzhina Petelin [Panteleev], a man of very special account among them for his wisdom and promptness in matters of policy. His pension is 150 rubles a year.

From these *chetverti,* or tetrarchies, is exempted the Emperor's inheritance, or *votchina,* as they call it, for that it pertained from ancient time to the house of Bela, which is the surname of the imperial blood. This standeth of thirty-six towns with their bounds or territories, besides divers peculiar jurisdictions, which are likewise deducted out of those *chetverti,* as the shire of Vaga, belonging to the Lord Boris Fedorovich Godunov, and suchlike.

These are the chief governors or officers of the provinces, not resident at their charge abroad but attending the Emperor

---

Andrei Shchelkalov administered the *Posolskii Prikaz* and a *Chetvert;* Vasilii Shchelkalov and later Sapun Abramov the *Rozriadnyi* and a *Chetvert;* Druzhina Petelin, the *Kazanskii Dvorets* and a *Chetvert;* and probably Elizar Vyluzgin, the *Pomestnyi Prikaz* and a *Chetvert.* This attachment of the *Chetvert* to the *prikazy,* quite incidental, depended upon the personality of the *diak* and became more commonplace during the reign of Fedor. Cf. Seredonin, *Sochinenie,* pp. 259–260; also cf. above, p. 6, and below, p. 52, for more on *Chetverti.*

The Government of Their Provinces

whithersoever he goeth, and carrying their offices about with them, which for the most part they hold at Moscow, as the Emperor's chief seat.

The parts and practice of these four offices is to receive all complaints and actions whatsoever that are brought out of their several *chetverti* and quarters and to inform them to the Emperor's council; likewise, to send direction again to those that are under them in their said provinces for all matters given in charge by the Emperor and his council to be done or put in execution within their precincts.

For the ordering of every particular province of these four *chetverti* there is appointed one of these dukes, which were reckoned before in the lowest degree of their nobility, which are resident in the head towns of the said provinces, whereof every one hath joined with him in commission a *diak*, or secretary, to assist him, or rather to direct him; for in the executing of their commission the *diak* doth all. The parts of their commission are these in effect: first, to hear and determine in all civil matters within their precinct. To which purpose they have under them certain officers, as *gubnye starosty*, or coroners, who, besides the trial of self murders, are to attach felons, and the *sudi*, or underjustices, who themselves also may hear and determine in all matters of the same nature among the country people of their own wards or bailiwicks; but so that in case either part dissent they may appeal and go farther to the duke and *diak* that reside within the head town. From whom also they may remove the matter to the higher court at Moscow of the Emperor's council, where lie all appeals. They have under them also *sotskie starosty*, that is, aldermen or bailiffs of the hundreds.[2]

Secondly, in all criminal matters, as theft, murder, treason, etc., they have authority to apprehend, to examine, and to imprison the malefactor; and so, having received perfect evidence and information of the cause, they are to send it ready-drawn

[2] Cf. below, pp. 47 and 70.

Of the Rus Commonwealth

and orderly digested up to the Moscow to the officer of the *chetvert* whereunto that province is annexed, by whom it is referred and propounded to the Emperor's council. But to determine in any matter criminal or to do execution upon the party offending is more than their commission will allow them to do.

Thirdly, if there be any public service to be done within that province, as the publishing of any law or common order by way of proclamation, collecting of taxes and impositions for the Emperor, mustering of soldiers and sending them forth at the day and to the place assigned by the Emperor or his council, all these and suchlike pertain to their charge.

These dukes and *diaki* are appointed to their place by the Emperor himself and are changed ordinarily at every year's end, except upon some special liking or suit the time be prorogued for a year or two more. They are men of themselves of no credit nor favor with the people where they govern, being neither born nor brought up among them, nor yet having inheritance of their own there or elsewhere. Only of the Emperor they have for that service 100 marks [3] a year, he that hath most; some fifty, some but thirty, which maketh them more suspected and odious to the people. Because being so bare and coming fresh and hungry upon them lightly [4] every year, they rack and spoil them without all regard of justice or conscience, which is easily tolerated by the chief officers of the *chetverti*, to the end they may rob them again and have a better booty when they call them to account, which commonly they do at the end of their service, making an advantage of their injustice and oppression over the poor people. There are few of them but they come to the *pytki*, or whip, when their time is ended, which themselves for the most part do make account of. And therefore they furnish themselves with all the spoil they can for the time of their government that they may have for both turns, as well for the Emperor and lord of the *chetvert*, as to reserve some good part for themselves.

[3] In England a mark equaled 13s.4d.   [4] Usually

The Government of Their Provinces

They that are appointed to govern abroad are men of this quality, save that in the four border towns that are of greatest importance are set men of more special valor and trust, two in every town,[5] whereof one is ever of the Emperor's privy council. These four border towns are Smolensk, Pskov, Novgorod, and Kazan, whereof three lie toward the Polonian and Sweden, one bordereth far off upon the Crim Tartar. These have larger commission than the other dukes of the provinces that I spake of before and may do execution in criminal matters, which is thought behooveful for the commonwealth for incident occasions that may happen upon the borders that are far off and may not stay for direction about every occurrent and particular matter from the Emperor and his council. They are changed every year, except as before, and have for their stipend seven hundred rubles a year, he that hath most; some have but four hundred. Many of these places that are of greatest importance, and almost the whole country, is managed at this time by the Godunovs and their clients.

The city of Moscow, that is the Emperor's seat, is governed altogether by the Emperor's council. All matters there, both civil and criminal, are heard and determined in the several courts held by some of the said council that reside there all the year long.

Only for their ordinary matters, as buildings, reparations, keeping of their streets decent and clean, collections, levying of taxes, impositions, and suchlike are appointed two gentlemen and two *diaki,* or secretaries, who hold a court together for the ordering of such matters. This is called the *Zemskii* House.[6] If any townsman suspect his servant of theft or like matter, hither he may bring him to have him examined upon the *pytki* or other torture. Besides these two gentlemen and secretaries that order the whole city, there are *starosty,* or aldermen, for every several company. The alderman hath his *sotskie,* or constable; and the

[5] Cf. below, p. 88.   [6] Or *Zemskii Dvor.*

constable hath certain *desiatskie,* or decurions, under him, which have the oversight of ten households apiece, whereby every disorder is sooner spied and the common service hath the quicker dispatch. The whole number of citizens, poor and rich, are reduced into companies. The chief officers, as the *diaki* and gentlemen, are appointed by the Emperor himself, the *starosta* by the gentlemen and *diaki,* the *sotskie* by the *starosta,* or alderman, and the *desiatskie* by the constables.

This manner of government of their provinces and towns, if it were as well set for the giving of justice indifferently to all sorts as it is to prevent innovations by keeping of the nobility within order and the commons in subjection, it might seem in that kind to be no bad nor unpolitic way for the containing of so large a commonwealth of that breadth and length as is the kingdom of Russia. But the oppression and slavery is so open and so great that a man would marvel how the nobility and people should suffer themselves to be brought under it while they had any means to avoid and repulse it; or, being so strengthened as it is at this present, how the emperors themselves can be content to practice the same with so open injustice and oppression of their subjects, being themselves of a Christian profession.

By this it appeareth how hard a matter it were to alter the state of the Rus government as now it standeth—first, because they have none of the nobility able to make head. As for the lords of the four *chetverti,* or tetrarchies, they are men of no nobility but *diaki* advanced by the Emperor, depending on his favor and attending only about his own person. And for the dukes that are appointed to govern under them, they are but men of a titular dignity, as was said before, of no power, authority, nor credit save that which they have out of the office for the time they enjoy it.[7] Which doth purchase them no favor but rather hatred of the people, forasmuch as they see that they are set over them not so much for any care to do them right and

---

[7] Cf. above, p. 46.

The Government of Their Provinces

justice as to keep them under in a miserable subjection and to take the fleece from them, not once in the year, as the owner from his sheep, but to poll and clip them all the year long. Besides, the authority and rule which they bear is rent and divided into many small pieces, being divers of them in every great shire, limited besides with a very short time; which giveth them no scope to make any strength, nor to contrive such an enterprise if happily they intended any matter of innovation. As for the common people (as may better appear in the description of their state and quality afterward set down), besides their want of armor and practice of war, which they are kept from of purpose, they are robbed continually both of their hearts and money, besides other means, sometimes by pretense of some service to be done for the common defense, sometimes without any show at all of any necessity of commonwealth or prince. So that there is no means either for nobility or people to attempt any innovation so long as the military forces of the Emperor, which are the number of 8,000 at the least in continual pay,[8] hold themselves fast and sure unto him and to the present state. Which needs they must do, being of the quality of soldiers and enjoying withal that free liberty of wronging and spoiling of the commons at their pleasure, which is permitted them of purpose to make them have a liking of the present state. As for the agreement of the soldiers and commons, it is a thing not to be feared, being of so opposite and contrary practice much one to the other. This desperate state of things at home maketh the people for the most part to wish for some foreign invasion, which they suppose to be the only means to rid them of the heavy yoke of this tyrannous government.

[8] This figure should read 80,000; cf. below, p. 77, where Fletcher refers again to these 80,000 troops.

Of the Rus Commonwealth

CHAPTER XI

Of the Emperor's Council

THE emperors of Russia give the name of councilor to divers of their chief nobility rather for honor's sake than for any use they make of them about their matters of state. These are called boiar without any addition and may be called councilors at large, for they are seldom or never called to any public consultation. They which are of his special and privy council indeed, whom he useth daily and ordinarily for all public matters pertaining to the state, have the addition of *dumnye* and are named *dumnye* boiars, or lords of the council, their office or sitting *boiarskaia duma*.

Their names at this present are these in their order: first, Kniaz Fedor Ivanovich Mstislavskii; 2) Kniaz Ivan Mikhailovich Glinskii; 3) Kniaz Vasilii Ivanovich Shuiskii Skopin [1] (these three are accounted to be of greater birth than wisdom, taken in, as may seem, for that end rather to furnish the place with their honors and presence than with their advice or counsel); 4) Kniaz Vasilii Ivanovich Shuiskii,[2] thought to be more wise than the other of his name; 5) Kniaz Fedor Mikhailovich;[3] 6) Kniaz Nikita Romanovich Trubetskoi; 7) Kniaz Timofei Romanovich Trubetskoi; 8) Kniaz Andrei Grigorievich Kurakin;[4] 9) Kniaz Dimitrii Ivanovich Khvorostinin; 10) Kniaz Fedor Ivanovich Khvorostinin; 11) Bogdan Ivanovich Saburov;[5] 12) Kniaz Ivan Vasilevich;[6] 13) Kniaz Fedor Di-

---

[1] Vasilii Fedorovich Skopin-Shuiskii.   [2] Tsar, 1606–1610.
[3] Fedor Mikhailovich Trubetskoi.
[4] Grigorii Andreevich instead of Andrei Grigorievich.
[5] Bogdan Iurevich instead of Bogdan Ivanovich.
[6] Apparently Ivan Vasilevich Sitskii.

The Emperor's Council

mitrievich Shestunov; 14) Kniaz Fedor Mikhailovich Troekurov; 15) Ivan Buturlin; [7] 16) Dimitrii Ivanovich Godunov; 17) Boris Fedorovich Godunov, brother to the Empress; 18) Stepan Vasilevich Godunov; 19) Grigorii Vasilevich Godunov; 20) Ivan Vasilevich Godunov; 21) Fedor Sheremetev; 22) Andrei Petrovich Kleshnin; 23) Ignatii Petrovich Tatishchev; 24) Roman Mikhailovich Pivov; 25) Dementii Ivanovich Cheremisinov; 26) Roman Vasilevich Alferev; 27) Andrei Shchelkalov; 28) Vasilii Shchelkalov; 29) Elizar Vyluzgin; 30) Druzhina Petelin; 31) Sapun Abramov.

The four last of these are called *dumnye diaki,* or lord secretaries. These are all of the Emperor's privy council, though but few of them are called to any consultation, for that all matters are advised and determined upon by Boris Fedorovich Godunov, brother to the Empress, with some five or six more whom it pleaseth him to call. If they come, they are rather to hear than to give counsel and do so demean themselves. The matters occurrent, which are of state done within the realm, are informed them at their sittings by the lords of the four *chetverti,* or tetrarchies, whereof mention is made in the chapter concerning the government of their provinces, who bring in all such letters as they receive from the dukes, *diaki,* captains, and other officers of the cities and castles pertaining to their several quarter, or *chetvert,* with other advertisements, and inform the council of them.

The like is done by the chief officer of every several office of record, who may come into the council chamber and inform them as occasion incident to his office doth require. Besides matters of state, they consider of many private causes, informed by way of supplication in very great numbers: whereof some they entertain and determine as the cause or means can procure favor; some they send to the offices whereto they pertain by common course of law. Their ordinary days for their sitting are

[7] Ivan Mikhailovich Buturlin.

Of the Rus Commonwealth

Mondays, Wednesdays, and Fridays. Their time of meeting is commonly seven o'clock in the morning. If there be any extraordinary occasion that requireth consultation on some other day, they have warning by the clerk of the council, called Dorofei Bushevoi, who receiveth order from the *Rozriadnyi,* or high constable of the realm, to call them together at the time appointed.[8]

CHAPTER XII

Of the Emperor's Customs and Other Revenues

FOR the receiving of customs and other rents belonging to the crown there are appointed divers underofficers, which deliver over the same into the head treasury. The first is the office of *Dvortsovyi Prikaz,* or steward of the household. The second is the office of the *Chetverti,*[1] which I comprehend under one though it be divided into four several parts, as was said before. The third is called *Bolshoi Prikhod,* or the great income.[2]

As touching the first, which is the office of the steward, it receiveth all the rents of the Emperor's inheritance or crown land, which they call *votchina.* The *votchina,* or crown land, containeth in it thirty-six towns, with the territories or hundreds belonging unto them, whereof the chief that yield the greatest rents are these: Aleksandrovskaia [Sloboda], Karelia, Tver, Slobody, Danilovo, Mosalsk, Cherkizovo, Semchinskoe, Staraia Rusa, Vorontsovo, etc.[3] The inhabitants or tenants of these and the other

[8] This is the only known reference to the meeting time of the sixteenth-century Moscow *duma.*

[1] Cf. above, pp. 6, n. 9, and 43, n. 1.

[2] Although Fletcher mentioned but three offices, others engaged in the collection of revenue in lands under their jurisdiction and then transferred the funds to the *Bolshoi Prikhod.* Cf. Seredonin, *Sochinenie,* p. 317.

[3] While many of these *votchiny* under the *Bolshoi Dvorets* were obscure villages in the vicinity of Moscow, this ministry's jurisdiction extended

The Emperor's Customs and Other Revenues

towns pay some rent money; some other, rent duties called *obrok*, as certain *chetverti* or measures of grain, wheat, rye, barley, oats, etc.; or of other victual, as oxen, sheep, swans, geese, hares, hens, wild fowl, fish, hay, wood, honey, etc. Some are bound to sow for the Emperor's provision certain acres of ground and to make the corn ready for his use, having for it an allowance of certain acres of ground for their own proper use.

This provision for the household—especially of grain served in by the tenants—is a great deal more than is spent in his house or in other allowance served out in livery, or for the Emperor's honor called *zhalovane*, for which use there is bestowed very much both in grain and other victual. This surplus of provision is sold by the steward to the best hand and runneth into the Emperor's treasury.

In the time of Ivan Vasilevich, father to this Emperor, who kept a more princely and bountiful house than the Emperor now doth, this overplus of grain and other incomes into the steward's office yielded to his treasury not past 60,000 rubles yearly but riseth now by good husbanding of the steward Grigorii Vasilevich Godunov to 230,000 rubles a year.[4] And this by the means of the Empress and her kindred, especially Boris Fedorovich Godunov, that account it all their own that runneth into the Emperor's treasury. Much of this surplusage that riseth out of the rent provision is employed to the payment of the wages of his household officers, which are very many attending at home and purveying abroad.

The second office of receipt, called the *Chetverti* (being divided into four several parts as before was said), hath four head officers, which besides the ordering and government of the shires contained within their several *chetverti* have this also as a

---

throughout Muscovy. Fletcher erred in placing Tver and Staraia Rusa in the *Dvorets* government; they belonged in the *Bolshoi Prikhod* (cf. p. 55 below). *Slobody* referred to the Moscow *slobody*, or settlements, or villages.

[4] Fletcher erred, as this sum is too high. Cf. Seredonin, *Sochinenie*, p. 326.

Of the Rus Commonwealth

part of their office: to receive the *tiaglo* and *podat* belonging to the Emperor, that riseth out of the four *chetverti*, or quarters. The *tiaglo* is a yearly rent or imposition raised upon every *vyt*, or measure, of grain that groweth within the land, gathered by sworn men and brought into the office. The *vyt* containeth sixty *chetverti*. Every *chetvert* is three bushels English, or little less. The *podat* is an ordinary rent of money imposed upon every soke, or hundred, within the whole realm.[5]

This *tiaglo* and *podat* bring in yearly to the offices of the *chetverti* a great sum of money, as may appear by the particulars here set down. The town and province [6] of Pskov pay yearly for *tiaglo* and *podat* about 18,000 rubles; Novgorod, about 35,000 rubles; Torzhok and Tver, 8,000 rubles: Riazan, 30,000 rubles; Murom, 12,000 rubles; Kholmogory and Dvina, 8,000 rubles; Vologda, 12,000 rubles; Kazan, 18,000 rubles; Ustiug, 30,000 rubles; Rostov, 50,000; the city of Moscow, 40,000 rubles; Siberia, 20,000 rubles; Kostroma, 12,000 rubles.[7] The total amounteth to 400,000 rubles or marks a year, which is brought in yearly the first day of September, that is reckoned by them the first day of the year.[8]

The third, that is called the *Bolshoi Prikhod*, or great income, receiveth all the customs that are gathered out of all the principal towns and cities within the whole realm, besides the fees

---

[5] Fletcher's use of "soke" is not clear. In England the term applied to a local division or district. In Russia a *sokha* was an old measure of tillable land or a unit of tax assessment.

[6] Fletcher did not clearly distinguish between cities and *oblasti* ("shires") of the same name. If he meant *oblasti*, he included Murom, Kostroma, and Vologda, which he failed to mention earlier (cf. above, p. 5). If he meant cities, then the amounts ascribed often were too high. Riazan must be regarded as a province in this instance.

[7] Seredonin's analysis (*Sochinenie*, pp. 329–331) has shown that Fletcher's figures for Pskov, Ustiug, and especially Rostov, were much too high. Since the conquest of Siberia had begun only a few years before Fletcher's arrival in Moscow, he could not have had access to reliable statistics here.

[8] The sum of these figures is 293,000 rubles; Fletcher assumed that about 107,000 rubles came from other cities.

The Emperor's Customs and Other Revenues

and other duties which rise out of divers smaller offices, which are all brought into this office of *Bolshoi Prikhod*. The towns of most trade that do yield greatest custom are these here set down: Moscow, Smolensk, Pskov, Novgorod Velikii, Staraia Rusa, Torzhok, Tver, Iaroslavl, Kostroma, Nizhnii Novgorod, Kazan, Vologda. This custom out of the great town is therefore more certain and easy to be reckoned, because it is set and rated precisely what they shall pay for the custom of the year. Which needs must be paid into the said office, though they receive not so much. If it fall out to be more, it runneth all into the Emperor's advantage.

The custom at Moscow for every year is 12,000 rubles; the custom of Smolensk, 8,000; Pskov, 12,000 rubles; Novgorod Velikii, 6,000 rubles; Staraia Rusa, by salt and other commodities, 18,000 rubles; Torzhok, 800 rubles; Tver, 700 rubles; Iaroslavl, 1,200 rubles; Kostroma, 1,800 rubles; Nizhnii Novgorod, 7,000 rubles; Kazan, 11,000 rubles; Vologda, 2,000 rubles. The custom of the rest that are towns of trade is sometimes more, sometimes less, as their traffic and dealings with commodities to and fro falleth out for the year.[9]

This may be said for certain, that the three tables of receipts belonging to this office of *Bolshoi Prikhod* when they receive least account for thus much, viz., the first table, 160,000 rubles; the second table, 90,000 rubles; the third, 70,000 rubles. So that there cometh into the office of *Bolshoi Prikhod* at the least reckoning, as appeareth by their books of customs, out of these and other towns, and maketh the sum of 340,000 rubles a year.[10]

---

[9] The amounts given for Novgorod Velikii, Kazan, and Pskov are disproportionately high when compared with other available figures. Seredonin, *Sochinenie*, p. 334, suspected that Fletcher in haste had duplicated all these *Bolshoi Prikhod* figures, having already included them in the *tiaglo* and *podat* from the cities noted above. There is no evidence to indicate that direct taxes (*Chetvert*) ever exceeded the customs duties (*Bolshoi Prikhod*) paid by the towns or provinces at this time.

[10] Fletcher is not clear, as he previously had mentioned only two sources

Of the Rus Commonwealth

Besides this custom out of the towns of trade there is received by this office of *Bolshoi Prikhod* the yearly rent of the common bathstoves and *kabaki*, or drinking houses, which pertain to the Emperor. Which, though it be uncertain for the just sum, yet because it is certain and an ordinary matter that the Rus will bathe himself as well within as without, yieldeth a large rent to the Emperor's treasury.

There is besides a certain mulct or penalty that groweth to the Emperor out of judgment or sentence that passeth in any of his courts of record in all civil matters. This penalty or mulct is 20 *dengi*, or pence, upon every ruble or mark, and so ten in the hundred, which is paid by the party that is convict by law. He hath besides for every name contained in the writs that pass out of these courts five *altyny*. An *altyn* is fivepence sterling or thereabouts. This is made good out of the office whence the writ is taken forth; thence it goeth to the office that keepeth the lesser seal, where it payeth as much more to the Emperor's use. This riseth commonly to 3,000 rubles a year or thereabouts. Farther also out of the office of *Razboinyi Prikaz*, where all felonies are tried, is received for the Emperor the half part of felons' goods; the other half goeth, the one part to the informer, the other to the officers.

All this is brought into the office of *Bolshoi Prikhod*, or great income. Besides the overplus or remainder that is saved out of the land rents allotted to divers other offices, as, namely, to the office called *Rozriad*, which hath lands and rents assigned unto it to pay the yearly salaries of the soldiers or horsemen that are kept still in pay. Which in time of peace, when they rest at home not employed in any service, is commonly cut off and paid

---

of revenue for the *Bolshoi Prikhod*; moreover, his total should here read 320,000 rubles. Since the sum of the customs was 80,500 rubles and included even such a small amount as 700 rubles from Tver, it is hard to conceive how the remainder of the 340,000 or 320,000 rubles was acquired by the *Bolshoi Prikhod*.

The Emperor's Customs and Other Revenues

them by half, sometimes not the half; so that the remainder out of the *Rozriad* office that is laid into the Emperor's treasury cometh for the most part every year to 250,000 rubles.

In like sort, though not so much, is brought in the surplus out of the *streletskii* offices, which hath proper lands for the payment of the *streltsy* men, or gunners, as well those at Moscow that are of the Emperor's guard—12,000 in ordinary—as on the borders and other garrison towns and castles. Likewise out of the office of *Prikaz Shishevoi Nemskii*, which hath set allowance of lands to maintain the foreign mercenary soldiers, as Poles, Swedens, Dutches, Scots, etc. So, out of the office of *Pusharskii*, which hath lands and rents allowed for the provision of munition, great ordnance, powder, shot, saltpeter, brimstone, lead, and suchlike, there is left somewhat at the year's end that runneth into the treasury. All these bring into the office of *Bolshoi Prikhod* that which remaineth in their hand at the year's end, whence it is delivered into the Emperor's treasury. So that the whole sum that groweth to this office of *Bolshoi Prikhod*, or the great income, as appeareth by the books of the said office, amounteth to 800,000 rubles a year or thereabouts.[11]

All these offices, to wit, the office of the steward, the four *Chetverti*, and the *Bolshoi Prikhod*, deliver in their receipts to the head treasury that lieth within the Emperor's house or castle at the Moscow, where lie all his moneys, jewels, crowns, scepters, plate, and suchlike, the chests, hutches, and bags being signed by the Emperors themselves with their own seal. Though at this time the Lord Boris Fedorovich Godunov his seal and oversight supplieth for the Emperor as in all other things. The underofficer at this time is one Stepan Vasilevich Godunov,

[11] Fletcher implied here that the military *prikazy* contributed not less than 400,000 rubles to the *Bolshoi Prikhod*. The assumption that their income totaled 800,000 rubles—they retained at least half for their own needs—is simply implausible. Seredonin concludes that Fletcher carelessly used some figures twice and that the total income paid into the *Chetvert* and *Bolshoi Prikhod* was about 400,000 rubles.

Of the Rus Commonwealth

cousin-german [12] to the said Boris, who hath two clerks allowed to serve under him in the office.

| The sum that groweth to the Emperor's treasury in money only for every year | 1. Out of the steward's office, above the expense of his house, 23,000 rubles
2. Out of the four *Chetverti* for soke and head money, 400,000 rubles
3. Out of the *Bolshoi Prikhod* office, or great income, for custom and other rents, 800,000 rubles | Sum: 1,430,000 [13] rubles clear, besides all charges for his house and ordinary salaries of his soldiers otherwise discharged |

But besides this revenue, that is paid all in money to the Emperor's treasury, he receiveth yearly in furs and other duties to a great value out of Siberia, Pechora, Perm, and other places, which are sold or bartered away for other foreign commodities to the Turkish, Persian, Armenian, Georgian, and Bukhara merchants that trade within his countries, besides others of Christendom. What it maketh in the whole, though the value cannot be set down precisely, as being a thing casual as the commodity may be got, it may be guessed by that which was gathered the last year out of Siberia for the Emperor's custom, viz., 466 timber [14] of sables, five timber of martens, 180 black foxes, besides other commodities.

To these may be added their seizures and confiscations upon such as are in displeasure, which riseth to a great sum, besides their other extraordinary impositions and exactions done upon their officers, monasteries, etc., not for any apparent necessity or use of the prince or commonwealth, but of will and custom. Yet

---

[12] First cousin.

[13] Aside from the dubious total recorded here, Fletcher made some simple errors in arithmetic. The "23,000" should read "230,000" in order for the sum to be "1,430,000." Cf. p. 53, n. 4.

[14] A certain number of fur skins; a package containing forty skins (i.e., 20 pairs of half skins) of martens, sables, and ermine.

The Emperor's Customs and Other Revenues

with some pretense of a Scythian, that is, gross and barbarous, policy, as may appear by these few *sophismata,* or counterfeit policies, put in practice by the Emperors of Russia, all tending to this end: to rob their people and to enrich their treasury. To this purpose this byword was used by the late Emperor Ivan Vasilevich: that his people were like to his beard—the oftener shaven, the thicker it would grow. Or like sheep that must needs be shorn once a year at the least to keep them from being overladen with their wool.

MEANS USED TO DRAW THE WEALTH OF THE LAND INTO THE EMPEROR'S TREASURY

To prevent no extortions, exactions, or briberies whatsoever done upon the commons by their dukes, *diaki,* or other officers in their provinces, but to suffer them to go on till their time be expired and to suck themselves full; then to call them to the *pravezh,* or whip, for their behavior and to beat out of them all or the most part of the booty, as the honey from the bee, which they have wrung from the commons, and to turn it into the Emperor's treasury, but never anything back again to the right owners, how great or evident soever the injury be. To this end the needy dukes and *diaki* that are sent into their provinces serve the turn very well, being changed so often, to wit, once a year; where, in respect of their own and the quality of the people, as before was said, they might be continued for some longer time without all fear of innovation. For coming still fresh upon the commons, they suck more eagerly, like Tiberius the Emperor's flies, that came new still upon all old sores and to whom he was wont to compare his praetors and other provincial officers.

2

To make of these officers that have robbed their people sometimes a public example, if any be more notorious than the rest,

Of the Rus Commonwealth

that the Emperor may seem to mislike the oppressions done to his people and transfer the fault to his ill officers.

As, among divers other, was done by the late Emperor Ivan Vasilevich to a *diak* in one of his provinces, that besides many other extortions and briberies had taken a goose ready dressed full of money. The man was brought to the market place in Moscow. The Emperor himself present made an oration. "These, good people, are they that would eat you up like bread," etc. Then asked he his *palachi*, or executioners, who could cut up a goose and commanded one of them first to cut off his legs about the midst of the shin, then his arms above his elbows (asking him still if goose flesh were good meat), in the end to chop off his head, that he might have the right fashion of a goose ready dressed. This might seem to have been a tolerable piece of justice, as justice goeth in Russia, except his subtle end to cover his own oppressions.

3

To make an open show of want when any great tax or imposition is toward. As was done by this Emperor Fedor Ivanovich by the advice of some about him at the beginning of his reign, when, being left very rich, as was thought, by his father, he sold most of his plate and stamped some into coin that he might seem to want money; whereupon presently out came a taxation.

4

To suffer their subjects to give freely to the monasteries, which for their superstition very many do, especially in their last wills, and to lay up their money and substance in them to keep it more safe. Which all is permitted them without any restraint or proviso, as was and is in some countries of Christendom. Whereby their monasteries grow to exceeding great wealth. This they do to have the money of the realm better stored together and more ready for their hand when they list to

The Emperor's Customs and Other Revenues

take it: which many times is done without any noise, the friars being content rather to part from somewhat as the increase groweth than to loose all at once—which they were made to doubt of in the other Emperor's days.

To this end Ivan Vasilevich, late Emperor, used a very strange practice that few princes would have done in their greatest extremities. He resigned his kingdom to one Velikii Kniaz Simeon, the Emperor's son of Kazan, as though he meant to draw himself from all public doings to a quiet private life.[15] Toward the end of the year he caused this new king to call in all charters granted to bishoprics and monasteries, which they had enjoyed many hundred years before and which were all cancelled.[16] This done, as in dislike of the fact and of the misgovernment of the new king, he resumed his scepter and so was content, as in favor to the Church and religious men, that they should renew their charters and take them of himself, reserving and annexing to the crown so much of their lands as himself thought good.

By this practice he wrung from the bishoprics and monasteries, besides the lands which he annexed to the crown, an huge mass of money. From some forty, from some fifty, from some an hundred thousand rubles.[17] And this as well for the increase of his treasury as to abate the ill opinion of his hard government by a show of worse in another man. Wherein his strange spirit is to be noted, that, being hated of his subjects, as himself knew well enough, yet would venture such a practice to set another in

---

[15] Fletcher referred to the temporary resignation of Ivan IV (probably in September or October, 1575) in favor of the Tartar Khan of Kasimov, Ssain Bulat, baptized Simeon Bekbulatovich. Cf. Jack M. Culpepper, "The Kremlin Executions of 1575 and the Enthronement of Simeon Bekbulatovich," *Slavic Review*, XXIV (1965), 503–506.

[16] That an old charter was reaffirmed in 1578 suggests that not all had been cancelled. Fletcher's assumption that Simeon's reign was but a device to procure more revenue does not suffice. As head of the *zemshchina*, Simeon must be counted a political as well as a financial tool of Ivan IV.

[17] This figure seems unreasonably high. Cf. Seredonin, *Sochinenie*, p. 61.

Of the Rus Commonwealth

his saddle that might have rid away with his horse while himself walked by on foot.

5

To send their messengers into the provinces or shires where the special commodities of their country grow, as furs, wax, honey, etc. There to forestall and engross [18] sometime one whole commodity, sometime two or more, taking them at small prices what themselves list and selling them again at an excessive rate to their own merchants and to merchants strangers. If they refuse to buy them, then to force them unto it.

The like is done when any commodity—either native or foreign, as cloth of gold, broadcloth, etc., thus engrossed by the Emperor and received into his treasury—happeneth to decay or mar by long lying or some other casualty; which is forced upon the merchants to be bought by them at the Emperor's price whether they will or no. This last year of 1589 was engrossed all the wax of the country, so that none might deal with that commodity but the Emperor only.

6

To take up and engross in like sort sometime foreign commodities, as silks, cloth, lead, pearl, etc., brought into his realm by Turkish merchants, Armenians, Bukharians, Poles, English, and other. And then to force his merchants to buy them of his officers at his own price.

7

To make a monopoly for the time of such commodities as are paid him for rent or custom and to enhance the price of them, as furs, corn, wood, etc. What time none must sell of the same kind of commodity till the Emperor's be all sold. By this means he maketh of his rent, corn, and other provision of victual, as

---

[18] To control by anticipatory measures and monopolize, particularly a marketable commodity. These terms in their sixteenth-century sense suggest the sin of avarice.

The Emperor's Customs and Other Revenues

before was said, about 200,000 rubles or marks a year. Of his rent, wood, hay, etc., 30,000 rubles or thereabouts.

8

In every great town of his realm he hath a *kabak*, or drinking house, where is sold aquavite [19]—which they call Rus wine—mead, beer, etc. Out of these he receiveth rent that amounteth to a great sum of money. Some yield 800, some 900, some 1,000, some 2,000 or 3,000 rubles a year. Wherein, besides the base and dishonorable means to increase his treasury, many foul faults are committed. The poor laboring man and artificer many times spendeth all from his wife and children. Some use to lay in twenty, thirty, forty rubles, or more into the *kabak* and vow themselves to the pot till all that be spent. And this, as he will say, for the honor of *hospodar*,[20] or the Emperor. You shall have many there that have drunk all away to the very skin and so walk naked, whom they call *nagie*. While they are in the *kabak*, none may call them forth, whatsoever cause there be, because he hindereth the Emperor's revenue.

9

To cause some of his boiars or nobles of his court, whom he useth upon trust, that have houses in the Moscow to feign themselves robbed; then to send for the *zemskie* men, or aldermen of the city, and to command them to find out the robbery. In default of not finding it, to prave,[21] or seize, the city for their misgovernment in 8,000, 9,000, or 10,000 rubles at a time. This is many times practiced.

10

In these extractions, to show their sovereignty, sometimes they use very plain and yet strange cavillations. As was that of Ivan

---

[19] Probably vodka.

[20] A word of Slavic origin, meaning "master" or "lord."

[21] Fletcher seems to have coined from the Russian word *pravezh* (see p. 72) a verb meaning to extort by beating, perhaps with some recollection of the English "prive," to deprive or rob.

Of the Rus Commonwealth

Vasilevich, father to this Emperor, after this sort. He sent into Perm for certain loads of cedar wood, whereof he knew that none grew in that country. The inhabitants returned answer they could find none there; whereupon he seized their country in 12,000 rubles, as if they concealed the commodity of purpose. Again he sent to the city of Moscow to provide for him a *kolpak*,[22] or measure, full of live fleas for medicine. They returned answer that the thing was impossible; and if they could get them, yet they could not measure them for leaping out; whereupon he praved, or beat out of their shins, 7,000 rubles for a mulct.[23]

By like cavillation he extorted from his nobility 30,000 rubles because he missed of his game when he went ahunting for the hare, as if their hunting and murdering of hares had been the cause of it. Which the nobility, as the manner is, praved presently again upon the *muzhiki,* or common people of the country. This may seem a strange kind of extortion by such pleasant cavils to fleece his poor subjects in good sadness, but that it agreeth with the quality of those emperors and the miserable subjection of that poor country. These and suchlike means are practiced by the Emperors of Russia to increase their treasury.

CHAPTER XIII

Of the State of the Commonalty, or Vulgar Sort of People, in the Country of Russia

THE condition of the commons and vulgar sort of people may partly be understood by that which already hath been said concerning the manner of their government and the state of the nobility, with the ordering of their provinces and chief towns of

---
[22] Literally, in Russian, a cap or cowl.
[23] A fine imposed for an offense.

Of the Commonalty

the land. And first, touching their liberty, how it standeth with them, it may appear by this: that they are reckoned in no degree at all nor have any suffrage nor place in their *sobor*, or high court of parliament, where their laws and public orders are concluded upon, which commonly tend to the oppression of the commons. For the other two degrees, viz., of the nobility and clergy, which have a vote in the parliaments, though far from that liberty that ought to be in common consultations for the public benefit, according to the measure and proportion of their degrees, are well contented that the whole burden shall light upon the commons; so they may ease their own shoulders by laying all upon them. Again, into what servile condition their liberty is brought not only to the prince but to the nobles and gentlemen of the country, who themselves also are but servile —especially of late years—it may further appear by their own acknowledgments in their supplications and other writings to any of the nobles or chief officers of the Emperor's.[1] Wherein they name and subscribe themselves *khlopy*, that is, their villeins, or bondslaves, as they of the nobility do unto the Emperor. This may truly be said of them: that there is no servant nor bondslave more awed by his master nor kept down in a more servile subjection than the poor people are, and that universally, not only by the Emperor but by his nobility, chief officers, and soldiers. So that when a poor *muzhik* meeteth with any of them upon the highway, he must turn himself about, as not daring to look him on the face, and fall down with knocking of his head to the very ground, as he doth unto his idol.[2]

Secondly, concerning the lands, goods, and other possessions of the commons, they answer the name and lie common indeed without any fence against the rapine and spoil not only of the highest but of his nobility, officers, and soldiers. Besides the

---

[1] There is no evidence of such petitions.
[2] Seredonin, *Sochinenie*, p. 202, has cited this statement as an example of Fletcher's tendency to generalize from isolated happenings.

taxes, customs, seizures, and other public exactions done upon them by the Emperor, they are so racked and pulled by the nobles, officers, and messengers sent abroad by the Emperor in his public affairs—especially in the *iamy* (as they call them) and thoroughfare towns—that you shall have many villages and towns of half a mile and a mile long stand all unhabited, the people being fled all into other places by reason of the extreme usage and exactions done upon them.³ So that in the way toward Moscow, betwixt Vologda and Iaroslavl (which is two nineties, after their reckoning, little more than an hundred miles English) there are in sight fifty *derevni,* or villages, at the least, some half a mile, some a mile long, that stand vacant and desolate without any inhabitant. The like is in all other places of the realm, as is said by those that have better traveled the country than myself had time or occasion to do.

The great oppression over the poor commons maketh them to have no courage in following their trades, for that the more they have the more danger they are in, not only of their goods but of their lives also. And if they have anything, they conceal it all they can—sometimes conveying it into monasteries, sometimes hiding it under the ground and in woods, as men are wont to do where they are in fear of invasion. Insomuch that many times you shall see them afraid to be known to any boiar or gentleman of such commodities as they have to sell. I have seen them sometimes when they have laid open their commodities for a liking, as their principal furs and suchlike, to look still behind them and toward every door, as men in some fear that looked to be set upon and surprised by some enemy. Whereof, asking the cause, I found it to be this: that they have doubted lest some nobleman, or *syn boiarskii,* of the Emperor had been in com-

³ *Iamy:* post stations. The Muscovite rulers controlled remote areas and obtained information by means of a unique mail service. Fletcher likely mistook a nest of villages for one large village.

Of the Commonalty

pany and so laid a train for them to prey upon their commodities perforce.[4]

This maketh the people, though otherwise hardened to bear any toil, to give themselves much to idleness and drinking, as passing for no more than from hand to mouth. And hereof it cometh that the commodities of Russia (as was said before), as wax, tallow, hides, flax, hemp, etc., grow and go abroad in far less plenty than they were wont to do, because the people, being oppressed and spoiled of their gettings, are discouraged from their labors. Yet this one thing is much to be noted: that in all this oppression there were three brethren merchants of late that traded together with one stock in common, that were found to be worth 300,000 rubles in money, besides lands, cattles, and other commodities.[5] Which may partly be imputed to their dwellings far off from the eye of the court, viz., in Vychegda, 1,000 miles from Moscow and more. The same are said by those that knew them to have set on work all the year long ten thousand men in making of salt, carriages by cart and boat, hewing of wood, and suchlike, besides five thousand bondslaves at the least to inhabit and till their land.

They had also their physicians, surgeons, apothecaries, and all manner of artificers, of Dutches and others, belonging unto them. They are said to have paid to the Emperor for custom to the sum of 23,000 rubles a year,[6] for which cause they were suffered to enjoy their trade, besides the maintaining of certain garrisons on the borders of Siberia which were near unto them. Wherein the Emperor was content to use their purse till such

---

[4] Seredonin, *Sochinenie*, p. 204, suggested that the merchants' anxiety resulted from their attempt to sell prohibited goods.

[5] This is a reference to the Stroganov family, so influential in Muscovy's expansion into Siberia.

[6] This sum seems wildly exaggerated. Seredonin, *Sochinenie*, pp. 208–209, has shown that the sum of 23,000 rubles was a hundred times more than in reality was paid.

time as they had got ground in Siberia and made it habitable by burning and cutting down woods from Vychegda to Perm above 1,000 versts and then took it all away from them perforce.

But this in the end being envied and disdained, as a matter not standing with their policy to have any so great, especially a *muzhik*, the Emperor began first to pull from them by pieces, sometimes 20,000 rubles at a time, sometime more, till in the end their sons that now are are well eased of their stock and have but small part of their father's substance, the rest being drawn all into the Emperor's treasury. Their names were Iakov, Grigorii, and Simeon, the sons of Anika.

For the quality of their people otherwise, though there seemeth to be in them some aptness to receive any art, as appeareth by the natural wits in the men and very children, yet they excel in no kind of common art, much less in any learning or literal kind of knowledge, which they are kept from of purpose, as they are also from all military practice, that they may be fitter for the servile condition wherein now they are, and have neither reason nor valor to attempt innovation. For this purpose also they are kept from traveling, that they may learn nothing nor see the fashions of other countries abroad. You shall seldom see a Rus a traveler except he be with some ambassador or that he make a scape out of his country, which hardly he can do, by reason of the borders that are watched so narrowly and the punishment for any such attempt, which is death if he be taken and all his goods confiscate. Only they learn to write and to read, and that very few of them. Neither do they suffer any stranger willingly to come into their realm out of any civil country for the same cause, farther than necessity of uttering their commodities and taking in of foreign doth enforce them to do.

And therefore this year 1589 they consulted about the removing of all merchants strangers to the border towns to abide and have their residency there and to be more wary in admitting other strangers hereafter into the inland parts of the realm, for

Of the Commonalty

fear of infection with better manners and qualities than they have of their own. For the same purpose also they are kept within the bounds of their degree by the laws of their country, so that the son of a *muzhik,* artificer, or husbandman is ever a *muzhik,* artificer, etc., and hath no means to aspire any higher except, having learned to write and read, he attain to the preferment of a priest or *diak.* Their language is all one with the Slavonian, which is thought to have been derived from the Rus tongue rather than the Rus from the Slavonian. For the people called Slavs are known to have had their beginning out of Sarmatia and to have termed themselves of their conquest Slavs, that is, "famous" or "glorious," of the word *slava,* which in the Rus and Slavonian tongue signifieth as much as "glory" or "fame." Though afterward, being subdued and trod upon by divers nations, the Italians, their neighbors, have turned the word to a contrary signification and term every servant or peasant by the name of *sclava,* as did the Romans by the Getes and Syrians for the same reason.[7] The Rus character or letter is no other than the Greek somewhat distorted.

Concerning their trades, diet, apparel, and suchlike, it is to be noted in a several chapter of their private behavior.

This order that bindeth every man to keep his rank and several degree wherein his forefathers lived before him is more meet to keep the subjects in a servile subjection, and so apt for this and like commonwealths, than to advance any virtue or to breed any rare or excellent quality in nobility or commons, as having no farther reward nor preferment whereunto they may bend their endeavors and employ themselves to advance their estate but rather procure more danger to themselves the more they excel in any noble or principal quality.

---

[7] Fletcher depended upon Martin Kromer for this erroneous account of the origin of the Slavic tongue. *Slava* does mean "glory" in Russian. "Getes" probably refers to the Getae, a Thracian tribe living on the lower Danube.

CHAPTER XIV

Of Their Public Justice and Manner of Proceeding in Civil and Criminal Matters

THEIR courts of civil justice for matter of contract and other of like sort are of three kinds, the one being subject unto the other by way of appeal. The lowest court, that seemeth to be appointed for some ease to the subjects, is the office of the *gubnyi starosta,* that signifieth an alderman, and of the *sotskii starosta,* or bailiff of the soke or hundred, whereof I spake before in the ordering of the provinces. These may end matters among their neighbors within their soke or several hundred, where they are appointed under the dukes and *diaki* of the provinces, to whom the parties may remove their matter if they cannot be agreed by the said *gubnyi* or *sotskii starosta.*[1]

The second is kept in the head towns of every province or shire by the said dukes and *diaki* that are deputies to the four lords of the *chetverti,* as before was said. From these courts they may appeal and remove their suits to the chief court that is kept at the Moscow, where are resident the officers of the four *chetverti.* These are the chief justices or judges, every of them in all civil matters that grow within their several *chetvert,* or quarter, and may be either commenced originally before them or prosecuted out of the inferior courts of the shires by way of appeal.[2]

Their commencing and proceeding in civil actions is on this manner. First, the plaintiff putteth up his supplication, wherein he declareth the effect of his cause or wrong done unto him; whereupon is granted unto him a *vypis,* or warrant, which he delivereth to the *pristav,* or sergeant, to do the arrest upon the

[1] See above, p. 45. [2] See above, p. 45.

Their Public Justice

party whom he meaneth to implead. Who upon the arrest is to put in sureties to answer the day appointed or else standeth at the sergeant's devotion [3] to be kept safe by such means as he thinketh good.

The sergeants are many and excel for their hard and cruel dealing toward their prisoners: commonly they clap irons upon them, as many as they can bear, to wring out of them some larger fees. Though it be but for sixpence, you shall see them go with chains on their legs, arms, and neck. When they come before the judge, the plaintiff beginneth to declare his matter after the content of his supplication. As for attorneys, counselors, procurators, and advocates to plead their cause for them, they have no such order; but every man is to tell his own tale and plead for himself so well as he can.[4]

If they have any witness or other evidence, they produce it before the judge. If they have none, or if the truth of the cause cannot so well be discerned by the plea or evidence on both parts, then the judge asketh either party which he thinketh good, plaintiff or defendant, whether he will kiss the cross upon that which he avoucheth or denieth. He that taketh the cross, being so offered by the judge, is accounted clear and carrieth away the matter. This ceremony is not done within the court or office, but the party is carried to the church by an officer and there the ceremony is done—the money in the meanwhile hanging upon a nail or else lying at the idol's feet, ready to be delivered to the party as soon as he hath kissed the cross before the said idol.

This kissing of the cross (called *krestnoe tselovanie*) is as their corporal oath and accounted with them a very holy thing, which no man will dare to violate or profane with a false allegation. If both parties offer to kiss the cross in a contradictory

---

[3] Is left to the sergeant's care.
[4] Fletcher erred, as there were judicial mediators in the Muscovite courts at this time.

matter, then they draw lots. The better lot is supposed to have the right and beareth away the matter.[5] So the party convicted is adjudged to pay the debt or penalty whatsoever and withal to pay the Emperor's fees, which is twenty pence upon every mark, as before hath been noted.

When the matter is thus ended, the party convicted is delivered to the sergeant, who hath a writ for his warrant out of the office to carry him to the *pravezh*, or righter of justice, if presently he pay not the money or content not the party. This *pravezh*, or righter, is a place near to the office, where such as have sentence passed against them and refuse to pay that which is adjudged are beaten with great cudgels on the shins and calves of their legs. Every forenoon from eight to eleven they are set on the *pravezh* and beat in this sort till the money be paid. The afternoon and nighttime they are kept in chains by the sergeant, except they put in sufficient sureties for their appearance at the *pravezh* at the hour appointed. You shall see forty or fifty stand together on the *pravezh* all on a row and their shins thus becudgeled and bebasted every morning with a piteous cry. If, after a year's standing on the *pravezh*, the party will not, or lack wherewithal to, satisfy his creditor, it is lawful for him to sell his wife and children, either outright or for a certain term of years. And if the price of them do not amount to the full payment, the creditor may take them to be his bondslaves for years or forever, according as the value of the debt requireth.[6]

Such kind of suits as lack direct evidence or stand upon conjectures and circumstances to be weighed by the judge draw of great length and yield great advantage to the judge and officers. If the suit be upon a bond, or bill, they have for the most part good and speedy justice. Their bonds, or bills, are drawn in a

[5] The casting of lots frequently determined only the order of kissing the cross or decided matters of little importance.

[6] Fletcher erred, as it was forbidden by law to sell a debtor into full serfdom, nor could a debtor request it as a means of avoiding payment. Cf. Seredonin, *Sochinenie*, p. 303.

Their Public Justice

very plain sort after this tenor: "I, Ivan Vasilev, have borrowed of Afonasii Dementiev the sum of one hundred rubles of going money of Moscow, from the *Kreshchenie,* or hallowing of the water, until the *Sobornoe voskresene,* or Council Sunday, without interest. And if this money rest unpaid after that day, then he shall give interest upon the said money after the common rate as it goeth among the people, viz., for every five the sixth ruble. Upon this there are witnesses, Nikita Sidorov, etc., subscribed. This bill have I written Gavrilko Iakovlev in the year 7096." [7] The witnesses and debtor, if he can write, endorse their names on the back side of the bill. Other signing or sealing have they none.

When any is taken for a matter of crime, as treason, murder, theft, and suchlike, he is first brought to the duke and *diak* that are for the province where the party is attached, by whom he is examined. The manner of examination in such cases is all by torture, as scourging with whips made of sinews or whitleather, called the *pytka,* as big as a man's finger, which giveth a sore lash and entereth into the flesh; or by tying to a spit and roasting at the fire; sometimes by breaking and wresting one of their ribs with a pair of hot tongs, or cutting their flesh under the nails, and suchlike.

The examination thus taken, with all the proofs and evidences that can be alleged against the party, it is sent up to the Moscow to the lord of the *chetvert,* or fourth part, under whom the province is, and by him is presented to the council table, to be read and sentenced there where only judgment is given in matter of life and death and that by evidence upon information, though they never saw nor heard the party, who is kept still in prison where the fact was committed and never sent up to the place where he is tried. If they find the party guilty, they give

---

[7] Into this typical document which Fletcher copied I have inserted the correct Russian names. *Kreshchenie* refers to Epiphany or Twelfth Day. The date 7096 may be translated 1588.

sentence of death according to the quality of the fact, which is sent down by the lord of the *chetvert* to the duke and *diak* to be put in execution. The prisoner is carried to the place of execution with his hands bound and a wax candle burning held betwixt his fingers. Their capital punishments are hanging, heading, knocking on the head, drowning, putting under the ice, setting on a stake, and suchlike. But for the most part the prisoners that are condemned in summer are kept for the winter to be knocked in the head and put under the ice. This is to be understood of common persons. For theft and murder, if they be committed upon a poor *muzhik* by one of nobility, are not lightly [8] punished, nor yet is he called to any account for it. Their reason is because they are accounted their *khlopy*, or bondslaves. If by some *synovia boiarskie*, or gentleman soldier, a murder or theft be committed, peradventure he shall be imprisoned at the Emperor's pleasure. If the manner of the fact be very notorious, he is whipped perchance; and this is commonly all the punishment that is inflicted upon them.[9]

If a man kill his own servant, little or nothing is said unto him, for the same reason, because he is accounted to be his *khlopy*, or bondslave, so to have right over his very head. The most is some small mulct to the Emperor if the party be rich, and so the quarrel is made rather against the purse than against the injustice. They have no written law save only a small book, that containeth the time and manner of their sitting, order in proceeding, and such other judicial forms and circumstances, but nothing to direct them to give sentence upon right or wrong. Their only law is their speaking law, that is, the pleasure of the prince and of his magistrates and officers, which showeth the miserable condition of this poor people, that are forced to have

---

[8] Usually.

[9] Seredonin, *Sochinenie*, p. 306, cites evidence that nobles guilty of crimes did not always go unpunished or receive light penalties. For previous comments by Fletcher on judicial procedure cf. pp. 45 and 65.

Their Forces for the Wars

them for their law and direction of justice against whose injustice and extreme oppression they had need to be armed with many good and strong laws.[10]

CHAPTER XV

Their Forces for the Wars, with the Chief Officers and Their Salaries

THE soldiers of Russia are called *synovia boiarskie*, or the sons of gentlemen, because they are all of that degree by virtue of their military profession. For every soldier in Russia is a gentleman, and none are gentlemen but only soldiers that take it by descent from their ancestors, so that the son of a gentleman which is born a soldier is ever a gentleman and a soldier withal and professeth nothing else but military matters. When they are of years able to bear arms, they come to the office of *Rozriadnyi*, or great constable, and there present themselves, who entereth their names and allotteth them certain lands to maintain their charges, for the most part the same that their fathers enjoyed.[1] For the lands assigned to maintain the army are ever certain, annexed to this office without improving or detracting one foot. But that if the Emperor have sufficient in wages, the room being full so far as the land doth extend already, they are many times deferred and have nothing allowed them except some one portion of the land be divided into two, which is a cause of great disorder within that country when a soldier that hath many children shall have sometimes but one entertained in the Emperor's pay. So that the rest, having nothing, are forced to live by unjust

---

[10] Fletcher apparently did not know about the law code of 1497 and the one of 1550 based on it.

[1] Fletcher exaggerated, for the *deti boiarskie* (cf. above, p. 44) often received holdings in newly annexed lands.

Of the Rus Commonwealth

and wicked shifts that tend to the hurt and oppression of the *muzhiki,* or common sort of people. The inconvenience groweth by maintaining his forces in a continual succession. The whole number of his soldiers in continual pay is this: first, he hath of his *dvoriane,* that is, pensioners or guard of his person, to the number of 15,000 horsemen, with their captains and other officers that are always in a readiness.

Of these 15,000 horsemen there are three sorts or degrees, that differ as well in estimation as in wages, one degree from another. The first sort of them is called *dvoriane bolshie,* or the company of head pensioners, that have some an hundred, some fourscore rubles a year, and none under seventy. The second sort are called *serednie dvoriane,* or the middle rank of pensioners. These have sixty or fifty rubles by the year, none under forty. The third and lowest sort are the *deti boiarskie,* that is, the low pensioners. Their salary is thirty rubles a year for him that hath most. Some have but five-and-twenty, some twenty, none under twelve—whereof the half part is paid them at the Moscow, the other half in the field by the general when they have any wars and are employed in service.[2] When they receive their whole pay, it amounteth to 55,000 rubles by the year.[3]

And this is their wages, besides lands allotted to every one of them, both to the greater and the less according to their degrees; whereof he that hath least hath to yield him twenty rubles or marks by the year. Besides these 15,000 horsemen that are of better choice, as being the Emperor's own guard when himself goeth to the wars, not unlike the Roman soldiers called *praetoriani,* are 110 men of special account for their nobility and

---

[2] Salaries were not always paid annually and in full. While most of the *deti boiarskie* received theirs within a year, there were instances of payment extending over ten years. In time of peace half-salary was not uncommon.

[3] This is a misprint, as the number should probably read 550,000 rubles. Moreover, Fletcher had an exaggerated notion of the number of troops, 15,000, in the Emperor's guard.

Their Forces for the Wars

trust, which are chosen by the Emperor and have their names registered, that find among them for the Emperor's wars to the number of 65,000 horsemen with all necessaries meet for the wars after the Rus manner.[4]

To this end they have yearly allowance made by the Emperor for themselves and their companies to the sum of 40,000 rubles.[5] And those 65,000 are to repair to the field every year on the borders toward the Crim Tartar, except they be appointed for some other service, whether there be wars with the Tartars or not. This might seem peradventure somewhat dangerous for some state, to have so great forces under the command of noblemen to assemble every year to one certain place. But the matter is so used as that no danger can grow to the Emperor or his state by this means: 1) because these noblemen are many, to wit, 110 in all, and changed by the Emperor so oft as he thinketh good; 2) because they have their livings of the Emperor, being otherwise but of very small revenue, and receive this yearly pay of 40,000 rubles when it is presently to be paid forth again to the soldiers that are under them; 3) because for the most part they are about the Emperor's person, being of his council, either special or at large; 4) they are rather as paymasters than captains to their companies, themselves not going forth ordinarily to the wars save when some of them are appointed by special order from the Emperor himself. So the whole number of horsemen that are ever in readiness and in continual pay are 80,000, a few more or less.

If he have need of a greater number, which seldom falleth out, then he entertaineth of those *synovia boiarskie* that are out of pay so many as he needeth. And if yet he want of his number, he giveth charge to his noblemen that hold lands of him to bring

[4] These 110 men were probably a fabrication by Fletcher. Cf. Seredonin, *Sochinenie*, p. 345.

[5] This salary figure was also too low. Fletcher simply exaggerated the numbers of troops, which in his 80,000 estimate included the people of the *deti boiarskie* as well.

Of the Rus Commonwealth

into the field every man a proportionable number of his servants, called *khlopy*, such as till his lands, with their furniture, according to the just number that he intendeth to make; which, the service being done, presently lay in their weapons and return to their servile occupations again.

Of footmen that are in continual pay he hath to the number of 12,000, all gunners, called *streltsy*, whereof 5,000 are to attend about the city of Moscow or any other place where the Emperor shall abide. And 2,000, which are called *stremiannye streltsy*, or gunners at the stirrup, are about his own person at the very court or house where himself lodgeth. The rest are placed in his garrison towns, till there be occasion to have them in the field, and receive for their salary or stipend every man seven rubles a year, besides twelve measures apiece of rye and oats.[6] Of mercenary soldiers that are strangers, whom they call *nemtsy*,[7] they have at this time 4,300 of Polonians; of Cherkasy, that are under the Polonians, about 4,000, whereof 3,500 are abroad in his garrisons; of Dutches and Scots, about 150; of Greeks, Turks, Danes, and Swedens, all in one band, 100 or thereabouts. But these they use only upon the Tartar side and against the Siberians, as they do the Tartar soldiers, whom they hire sometimes, but only for the present, on the other side against the Polonian and Sweden, thinking it best policy so to use their service upon the contrary border.

The chief captains or leaders of these forces, according to their names and degrees, are these which follow: first, the *bolshoi voevoda*, that is, the great captain or lieutenant general under the Emperor. This commonly is one of the four houses of the chief nobility of the land but so chosen otherwise as that he is of small valor or practice in martial matters, being thought to serve that turn so much the better if he bring no other parts

---

[6] Fletcher's estimate was high. Cf. Seredonin, *Sochinenie*, p. 356.

[7] *Nemtsy* literally means "German" but is a general label for "foreigner."

Their Forces for the Wars

with him save the countenance of his nobility to be liked of by the soldiers for that and nothing else. For in this point they are very wary that these two, to wit, nobility and power, meet not both in one, especially if they see wisdom withal or aptness for policy.

Their great *voevoda,* or general, at this present in their wars is commonly one of these four: Kniaz Fedor Ivanovich Mstislavskii, Kniaz Ivan Mikhailovich Glinskii, Cherkasskii, and Trubetskoi—all of great nobility but of very simple quality otherwise, though in Glinskii, as they say, there is somewhat more than in the rest.[8] To make up this defect in the *voevoda,* or general, there is some other joined with him as lieutenant general, of far less nobility but of more valor and experience in the wars than he who ordereth all things that the other countenanceth. At this time their principal man and most used in their wars is one Kniaz Dimitrii Ivanovich Khvorostinin, an ancient and expert captain and one that hath done great service, as they say, against the Tartar and Polonian. Next under the *voevoda* and his lieutenant general are four other that have the marshaling of the whole army divided among them and may be called the marshals of the field.

Every man hath his quarter or fourth part under him, whereof the first is called the *pravyi polk,* or right wing. The second is the *levyi polk,* or left wing. The third is *rusnyi polk,* or the broken band, because out of this there are chosen to send abroad upon any sudden exploit or to make a rescue or supply as occasion doth require. The fourth, *storozhevoi polk,* or the warding band.[9] Every one of these four marshals have two other under them, eight in all, that twice every week at the least must muster and train their several wings or bands and hold and give justice for all faults and disorders committed in the camp.

---
[8] Fletcher's previous estimate of Glinskii appears on pp. 41–42 above.
[9] *Polk* means regiment in Russian. Fletcher omitted a fifth *polk,* the Bolshoi.

Of the Rus Commonwealth

And these eight are commonly chosen out of the 100 which I spake of before, that receive and deliver the pay to the soldiers. Under these eight are divers other captains, as the *golovy*, captains of thousands, five hundreds, and 100; the *piatidesiatskie*, or captains of fifties; and the *desiatskie*, or captains of tens.

Besides the *voevoda*, or general of the army, spoken of before, they have two other that bear the name of *voevoda*, whereof one is the master of the great ordnance, called *nariadnyi voevoda*, who hath divers underofficers necessary for that service. The other is called the *voevoda gulevoi*, or the walking captain, that hath allowed him 1,000 good horsemen of principal choice to range and spy abroad and hath the charge of the running castle which we are to speak of in the chapter following.[10] All these captains and men of charge must once every day resort to the *bolshoi voevoda*, or general of the army, to know his pleasure and to inform him if there be any requisite matter pertaining to their office.[11]

CHAPTER XVI

Of Their Mustering and Levying of Forces, Manner of Armor, and Provision of Victual for the Wars

WHEN wars are toward, which they fail not of lightly every year with the Tartar and many times with the Polonian and Sweden, the four lords of the *chetverti* send forth their summons in the Emperor's name to all the dukes and *diaki* of the provinces to be proclaimed in the head towns of every shire that all the *synovia*

---

[10] Apparently Fletcher confused the word *guliai* (walking) with *gulevoi* (rear-guard), thus concluding that the rear-guard *voevoda* commanded the "walking castle." For more on the "walking castle" see below, p. 84.

[11] Fletcher was too restrictive in his use of the term *voevoda*. Besides the *voevody* noted, one commanded each *polk*, or regiment.

Their Manner of Mustering

boiarskie, or sons of gentlemen, make their repair to such a border where the service is to be done, at such a place and by such a day, and there present themselves to such and such captains. When they come to the place assigned them in the summons or proclamation, their names are taken by certain officers that have commission for that purpose from the *Rozriadnyi*, or high constable, as clerks of the bands. If any make default and fail at the day, he is mulcted and punished very severely. As for the general and other chief captains, they are sent thither from the Emperor's own hand with such commission and charge as he thinketh behooveful for the present service. When the soldiers are assembled, they are reduced into their bands and companies under their several captains of tens, fifties, hundreds, thousands, etc., and these bands into four *polki,* or legions (but of far greater numbers than the Roman legions were), under their four great leaders, which also have the authority of marshals of the field, as was said before.

Concerning their armor, they are but slightly appointed. The common horseman hath nothing else but his bow in his case under his right arm and his quiver and sword hanging on the left side, except some few that bear a case of dags [1] or a javelin or short staff along their horse side. The undercaptains will have commonly some piece of armor besides, as a shirt of mail or suchlike. The general, with the other chief captains and men of nobility, will have their horse very richly furnished, their saddles of cloth of gold, their bridles fair bossed and tasseled with gold and silk fringe, bestudded with pearl and precious stones, themselves in very fine armor which they call *bulatnyi*,[2] made of fair shining steel yet covered commonly with cloth of gold and edged round with ermine fur, his steel helmet on his head of a very great price, his sword, bow, and arrows at his side, his spear in his hand, with another fair helmet and his *shestoper*, or

[1] Probably daggers, although it could be a reference to handguns.
[2] *Bulat:* a damask steel.

Of the Rus Commonwealth

horseman's scepter, carried before him. Their swords, bows, and arrows are of the Turkish fashion. They practice like the Tartar to shoot forward and backward as they fly and retire.

The *strelets*, or footman, hath nothing but his piece in his hand, his striking hatchet at his back, and his sword by his side. The stock of his piece is not made caliverwise [3] but with a plain and straight stock, somewhat like a fowling piece. The barrel is rudely and unartificially made, very heavy, yet shooteth but a very small bullet.

As for their provision of victual, the Emperor alloweth none, either for captain or soldier, neither provideth any for them except peradventure some corn for their money.[4] Every man is to bring sufficient for himself to serve his turn for four months and if need require to give order for more to be brought unto him to the camp from his tenant that tilleth his land or some other place. One great help they have, that for lodging and diet every Rus is prepared to be a soldier beforehand. Though the chief captains and other of account carry tents with them after the fashion of ours, with some better provision of victual than the rest. They bring with them commonly into the camp for victual a kind of dried bread which they call *sukhar*, with some store of meal, which they temper with water and so make it into a ball or small lump of dough called *tolokno;* and this they eat raw instead of bread. Their meat is bacon or some other flesh or fish dried after the Dutch manner. If the Rus soldier were as hardy to execute an enterprise as he is hard to bear out toil and travail, or were otherwise as apt and well-trained for the wars as he is indifferent for his lodging and diet, he would far exceed the soldiers of our parts; whereas now he is far meaner of courage and execution in any warlike service, which cometh partly

---

[3] A caliver was a special, light pistol or firearm of the sixteenth century.

[4] Again Fletcher exaggerated. The Tsar in certain instances did assume responsibility for victualing of troops. Cf. Seredonin, *Sochinenie*, pp. 357–358.

Their Martial Discipline

of his servile condition, that will not suffer any great courage or valor to grow in him, partly for lack of due honor and reward, which he hath no great hope of, whatsoever service or execution he do.

CHAPTER XVII

Of Their Marching, Charging, and Other Martial Discipline

THE Rus trusteth rather to his number than to the valor of his soldiers or good ordering of his forces. Their marching or leading is without all order, save that the four *polki,* or legions, whereinto their army is divided, keep themselves several under their ensigns and so thrust all on together in a hurry as they are directed by their general. Their ensign is the image of St. George. The *bolshie dvoriane,* or chief horsemen, have every man a small drum of brass at his saddle bow, which he striketh when he giveth the charge or onset.

They have drums besides of a huge bigness, which they carry with them upon a board laid on four horses that are sparred [1] together with chains, every drum having eight strikers or drummers, besides trumpets and shawms,[2] which they sound after a wild manner much different from ours. When they give any charge or make any invasion, they make a great hallow or shout altogether as loud as they can, which, with the sound of their trumpets, shawms, and drums, maketh a confused and horrible noise. So they set on, first discharging their arrows, then dealing with their swords, which they use in a bravery to shake and brandish over their heads before they come to strokes.

Their footmen, because otherwise they want order in leading, are commonly placed in some ambush or place of advantage

---

[1] Fastened.   [2] An obsolete wind instrument of the oboe class.

Of the Rus Commonwealth

where they may most annoy the enemy with least hurt to themselves. If it be a set battle, or if any great invasion be made upon the Rus borders by the Tartar, they are set within the running or moving castle, called *vezha* or *guliai-gorod*, which is carried about with them by the *voevoda gulevoi*, or the walking general, whom I spake of before.[3] This walking or moving castle is so framed that it may be set up in length, as occasion doth require, the space of one, two, three, four, five, six, or seven miles, for so long it will reach. It is nothing else but a double wall of wood to defend them on both sides behind and before, with a space of three yards or thereabouts betwixt the two sides, so that they may stand within it and have room enough to charge and discharge their pieces and to use their other weapons. It is closed at both ends and made with loopholes on either side to lay out the nose of their piece or to push forth any other weapon. It is carried with the army wheresoever it goeth, being taken into pieces and so laid on carts sparred together and drawn by horse that are not seen by reason that they are covered with their carriage as with a shelf or penthouse. When it is brought to the place where it is to be used, which is devised and chosen out before by the walking *voevoda*, it is planted so much as the present use requireth—sometimes a mile long, sometimes two, sometimes three, or more. Which is soon done without the help of any carpenter or instrument, because the timber is so framed to clasp together one piece within another, as is easily understood by those that know the manner of the Rus building.

In this castle standeth their shot, well fenced for advantage, especially against the Tartar, that bringeth no ordnance nor other weapon into the field with him save his sword and bow and arrows. They have also within it divers fieldpieces, which they use as occasion doth require. Of pieces for the field they carry no great store when they war against the Tartar; but when

[3] Cf. above, p. 80.

Of Their Colonies

they deal with the Polonian, of whose forces they make more account, they go better furnished with all kind of munition and other necessary provisions. It is thought that no prince of Christendom hath better store of munition than the Rus emperor. And it may partly appear by the artillery house at Moscow, where are of all sorts of great ordnance, all brass pieces, very fair, to an exceeding great number.

The Rus soldier is thought to be better at his defense within some castle or town than he is abroad at a set pitched field, which is ever noted in the practice of his wars—and namely, at the siege of Pskov, about eight years since, where he repulsed the Polonian King Stephen Bathory with his whole army of 100,000 men and forced him in the end to give over his siege with the loss of many of his best captains and soldiers. But in a set field the Rus is noted to have ever the worse of the Polonian and Sweden.

If any behave himself more valiantly than the rest or do any special piece of service, the Emperor sendeth him a piece of gold stamped with the image of St. George on horseback, which they hang on their sleeves and set in their caps. And this is accounted the greatest honor they can receive for any service they do.

CHAPTER XVIII

Of Their Colonies and Maintaining of Their Conquests, or Purchases by Force

THE Rus emperors of late years have very much enlarged their dominions and territories. Their first conquest after the dukedom of Moscow (for before that time they were but dukes of Vladimir, as before was said) was the city and dukedom of Novgorod on the west and northwest side, which was no small

Of the Rus Commonwealth

enlargement of their dominion and strengthening to them for the winning of the rest. This was done by Ivan, great-grandfather to Fedor, now Emperor, about the year 1480.[1] The same began likewise to encroach upon the countries of Lithuania and Livonia; but the conquest, only intended and attempted by him upon some part of those countries, was pursued and performed by his son Vasilii, who first won the city and dukedom of Pskov, afterward the city and dukedom of Smolensk, and many other fair towns with a large territory belonging unto them, about the year 1514.[2] These victories against the Letts, or Lithuanians, in the time of Alexander their duke, he achieved rather by advantage of civil dissensions and treasons among themselves than by any great policy or force of his own.[3] But all this was lost again by his son, Ivan Vasilevich, about eight or nine years past, upon composition with the Polonian King Stephen Bathory, whereunto he was forced by the advantages which the Pole had then of him by reason of the foil he had given him before and the disquietness of his own state at home. Only the Rus emperor at this time hath left him on that side his country the cities of Smolensk, Vitebsk, Chernigov, and Belgorod in Lithuania; in Livonia not a town nor one foot of ground.

When Vasilii first conquered those countries, he suffered the natives to keep their possessions and to inhabit all their towns, only paying him a tribute, under the government of his Rus captains;[4] but by their conspiracies and attempts not long after he was taught to deal more surely with them. And so, coming

[1] Novgorod submitted to Moscow in 1478. Ivan III, the Great, was Fedor's great-grandfather.
[2] Pskov was annexed in 1510 and Smolensk in 1514.
[3] Alexander I was Grand Duke of Lithuania (1492–1506) and King of Poland (1501–1506). Alexander's losses at the end of his reign were to Ivan III, not Vasilii III.
[4] Fletcher means Vasilii II (1425–1462), father of Ivan III.

Of Their Colonies

upon them the second time, he killed and carried away with him three parts of four, which he gave or sold to the Tartars that served him in those wars, and instead of them placed there his Rus, so many as might overmatch the rest, with certain garrisons of strength besides. Wherein notwithstanding, this oversight was committed: for that, taking away with him the upland or country people that should have tilled the ground and might easily have been kept in order without any danger by other good policies, he was driven afterward many years together to victual the country, especially the great towns, out of his own country of Russia, the soil lying there in the meanwhile waste and untilled.

The like fell out at the port of Narva in Liefland, where his son, Ivan Vasilevich, devised to build a town and a castle on the other side the river called Ivangorod to keep the town and country in subjection.[5] The castle he caused to be so built and fortified that it was thought to be invincible. And when it was finished, for reward to the architect, that was a Polonian, he put out both his eyes, to make him unable to build the like again.[6] But having left the natives all within their own country without abating their number or strength, the town and castle not long after was betrayed and surrendered again to the King of Sweden.

On the southeast side they have got the kingdom of Kazan and Astrakhan. These were won from the Tartar by the late Emperor Ivan Vasilevich, father of the Emperor that now is, the one about thirty-five, the other about thirty-three years ago. Northward out of the country of Siberia he hath laid unto his

[5] Ivangorod was founded opposite the German town of Narva in 1492 by Ivan III.

[6] This tale of the architect of the Ivangorod kremlin is a myth similar to one told about the designers of the Cathedral of St. Vasilii in Red Square, Moscow. Ivangorod, an important model for kremlin architecture of this period, still stands.

realm a great breadth and length of ground from Vychegda to the river of Ob, about 1,000 miles' space, so that he is bold to write himself now "the great commander of Siberia." [7]

The countries likewise of Perm and Pechora are a divers people and language from the Rus, overcome not long since, and that rather by threatening and shaking of the sword than by any actual force, as being a weak and naked [8] people without means to resist.

That which the Rus hath in his present possession he keepeth on this sort. In his four chief border towns of Pskov, Smolensk, Astrakhan, and Kazan he hath certain of his council, not of greatest nobility but of greatest trust, which have more authority within their precincts for the countenancing and strengthening of government there than the other dukes that are set to govern in other places, as was noted before, in the manner of ordering their provinces. These he changeth sometime every year, sometime every second or third year, but exceedeth not that time except upon very special trust and good liking of the party and his service, lest by enlarging of their time they might grow into some familiarity with the enemy, as some have done, being so far out of sight.

The towns besides are very strongly fenced with trenches, castles, and store of munition and have garrisons within them to the number of two or three thousand apiece. They are stored with victual, if any siege should come upon them, for the space of two or three years beforehand. The four castles of Smolensk, Pskov, Kazan, and Astrakhan he hath made very strong to bear out any siege, so that it is thought that those towns are impregnable.

As for the countries of Pechora and Perm and that part of Siberia which he hath now under him, they are kept by as easy

[7] The conquest of Siberia was largely achieved in 1581–1584 by the Cossack Ermak in the service of the Stroganovs. Fletcher again meant the Kama rather than the Vychegda. Cf. p. 11, n. 5, above.

[8] Unarmed.

Of Their Colonies

means as they were first got, viz., rather by showing than by using of arms. First, he hath stored the country with as many Rus as there are natives and hath there some few soldiers in garrison, enough to keep them under. Secondly, his officers and magistrates there are of his own Rus people, and he changeth them very often, viz., every year twice or thrice, notwithstanding there be no great fear of any innovation. Thirdly, he divideth them into many small governments, like a staff broke in many small pieces, so that they have no strength being severed, which was but little neither when they were all in one. Fourthly, he provideth that the people of the country have neither armor nor money, being taxed and pilled [9] so often as he thinketh good, without any means to shake off that yoke or to relieve themselves.

In Siberia, where he goeth on in pursuing his conquest, he hath divers castles and garrisons to the number of six thousand soldiers of Rus and Polonians and sendeth many new supplies thither to plant and to inhabit as he winneth ground. At this time besides he hath gotten the king's brother of Siberia, allured by certain of his captains, to leave his own country by offers of great entertainment and pleasanter life with the Rus emperor than he had in Siberia. He was brought in this last year and is now with the Emperor at Moscow well entertained.

This may be said of the Rus practice, wheresoever he ruleth either by right of inheritance or by conquest: first he bereaveth the country of armor and other means of defense, which he permitteth to none but to his boiars only; secondly, he robbeth them continually of their money and commodities and leaveth them bare with nothing but their bodies and lives within certain years' compass; thirdly, he renteth and divideth his territories into many small pieces by several governments, so that none hath much under him to make any strength though he had other opportunities; fourthly, he governeth his countries by men

[9] Pillaged.

of small reputation and no power of themselves and strangers in those places where their government lieth; fifthly, he changeth his governors once a year ordinarily, that there grow no great liking nor entireness [10] betwixt the people and them nor acquaintance with the enemy if they lie toward the borders; sixthly, he appointeth in one and the same place adversary governors, the one to be as controller of the other, as the dukes and *diaki*, where, by means of their envies and emulations, there is less hurt to be feared by their agreement and himself is better informed what is done amiss; seventhly, he sendeth many times into every province secret messengers of special trust about him as intelligences to pry and harken out what is doing and what is amiss there. And this is ordinary, though it be sudden and unknown what time they will come.

CHAPTER XIX

Of the Tartars and Other Borderers to the Country of Russia with Whom They Have Most to Do in War and Peace

THEIR neighbors with whom they have greatest dealings and intercourse both in peace and war are, first, the Tartar; secondly, the Polonian, whom the Rus calleth Liakhi, noting the first author or founder of the nation, who was called Liakh or Lekh, whereunto is added *po*, which signifieth "people." And so is made Poliakhi, that is, "the people or posterity of Liakhi," which the Latins after their manner of writing call Polanos.[1] The third are the Swedens. The Polonians and Swedens are better known to these parts of Europe than are the Tartars, that are farther off

---

[10] Intimacy.

[1] Fletcher was led into this error by Martin Kromer, who had an almost identical statement in his work. Fletcher's spelling was *Polaches*.

The Borderers of Russia

from us, as being of Asia, and divided into many tribes different both in name and government one from another.[2] The greatest and mightiest of them is the Crim Tartar, whom some call the Great Khan, that lieth south and southeastward from Russia and doth most annoy the country by often invasions, commonly once every year, sometimes entering very far within the inland parts. In the year 1571 he came as far as the city of Moscow, with an army of 200,000 men, without any battle or resistance at all; for that the Rus emperor, then Ivan Vasilevich, leading forth his army to encounter with him, marched a wrong way, but, it was thought, of very purpose, as not daring to adventure the field, by reason that he doubted his nobility and chief captains of a meaning to betray him to the Tartar.

The city he took not but fired the suburbs, which by reason of the building, which is all of wood without any stone, brick, or lime save certain outrooms, kindled so quickly and went on with such rage as that it consumed the greatest part of the city almost within the space of four hours, being of thirty miles or more of compass. Then might you have seen a lamentable spectacle: besides the huge and mighty flame of the city all on light fire, the people burning in their houses and streets, but most of all of such as labored to pass out of the gates farthest from the enemy, where, meeting together in a mighty throng and so pressing, every man to prevent another wedged themselves so fast within the gate and streets near unto it as that three ranks walked one upon the other's head, the uppermost treading down those that were lower, so that there perished at that time, as was said, by the fire and the press the number of 800,000 people or more.[3]

The Crim, thus having fired the city and fed his eyes with the

[2] Fletcher failed to mention Lithuanians, Livonians (Latvians), and Germans in the West.

[3] Although Fletcher's description of the raid of 1571 has become a classic, his estimate of Muscovite casualties was excessive. Cf. Seredonin, *Sochinenie*, pp. 75–76.

91

sight of it all on a light flame, returned with his army and sent to the Rus emperor a knife, as was said, to stick himself withal, upbraiding this loss and his desperate case, as not daring either to meet his enemy in the field nor to trust his friends or subjects at home. The principal cause of this continual quarrel betwixt the Rus and the Crim is for the right of certain border parts claimed by the Tartar but possessed by the Rus. The Tartar allegeth that besides Astrakhan and Kazan, that are the ancient possession of the East Tartar, the whole country from his bounds north and westward so far as the city of Moscow, and Moscow itself, pertaineth to his right. Which seemeth to have been true by the report of the Rus themselves, that tell of a certain homage that was done by the Rus emperor every year to the Great Crim, or Khan: the Rus emperor standing on foot and feeding the Crim's horse, himself sitting on his back, with oats out of his own cap instead of a bowl or manger, and that within the castle of Moscow. And this homage, they say, was done till the time of Vasilii, grandfather to this man, who, surprising the Crim emperor by a stratagem done by one of his nobility called Ivan Dimitrievich Belskii, was content with this ransom, viz., with the changing of this homage into a tribute of furs, which afterward also was denied to be paid by this Emperor's father.

Hereupon they continue the quarrel—the Rus defending his country and that which he hath won, the Crim Tartar invading him once or twice every year, sometime about Whitsuntide,[4] but oftener in harvest, what time, if the Great Khan, or Crim, come in his own person, he bringeth with him a great army of 100,000 or 200,000 men. Otherwise they make short and sudden roads into the country with lesser numbers, running about the list of the border as wild geese fly, invading and retiring where they see advantage.

[4] The week beginning with Whitsunday, the seventh Sunday and fiftieth day after Easter. It is the festival commemorating the descent of the Holy Spirit on the day of Pentecost.

The Borderers of Russia

Their common practice, being very populous, is to make divers armies and so, drawing the Rus to one or two places of the frontiers, to invade at some other place that is left without defense. Their manner of fight or ordering of their forces is much after the Rus manner (spoken of before), save that they are all horsemen and carry nothing else but a bow, a sheaf of arrows, and a falcon sword after the Turkish fashion. They are very expert horsemen and use to shoot as readily backward as forward. Some will have a horseman's staff like to a boar-spear, besides their other weapons. The common soldier hath no other armor than his ordinary apparel, viz., a black sheep's skin with the wool side outward in the daytime and inward in the nighttime, with a cap of the same. But their *murzy*, or noblemen, imitate the Turk both in apparel and armor. When they are to pass over a river with their army, they tie three or four horses together and, taking long poles or pieces of wood, bind them fast to the tails of their horse; so, sitting on the poles, they drive their horse over. At handy strokes, when they come to join battle, they are accounted far better men than the Rus people, fierce by nature but more hardy and bloody by continual practice of war, as men knowing no arts of peace nor any civil practice.

Yet their subtlety is more than may seem to agree with their barbarous condition, by reason they are practiced to invade continually and to rob their neighbors that border about them. They are very pregnant and ready-witted to devise stratagems upon the sudden for their better advantage, as in their war against Bela the Fourth, King of Hungary, whom they invaded with 500,000 men and obtained against him a great victory. Where, among others, having slain his chancellor, called Nicholas Schinick, they found about him the King's privy seal. Whereupon they devised presently to counterfeit letters in the King's name to the cities and towns next about the place where the field was fought, with charge that in no case they should convey

Of the Rus Commonwealth

themselves and their goods out of their dwellings, where they might abide safely without all fear of danger and not leave the country desolate to the possession of so vile and barbarous an enemy as was the Tartar nation, terming themselves in all reproachful manner. For notwithstanding he had lost his carriages, with some few stragglers that had marched disorderly; yet he doubted not but to recover that loss with the access of a notable victory, if the savage Tartar durst abide him in the field. To this purpose, having written their letters in the Polish character by certain young men whom they took in the field, and signed them with the King's seal, they dispatched them forth to all the quarters of Hungary that lay near about the place; whereupon the Hungarians, that were now flying away with their goods, wives, and children upon the rumor of the King's overthrow, taking comfort of these counterfeit letters, stayed at home, and so were made a prey, being surprised on the sudden by this huge number of these Tartars that had compassed them about before they were aware.

When they besiege a town or fort, they offer much parle and send many flattering messages to persuade a surrender, promising all things that the inhabitants will require. But being once possessed of the place, they use all manner of hostility and cruelty. This they do upon a rule they have, viz., that justice is to be practiced but toward their own. They encounter not lightly but they have some ambush, whereunto, having once showed themselves and made some short conflict, they retire as repulsed for fear and so draw the enemy into it if they can. But the Rus, being well acquainted with their practice, is more wary of them. When they come aroving with some small number, they set on horseback counterfeit shapes of men, that their number may seem greater.

When they make any onset, their manner is to make a great shout, crying all out together, "*Olla Billa, Olla Billa,* God help us, God help us." They contemn death so much as that they

The Borderers of Russia

choose rather to die than to yield to their enemy and are seen when they are slain to bite the very weapon when they are past striking or helping of themselves. Wherein appeareth how different the Tartar is in his desperate courage from the Rus and Turk. For the Rus soldier, if he begin once to retire, putteth all his safety in his speedy flight. And if once he be taken by his enemy, he neither defendeth himself nor entreateth for his life, as reckoning straight to die. The Turk commonly, when he is past hope of escaping, falleth to entreaty and casteth away his weapon, offereth both his hands, and holdeth them up as it were to be tied, hoping to save his life by offering himself bondslave.

The chief booty the Tartars seek for in all their wars is to get store of captives, especially young boys and girls, whom they sell to the Turks or other their neighbors. To this purpose they take with them great baskets made like bakers' panniers to carry them tenderly. And if any of them happen to tire or be sick on the way, they dash him against the ground or some tree and so leave him dead. The soldiers are not troubled with keeping the captives and the other booty, for hindering the execution of their wars, but they have certain bands that intend nothing else, appointed of purpose to receive and keep the captives and the other prey.

The Rus borders, being used to their invasions lightly every year in the summer, keep few other cattle on the border parts save swine only, which the Tartar will not touch nor drive away with him, for that he is of the Turkish religion and will eat no swines' flesh. Of Christ our Savior they confess as much as doth the Turk in his Koran, viz.: that He came of the Angel Gabriel and the Virgin Mary; that He was a great prophet and shall be the judge of the world at the last day. In other matters likewise they are much ordered after the manner and direction of the Turk, having felt the Turkish forces when he won from them Azov and Kaffa, with some other towns about the Euxine or Black Sea, that were before tributaries to the Crim Tartar. So

Of the Rus Commonwealth

that now the Emperor of the Crims for the most part is chosen some one of the nobility whom the Turk doth commend: whereby it is brought now to that pass that the Crim Tartar giveth to the Turk the tenth part of the spoil which he getteth in his wars against the Christians.

Herein they differ from the Turkish religion, for that they have certain idol puppets, made of silk or like stuff, of the fashion of a man, which they fasten to the door of their walking houses to be Januses or keepers of their house.[5] And these idols are made not by all but by certain religious women which they have among them for that and like uses. They have, besides, the image of their king or great Khan of an huge bigness, which they erect at every stage when the army marcheth. And this everyone must bend and bow unto as he passeth by it, be he Tartar or stranger. They are much given to witchcraft and ominous conjectures upon every accident which they hear or see.

In making of marriages, they have no regard of alliance or consanguinity. Only with his mother, sister, and daughter a man may not marry; and though he take the woman into his house and accompany with her, yet he accounteth her not for his wife till he have a child by her. Then he beginneth to take a dowry of her friends—of horse, sheep, kine, etc. If she be barren after a certain time, he turneth her home again.

Under the Emperor they have certain dukes whom they call *murzy* or *divei-murzy*, that rule over a certain number of 10,000, 20,000, or 40,000 apiece which they call hordes. When the Emperor hath any use of them to serve in his wars, they are bound to come and to bring with them their soldiers to a certain number, every man with his two horse at the least, the one to ride on, the other to kill, when it cometh to his turn to have his horse eat. For their chief victual is horse flesh, which they eat without bread or any other thing with it. So that if a Tartar be

[5] Janus was an ancient Italian deity regarded as doorkeeper of heaven.

The Borderers of Russia

taken by a Rus, he shall be sure lightly to find a horse leg or some other part of him at his saddlebow.

This last year, when I was at the Moscow, came in one Kiriak Murza, nephew to the Emperor of the Crims that now is, whose father was Emperor before, accompanied with three hundred Tartars and his two wives, whereof one was his brother's widow. Where being entertained in very good sort after the Rus manner, he had sent unto his lodging for his welcome to be made ready for his supper and his companies two very large and fat horses, ready flayed in a sled. They prefer it before other flesh, because the meat is stronger, as they say, than beef, mutton, and suchlike. And yet, which is marvel, though they serve all as horsemen in the wars and eat all of horse flesh, there are brought yearly to the Moscow to be exchanged for other commodities thirty or forty thousand Tartar horse which they call *koni*.[6] They keep also great herds of kine and flocks of black sheep, rather for the skins and milk, which they carry with them in great bottles, than for the use of the flesh, though they sometimes eat of it. Some use they have of rice, figs, and other fruits. They drink milk or warm blood and for the most part card [7] them both together. They use sometimes as they travel by the way to let their horse blood in a vein and to drink it warm as it cometh from his body.

Towns they plant none nor other standing buildings but have walking houses, which the Latins call *veij*,[8] built upon wheels like a shepherd's cottage. These they draw with them whithersoever they go, driving their cattle with them. And when they come to their stage or standing place, they plant their cart houses very orderly in a rank and so make the form of streets and of a large town. And this is the manner of the Emperor

---

[6] In Russian, *kon* means "horse" or "steed."   [7] Mix.

[8] Fletcher may have meant the Latin word *vinea:* "a kind of penthouse, shed, or mantlet, built like an arbor, for sheltering besiegers" (*Harper's Latin Dictionary*).

Of the Rus Commonwealth

himself, who hath no other seat of his empire but an *agora*, or town, of wood that moveth with him whithersoever he goeth. As for the fixed and standing building used in other countries, they say they are unwholesome and unpleasant.

They begin to move their houses and cattle in the springtime from the south part of their country toward the north parts. And so, driving on till they have grazed all up to the farthest part northward, they return back again toward their south country, where they continue all the winter, by ten or twelve miles a stage; in the meanwhile the grass being sprung up again to serve for their cattle as they return. From the border of the Shchelkaly toward the Caspian Sea to the Rus frontiers they have a goodly country, especially on the south and southeast parts, but lost for lack of tillage.

Of money they have no use at all and therefore prefer brass and steel before other metals, especially *bulat*, which they use for swords, knives, and other necessaries. As for gold and silver, they neglect it of very purpose, as they do all tillage of their ground, to be more free for their wandering kind of life and to keep their country less subject to invasions—which giveth them great advantage against all their neighbors, ever invading and never being invaded. Such as have taken upon them to invade their country, as of old time Cyrus and Darius Hystaspes on the east and southeast side, have done it with very ill success, as we find in the stories written of those times. For their manner is, when any will invade them, to allure and draw them on by flying and reculing [9] as if they were afraid, till they have drawn them some good way within their country; then when they begin to want victual and other necessaries, as needs they must where nothing is to be had, to stop up the passages and enclose them with multitudes. By which stratagem, as we read in Laonikos Chalcondyles in his Turkish story, they had well-nigh surprised the great and huge army of Tamerlane but that he re-

[9] Recoiling.

The Borderers of Russia

tired with all speed he could toward the river Tanais, or Don, not without great loss of his men and carriages.

In the story of Pachymeres the Greek, which he wrote of the emperors of Constantinople from the beginning of the reign of Michael Palaeologus to the time of Andronicus the Elder,[10] I remember he telleth to the same purpose of one Nogas, a Tartarian captain, under Kazan, the Emperor of the East Tartars (of whom the city and kingdom of Kazan may seem to have taken the denomination), who refused a present of pearl and other jewels sent unto him from Michael Palaeologus, asking withal for what use they served and whether they were good to keep away sickness, death, or other misfortunes of this life, or no. So that it seemeth they have ever, or long time, been of that mind to value things no further than by the use and necessity for which they serve.

For person and complexion they have broad and flat visages, of a tanned color into yellow and black, fierce and cruel looks, thin-haired upon the upper lip and pit of the chin, light and nimble-bodied, with short legs, as if they were made naturally for horsemen, whereto they practice themselves from their childhood, seldom going about any business. Their speech is very sudden and loud, speaking as it were out of a deep hollow throat. When they sing, you would think a cow lowed or some great bandog[11] howled. Their greatest exercise is shooting, wherein they train up their children from their very infancy, not suffering them to eat till they have shot near the mark within a certain scantling.[12] They are the very same that sometimes were called Scythae Nomads, or the Scythian shepherds, by the Greeks and Latins. Some think that the Turks took their beginning from the nation of the Crim Tartars, of which opinion is

[10] Michael VIII (1259–1282) was first of the Palaeologi; Andronicus II Palaeologus "the Elder" (1282–1328).
[11] A dog tied either to serve as a watchdog or because of its ferocity.
[12] A pattern.

Of the Rus Commonwealth

Laonikos Chalcondyles the Greek historiographer in his first book of his Turkish story, wherein he followeth divers very probable conjectures. The first, taken from the very name itself, for that the word Turk signifieth a shepherd or one that followeth a vagrant and wild kind of life. By which name these Scythian Tartars have ever been noted, being called by the Greeks Σκύφαι νόμαδες, or the Scythian shepherds. His second reason, because the Turks in his time that dwelt in Asia the Less, to wit, in Lydia, Caria, Phrygia, and Cappadocia, spake the very same language that these Tartars did that dwelt betwixt the river Tanais, or Don, and the country of Sarmatia, which as is well known are these Tartars called Crims. At this time also the whole nation of the Turks differ not much in their common speech from the Tartar language. Thirdly, because the Turk and the Crim Tartar agree so well together, as well in religion as in matter of traffic, never invading or injuring one another save that the Turk since Laonikos his time hath encroached upon some towns upon the Euxine Sea that before pertained to the Crim Tartar. Fourthly, because Urtoghrul, son to Oguzalpes and father to Ottoman,[13] the first of name of the Turkish nation, made his first roads out of those parts of Asia upon the next borderers till he came toward the countries about the hill Taurus, where he overcame the Greeks that inhabited there and so enlarged the name and territory of the Turkish nation till he came to Euboea and Attica and other parts of Greece. This is the opinion of Laonikos, who lived among the Turks in the time of Murad, the sixth Turkish emperor, about the year 1400, when the memory of their original was more fresh and therefore the likelier he was to hit the truth.[14]

[13] The reference here is to first Sultan Osman (1288–1326) from whom Osmanli or Ottoman is derived. "The countries about the hill Taurus" is a reference to the Tauride or Crimea.

[14] Murad II (1421–1451), sixth Ottoman ruler, added Corinth, Patras, and the north of the Morea to Turkish dominions. Fletcher erred in dating Murad about 1400. Laonikos refers to Chalcondyles.

The Borderers of Russia

There are divers other Tartars that border upon Russia, as the Nogais, the Cheremisians, the Mordvinians, the Cherkasy, and the Shchelkaly, which all differ in name more than in regiment or other condition from the Crim Tartar, except the Cherkasy, that border southwest toward Lithuania and are far more civil than the rest of the Tartars—of a comely person and of a stately behavior, as applying themselves to the fashion of the Polonian. Some of them have subjected themselves to the kings of Poland and profess Christianity. The Nogai lieth eastward and is reckoned for the best man of war among all the Tartars but very savage and cruel above all the rest. The Cheremisian Tartar, that lieth betwixt the Rus and the Nogai, are of two sorts: the *lugovoi*, that is, of the valley, and the *nagornyi*, or of the hilly country. These have much troubled the emperors of Russia, and therefore they are content now to buy peace of them under pretense of giving a yearly pension of Rus commodities to their *murzy* or *divei-murzy*, that are chief of their tribes, for which also they are bound to serve them in their wars under certain conditions. They are said to be just and true in their dealings, and for that cause they hate the Rus people, whom they account to be double and false in all their dealing. And therefore the common sort are very unwilling to keep agreement with them but that they are kept in by their *murzy*, or dukes, for their pensions' sake.

The most rude and barbarous is counted the Mordvinian Tartar, that hath many self fashions and strange kinds of behavior differing from the rest. For his religion, though he acknowledge one god, yet his manner is to worship for god that living thing that he first meeteth in the morning and to swear by it all that whole day, whether it be horse, dog, cat, or whatsoever else it be. When his friend dieth, he killeth his best horse, and, having flayed off the skin, he carrieth it on high upon a long pole before the corpse to the place of burial. This he doth, as the Rus saith, that his friend may have a good horse to carry him to heaven;

Of the Rus Commonwealth

but it is likelier to declare his love toward his dead friend, in that he will have to die with him the best thing that he hath.

Next to the kingdom of Astrakhan, that is the farthest part southeastward of the Rus dominion, lieth the Shchelkaly and the country of Media, whither the Rus merchants trade for raw silks, sindon, saffian, skins, and other commodities.[15] The chief towns of Media, where the Rus tradeth, are Derbent, built by Alexander the Great, as the inhabitants say, and Shemakha, where the staple is kept for raw silks.[16] Their manner is in the springtime to revive the silkworms, that lie dead all the winter, by laying them in the warm sun and, to hasten their quickening that they may sooner go to work, to put them into bags and so to hang them under their children's arms. As for the worm called *chrinisin* (as we call it, "crimson"), that maketh colored silk, it is bred not in Media but in Assyria.[17] This trade to Derbent and Shemakha for raw silks and other commodities of that country, as also into Persia and Bukhara down the river Volga and through the Caspian Sea, is permitted as well to the English as to the Rus merchants by the Emperor's last grant at my being there, which he accounteth for a very special favor and might prove indeed very beneficial to our English merchants if the trade were well and orderly used.

The whole nation of the Tartars are utterly void of all learning and without written law. Yet certain rules they have which they hold by tradition common to all the hordes for the practice of their life—which are of this sort. First, to obey their emperor and other magistrates whatsoever they command about the public service. 2) Except for the public behoove every man to be

[15] Sindon is a fine thin fabric of linen; a kind of cambric or muslin. Saffian is a leather made from goatskins or sheepskins, tanned with sumac and dyed in bright colors. The Russian word is *safian*.

[16] Derbent is on the west central coast of the Caspian; Shemakha is south of Derbent, though not on the coast.

[17] Crimson is derived from the sanskrit *krmi*, worm, or insect. Cf. *kermes*, the pregnant female of the insect *Coccus ilicis*, formerly supposed to be a berry and gathered in large quantities for use in dyeing.

The Permians, Samoyeds, and Lapps

free and out of controlment. 3) No private man to possess any lands but the whole country to be as a common. 4) To neglect all daintiness and variety of meats and to content themselves with that which cometh next to hand for more hardness and readiness in the executing of their affairs. 5) To wear any base attire and to patch their clothes whether there be any need or not; that when there is need, it be no shame to wear a patched coat. 6) To take or steal from any stranger whatsoever they can get, as being enemies to all men save to such as will subject themselves to them. 7) Toward their own horde and nation to be true in word and deed. 8) To suffer no stranger to come within the realm. If any do, the same to be bondslave to him that first taketh him, except such merchants and other as have the Tartar bull, or passport, about them.

CHAPTER XX

Of the Permians, Samoyeds, and Lapps

THE Permians and Samoyeds, that lie from Russia north and northeast, are thought likewise to have taken their beginning from the Tartar kind. And it may partly be guessed by the fashion of their countenance, as having all broad and flat faces, as the Tartars have, except the Cherkasy. The Permians are accounted for a very ancient people.[1] They are now subject to the Rus. They live by hunting and trading with their furs, as doth also the Samoyed, that dwelleth more toward the North Sea. The Samoyed hath his name, as the Rus saith, of eating himself, as if in times past they lived as the cannibals, eating one another,[2] which they make more probable because at this time they eat all kind of raw flesh, whatsoever it be, even the very

[1] By Permians, Fletcher probably meant Finns.
[2] This highly improbable explanation was derived from Herberstein, *Notes*, II, 39.

Of the Rus Commonwealth

carrion that lieth in the ditch. But as the Samoyeds themselves will say, they were called Samoyed, that is, of themselves, as though they were indigenous or people bred upon that very soil, that never changed their seat from one place to another as most nations have done. They are subject at this time to the Emperor of Russia.

I talked with certain of them and find that they acknowledge one god but represent him by such things as they have most use and good by. And therefore they worship the sun, the *olen*, the *los*, and suchlike. As for the story of Zolotaia Baba, or the golden hag, which I have read in some maps and descriptions of these countries to be an idol after the form of an old woman, that, being demanded by the priest, giveth them certain oracles concerning the success and event of things, I found it to be but a very fable.[3] Only, in the province of Obdorsk upon the seaside near to the mouth of the great river Ob, there is a rock which naturally, being somewhat helped by imagination, may seem to bear the shape of a ragged woman with a child in her arms, as the rock by the North Cape the shape of a friar, where the Obdorian Samoyeds use much to resort by reason of the commodity of the place for fishing. And there sometimes, as their manner is, conceive and practice their sorceries and ominous conjecturings about the good or bad speed of their journeys, fishings, huntings, and suchlike.

They are clad in sealskins with the hairy side outward down as low as the knees, with their breeches and netherstocks of the same, both men and women. They are all black-haired, naturally beardless; and therefore the men are hardly discerned from the women by their looks, save that the women wear a lock of hair down along both their ears. They live in a manner a wild and a savage life, roving still from one place of the country to another, without any property of house or land more to one

[3] *Ibid.*, p. 41, has a map of sixteenth-century Muscovy that depicts the Zolotaia Baba.

The Permians, Samoyeds, and Lapps

than to another. Their leader or director in every company is their *pop,* or priest.

On the north side of Russia, next to Karelia, lieth the country of Lappia, which reacheth in length from the farthest point northward toward the North Cape to the farthest part southeast, which the Rus calleth Sweetness, or Holy Nose, the Englishmen Cape Grace, about 345 versts or miles.[4] From Sviatoi Nos to Kandalaksha by the way of Varzuga, which measureth the breadth of that country, is ninety miles or thereabouts. The whole country in a manner is either lakes or mountains, which toward the seaside are called tundra, because they are all of hard and craggy rock;[5] but the inland parts are well furnished with woods that grow on the hillsides, the lakes lying between. Their diet is very bare and simple. Bread they have none but feed only upon fish and fowl. They are subject to the Emperor of Russia and the two Kings of Sweden and Denmark, which all exact tribute and custom of them, as was said before; but the Emperor of Russia beareth the greatest hand over them and exacts of them far more than the rest. The opinion is that they were first termed Lapps of their brief and short speech. The Rus divideth the whole nation of the Lapps into two sorts. The one they call *Novremanskie Lopari,* that is, the Norwegian Lapps, because they be of the Danish religion; for the Danes and Norwegians they account for one people. The other, that have no religion at all but live as brute and heathenish people without God in the world, they call *Dikie Lopari,* or the Wild Lapps.[6]

The whole nation is utterly unlearned, having not so much as the use of any alphabet or letter among them. For practice of

[4] Really Sviatoi Nos, or Holy Nose, on the Kola peninsula.

[5] Fletcher was confused. The tundra, of course, refers to the level or undulating treeless plains of the northern Arctic regions.

[6] *Novremanskie* does not correspond to Norwegian. Fletcher in error called the Wild Lapps living on the Murmansk coast Norwegian. There were in this region several monasteries, notably the one at Pechenga, to convert the Wild Lapps.

Of the Rus Commonwealth

witchcraft and sorcery they pass all nations in the world. Though, for the enchanting of ships that sail along their coast, as I have heard it reported, and their giving of winds good to their friends and contrary to other whom they mean to hurt, by tying of certain knots upon a rope, somewhat like to the tale of Aeolus his windbag, [it] is a very fable devised, as may seem, by themselves to terrify sailors for coming near their coast. Their weapons are the longbow and handgun, wherein they excel as well for quickness to charge and discharge as for nearness at the mark, by reason of their continual practice, whereto they are forced, of shooting at wild fowl. Their manner is in summertime to come down in great companies to the seaside, to Wardhouse, Kola, Koger, and the bay of Vitia-Guba and there to fish for cod, salmon, and buttfish,[7] which they sell to the Rus, Danes, and Norwegians and now of late to the Englishmen that trade thither with cloth, which they exchange with the Lapps and Karelians for their fish, oil, and furs, whereof also they have some store. They hold their mart at Kola on St. Peter's Day, what time the captain of Wardhouse, that is resiant there for the King of Denmark, must be present, or at least send his deputy to set prices upon their stockfish, train oil, furs, and other commodities, as also the Rus emperor's customer or tribute taker to receive his custom, which is ever paid before anything can be bought or sold.[8] When their fishing is done, their manner is to draw their carabus, or boats, on shore and there to leave them with the keel turned upward till the next spring tide.[9] Their travel to and fro is upon sleds drawn by the *olen* deer, which they use to turn agrazing all the summertime in an island called Kildin, of a very good soil compared with other parts of that country, and toward the wintertime, when the snow beginneth to fall, they fetch them home again for the use of their sled.

[7] A flounder or flatfish, especially the halibut.
[8] St. Peter's Day is June 29. "Resiant" means "resident."
[9] A carabus was a small ship. Cf. caravel.

Their Ecclesiastical State

CHAPTER XXI

Of Their Ecclesiastical State, with Their Church Offices

CONCERNING the government of their church, it is framed altogether after the manner of the Greek, as being a part of that church and never acknowledging the jurisdiction of the Latin Church usurped by the Pope. That I may keep a better measure in describing their ceremonies than they in the using them, wherein they are infinite, I will note briefly: first, what ecclesiastical degrees or offices they have, with the jurisdiction and practice of them; secondly, what doctrine they hold in matter of religion; thirdly, what liturgy or form of service they use in their churches, with the manner of their administering the sacraments; fourthly, what other strange ceremonies and superstitious devotions are used among them.

Their offices or degrees of churchmen are as many in number and the same in a manner both in name and degree that were in the western churches. First they have their patriarch, then their metropolites, their archbishops, their *vladyki*, or bishops, their *protopopy*, or archpriests, their *popy*, or priests, their deacons, friars, monks, nuns, and eremites.[1]

Their patriarch, or chief director in matter of religion, until this last year was of the city of Constantinople, whom they called the Patriarch of Scio, because, being driven by the Turk out of Constantinople, the seat of his empire, he removed to the isle Scio, sometimes called Chios, and there placed his patriarchal see.[2] So that the emperors and clergy of Russia were wont yearly to send gifts thither and to acknowledge a spiritual kind of homage and subjection due to him and to that church, which custom they have held, as it seemeth, ever since they professed

[1] Hermits.   [2] Cf. below, p. 109.

the Christian religion. Which how long it hath been I could not well learn, for that they have no story or monument of antiquity that I could hear of to show what hath been done in times past within their country concerning either church or commonwealth matters.[3] Only I hear a report among them that about three hundred years since there was a marriage betwixt the Emperor of Constantinople and the king's daughter of that country, who at the first denied to join his daughter in marriage with the Greek emperor because he was of the Christian religion. Which agreeth well with that I find in the story of Laonikos Chalcondyles concerning Turkish affairs in his fourth book, where he speaketh of such a marriage betwixt John, the Greek emperor, and the king's daughter of Sarmatia.[4] And this argueth out of their own report that at that time they had not received the Christian religion, as also that they were converted to the faith and withal perverted at the very same time, receiving the doctrine of the gospel corrupted with superstitions even at the first when they took it from the Greek Church, which itself then was degenerate and corrupted with many superstitions and foul errors both in doctrine and discipline, as may appear by the story of Nicephorus Gregoras in his eighth and ninth books. But as touching the time of their conversion to the Christian faith, I suppose rather that it is mistaken by the Rus for that which I find in the Polonian story, the second book, the third chapter, where is said that about the year 990 Vladimirus, duke of Russia, married one Anne, sister to Basileus and Constantinus, brothers and Emperors of Constantinople.[5] Whereupon the Rus received the faith and profession of Christ, which, though it be somewhat more

[3] The traditional date for the conversion of Russia to Greek Christianity was 988, when the Kievan Prince Vladimir married Anna, daughter of the Byzantine Emperor Romanus II.
[4] Fletcher here referred to the marriage of John VIII, son of the Byzantine Manuel II Palaeologus, with Anna, daughter of Grand Duke Vasilii I of Moscow.
[5] This reference to Martin Kromer should be to bk. 3, ch. 2.

Their Ecclesiastical State

ancient than the time noted before out of the Rus report, yet it falleth out all to one reckoning, touching this point, viz., in what truth and sincerity of doctrine the Rus received the first stamp of religion, forasmuch as the Greek Church at that time also was many ways infected with error and superstition.

At my being there the year 1588 came unto the Moscow the Patriarch of Constantinople, or Scio, called Hieronimo, being banished, as some said, by the Turk, or, as some other reported, by the Greek clergy deprived. The Emperor, being given altogether to superstitious devotions, gave him great entertainment. Before his coming to Moscow he had been in Italy with the Pope, as was reported there by some of his company. His errand was to consult with the Emperor concerning these points: first, about a league to pass betwixt him and the King of Spain, as the meetest prince to join with him in opposition against the Turk, to which purpose also embassages had passed betwixt the Rus and the Persian; likewise from the Georgians to the Emperor of Russia to join league together for the invading of the Turk on all sides of his dominion, taking the advantage of the simple quality of the Turk that now is. This treaty was helped forward by the Emperor's ambassador of Almaine sent at the same time to solicit an invasion upon the parts of Polonia that lie toward Rusland and to borrow money of the Rus emperor to pursue the war for his brother Maximilian against the Sweden's son, now King of Poland.[6] But this consultation concerning a league betwixt the Rus and the Spaniard, which was in some forwardness at my coming to Moscow and already one appointed for embassage into Spain, was marred by means of the overthrow given to the Spanish king by Her Majesty the Queen of England this last year. Which made the Rus emperor and his council to give a sadder countenance to the English ambassador at that

---

[6] Almaine = Allemagne, the French for Germany, or the Holy Roman Empire in this instance. The Swedish king of Poland mentioned was Sigismund III Vasa (1587–1632).

time, for that they were disappointed of so good a policy as was this conjunction supposed to be betwixt them and the Spanish.

His second purpose, whereto the first served as an introduction, was, in revenge of the Turk and the Greek clergy that had thrust him from his seat, to treat with them about the reducing of the Rus Church under the Pope of Rome. Wherein it may seem that, coming lately from Rome, he was set on by the Pope, who hath attempted the same many times before, though all in vain, and, namely, in the time of the late Emperor Ivan Vasilevich, by one Anthony, his legate, but thought this belike a far better mean to obtain his purpose by treaty and mediation of their own patriarch.[7] But this not succeeding, the Patriarch fell to a third point of treaty concerning the resignation of his patriarchship and translation of the see from Constantinople, or Scio, to the city of Moscow. Which was so well liked and entertained by the Emperor as a matter of high religion and policy that no other treaty, especially of foreign embassages, could be heard or regarded till that matter was concluded.

The reasons wherewith the Patriarch persuaded the translating of his see to the city of Moscow were these in effect: first, for that the see of the Patriarch was under the Turk, that is enemy to the faith, and therefore to be removed into some other country of Christian profession; secondly, because the Rus Church was the only natural daughter of the Greek at this time and holdeth the same doctrine and ceremonies with it, the rest being all subject to the Turk and fallen away from the right profession, wherein the subtle Greek to make the better market of his broken ware advanced the honor that would grow to the Emperor and his country to have the Patriarch's seat translated into the chief city and seat of his empire. As for the right of translating the see and appointing his successor, he made no doubt of it but that it pertained wholly to himself.

---

[7] The Jesuit Antonio Possevino was sent by Pope Gregory XIII to mediate between Stephen Bathory and Ivan IV in 1581.

Their Ecclesiastical State

So the Emperor and his council with the principal of his clergy being assembled at the Moscow, it was determined that the Metropolite of Moscow should become Patriarch of the whole Greek Church and have the same full authority and jurisdiction that pertained before to the Patriarch of Constantinople or Scio. And that it might be done with more order and solemnity, the twenty-fifth of January, 1588, the Greek Patriarch, accompanied with the Rus clergy, went to the great church of Prechistaia, or Our Lady, within the Emperor's castle,[8] having first wandered through the whole city in manner of a procession and blessing the people with his two fingers, where he made an oration and delivered his resignation in an instrument of writing and so laid down his patriarchal staff, which was presently received by the Metropolite of Moscow and divers other ceremonies used about the inauguration of this new Patriarch.[9] The day was holden very solemn by the people of the city, who were commanded to forbear works and to attend this solemnity. The great Patriarch that day was honored with rich presents sent him from the Emperor and Empress, of plate, cloth of gold, furs, etc., carried with great pomp through the streets of Moscow and at his departing received many gifts more both from the Emperor, nobility, and clergy. Thus the patriarchship of Constantinople, or Scio, which hath continued since the Council of Nicaea, is now translated to Moscow, or they made believe that they have a patriarch with the same right and authority that the other had. Wherein the subtle Greek hath made good advantage of their superstition and is now gone away with a rich booty into Poland, whether their patriarchship be current or not.

The matter is not unlike to make some schism betwixt the Greek and Rus Church, if the Rus hold this patriarchship that

---

[8] This is possibly a reference to the Cathedral of the Assumption (Uspenskii Sobor) in the Moscow kremlin. See above, p. 27.

[9] The new Patriarch of Moscow was Job.

he hath so well paid for and the Greeks elect another withal, as likely they will, whether this man were banished by the Turk or deprived by order of his own clergy. Which might happen to give advantage to the Pope and to bring over the Rus Church to the see of Rome, to which end peradventure he devised this stratagem and cast in this matter of schism among them, but that the emperors of Russia know well enough by the example of other Christian princes what inconvenience would grow to their state and country by subjecting themselves to the Romish see. To which end the late Emperor Ivan Vasilevich was very inquisitive of the Pope's authority over the princes of Christendom and sent one of very purpose to Rome to behold the order and behavior of his court.

With this Patriarch Hieronimo was driven out at the same time by the great Turk one Demitrio, Archbishop of Larissa, who is now in England and pretendeth the same cause of their banishment by the Turk, to wit, their not admitting of the Pope's new calendar for the alteration of the year.[10] Which how unlikely it is may appear by these circumstances: first, because there is no such affection nor friendly respect betwixt the Pope and the Turk as that he should banish a subject for not obeying the Pope's ordinance, especially in a matter of some sequel for the alteration of times within his own countries; secondly, for that he maketh no such scruple in deducting of times and keeping of a just and precise account from the Incarnation of Christ, whom he doth not acknowledge otherwise than I noted before; thirdly, for that the said Patriarch is now at Naples in Italy where, it may be guessed, he would not have gone within the Pope's reach and so near to his nose if he had been banished for opposing himself against the Pope's decree.

This office of patriarchship now translated to Moscow beareth a superior authority over all the churches, not only of Russia and other the Emperor's dominions, but throughout all the

[10] The Gregorian calendar introduced by Pope Gregory XIII in 1582.

Their Ecclesiastical State

churches of Christendom that were before under the Patriarch of Constantinople, or Scio. Or at least the Rus patriarch imagineth himself to have the same authority. He hath under him as his proper diocese the province of Moscow, besides other peculiars. His court or office is kept at the Moscow.

Before the creation of this new Patriarch they had but one metropolite that was called the Metropolite of Moscow. Now for more state to their church and new Patriarch they have two metropolites—the one of Novgorod Velikii, the other of Rostov.[11] Their office is to receive of the Patriarch such ecclesiastical orders as he thinketh good and to deliver the charge of them over to the archbishops, besides the ordering of their own diocese.

Their archbishops are four: of Smolensk, Kazan, Pskov, and Vologda.[12] The parts of their office is all one with the metropolites, save that they have an underjurisdiction as suffragans to the metropolites and superiors to the bishops. The next are the *vladyki*, or bishops, that are but six in all: of Krutitsk, of Riazan, of Tver and Torzhok, of Kolomenskoe, of Vladimir, of Suzdal.[13] These have every one a very large diocese, as dividing the rest of the whole country among them.

The matters pertaining to the ecclesiastical jurisdiction of the metropolites, archbishops, and bishops are the same in a manner that are used by the clergy in other parts of Christendom. For besides their authority over the clergy and ordering such matters as are mere ecclesiastical, their jurisdiction extendeth to all testamentary causes, matters of marriage and divorcements, some pleas of injuries, etc. To which purpose also they have their officials or commissaries, which they call *boiare vladychnye*, that are laymen of the degree of dukes or gentlemen that

[11] Kazan and Moscow were also seats of metropolitans.
[12] There were five archbishoprics: Smolensk, Vologda, Suzdal, Riazan, and Tver. Another was established in Astrakhan in 1602.
[13] There were but two bishoprics: Pskov and Kolomna. A bishopric in Karelia is mentioned from 1598.

Of the Rus Commonwealth

keep their courts and execute their jurisdiction.[14] Which, besides their other oppressions over the common people, reign over the priests as the dukes and *diaki* do over the poor people within their precincts. As for the archbishop or bishop himself, he beareth no sway in deciding those causes that are brought into his court. But if he would moderate any matter, he must do it by entreaty with his gentleman official. The reason is because these boiars, or gentlemen officials, are not appointed by the bishops but by the Emperor himself or his council and are to give account of their doings to none but to them. If the bishop can entreat at his admission to have the choice of his own official, it is accounted for a special great favor. But to speak it as it is, the clergy of Russia, as well concerning their lands and revenues as their authority and jurisdiction, are altogether ordered and overruled by the Emperor and his council and have so much and no more of both as their pleasure doth permit them.[15] They have also their assistants, or several counsels, as they call them, of certain priests that are of their diocese, residing within their cathedral cities, to the number of four-and-twenty apiece. These advise with them about the special and necessary matters belonging to their charge.

Concerning their rents and revenues to maintain their dignities, it is somewhat large. The Patriarch's yearly rents out of his lands, besides other fees, is about 3,000 rubles or marks; the metropolites and archbishops, about 2,500; the bishops, some 1,000, some 800, some 500, etc. They have had, some of them, as I have heard say, ten or twelve thousand rubles a year, as had the Metropolite of Novgorod.

Their habits or apparel when they show themselves in their *pontificalibus* after their solemnest manner is a miter on their

---

[14] The Russian word *vladyka*, used above as archbishop, may also mean "lord" or "ruler."

[15] Fletcher exaggerated this dependence of church on state. Seredonin discusses this secular influence in church affairs (*Sochinenie*, pp. 294–296).

Their Ecclesiastical State

heads after the popish fashion, set with pearl and precious stone, a cope on their backs, commonly of cloth of gold embroidered with pearl, and a crosier's staff in their hands laid over all with plate of silver double gilt, with a cross or shepherd's crook at the upper end of it. Their ordinary habit otherwise when they ride or go abroad is a hood on their heads of black color that hangeth down their back and standeth out like a bongrace [16] before. Their upper garment, which they call *riasa,* is a gown or mantle of black damask, with many lists, or guards, of white satin laid upon it, every guard about two fingers broad, and their crosier's staff carried before them. Themselves follow after, blessing the people with their two forefingers with a marvelous grace.

The election and appointing of the bishops and the rest pertaineth wholly to the Emperor himself. They are chosen ever out of the monasteries, so that there is no bishop, archbishop, nor metropolite but hath been a monk or friar before. And by that reason they are and must all be unmarried men, for their vow of chastity when they were first shorn. When the Emperor hath appointed whom he thinketh good, he is invested in the cathedral church of his diocese with many ceremonies, much after the manner of the popish inauguration. They have also their deans and their archdeacons.

As for preaching the word of God or any teaching or exhorting such as are under them, they neither use it nor have any skill of it, the whole clergy being utterly unlearned both for other knowledge and in the word of God. Only their manner is twice every year—viz., the first of September, which is the first day of their year, and on St. John Baptist's Day [17]—to make an ordinary speech to the people, every metropolite, archbishop, and bishop in his cathedral church to this or like effect: that if

---

[16] A shade or curtain formerly worn on the front of women's bonnets or caps for protection against sun.
[17] August 29.

Of the Rus Commonwealth

any be in malice toward his neighbor, he shall leave off his malice; if any thought of treason or rebellion against his prince, he beware of such practice; if he have not kept his fasts and vows nor done his other duties to the holy Church, he shall amend that fault, etc. And this is a matter of form with them, uttered in as many words and no more in a manner than I have here set down. Yet the matter is done with that grace and solemnity, in a pulpit of purpose set up for this one act, as if he were to discourse at large of the whole substance of divinity. At the Moscow the Emperor himself is ever present at this solemn exhortation.

As themselves are void of all manner of learning, so are they wary to keep out all means that might bring any in, as fearing to have their ignorance and ungodliness discovered. To that purpose they have persuaded the emperors that it would breed innovation and so danger to their state to have any novelty of learning come within the realm. Wherein they say but truth, for that a man of spirit and understanding, helped by learning and liberal education, can hardly endure a tyrannical government. Some years past in the other Emperor's time there came a press and letters out of Polonia to the city of Moscow, where a printing house was set up with great liking and allowance of the Emperor himself.[18] But not long after the house was set on fire in the nighttime and the press and letters quite burnt up, as was thought, by the procurement of the clergymen.

Their priests, whom they call *popy*, are made by the bishops without any great trial for worthiness of gifts before they admit them or ceremonies in their admission save that their heads are shorn—not shaven, for that they like not—about an handbreadth or more in the crown and that place anointed with oil

---

[18] According to Karamzin (*Histoire*, IX, 57–58), Ivan IV initially sought printers from Germany; in 1553 a printing establishment was opened in Moscow under the direction of Ivan Fedorov and Petr Matislavets, who published the first book in Moscow eleven years later.

Their Ecclesiastical State

by the bishop. Who in his admission putteth upon the priest first his surplice and then setteth a white cross on his breast, of silk or some other matter, which he is to wear eight days and no more, and so giveth him authority to say and sing in the church and to administer the sacraments.

They are men utterly unlearned, which is no marvel, forasmuch as their makers, the bishops themselves, as before was said, are clear of that quality and make no farther use at all of any kind of learning—no, not of the Scriptures themselves, save to read and to sing them. Their ordinary charge and function is to say the liturgy, to administer the sacraments after their manner, to keep and deck their idols, and to do the other ceremonies usual in their churches. Their number is great, because their towns are parted into many small parishes, without any discretion for dividing them into competent numbers of households and people for a just congregation, as the manner [is] in all places where the means is neglected for increasing of knowledge and instruction toward God. Which cannot well be had where, by means of an unequal partition of the people and parishes, there followeth a want and inequality of stipend for a sufficient ministry.

For their priests, it is lawful to marry for the first time. But if the first wife die, a second he cannot take but he must lose his priesthood and his living withal. The reason they make out of that place of St. Paul to Timothy, I. iii. 2, not well understood, thinking that to be spoken of divers wives successively that the apostle speaketh of at one and the same time. If he will needs marry again after his first wife is dead, he is no longer called *pop*, but *razpop*, or priest quondam. This maketh the priests to make much of their wives, who are accounted as the matrons and of best reputation among the women of the parish.

For the stipend of the priest, their manner is not to pay him any tenths of corn or aught else; but he must stand at the devo-

Of the Rus Commonwealth

tion of the people of his parish and make up the incomes toward his maintenance so well as he can by offerings, shrifts,[19] marriages, burials, dirges, and prayers for the dead and the living, which they call *molitva*. For besides their public service within their churches, their manner is for every private man to have a prayer said for him by the priest upon any occasion of business whatsoever, whether he ride, go, sail, plow, or whatsoever else he doth. Which is not framed according to the occasion of his business but at random, being some of their ordinary and usual church prayers. And this is thought to be more holy and effectual if it be repeated by the priest's mouth rather than by his own. They have a custom besides to solemnize the saint's day that is patron to their church once every year. What time all their neighbors of their country and parishes about come in to have prayers said to that saint for themselves and their friends and so make an offering to the priest for his pains. This offering may yield them some ten pounds a year, more or less, as the patron or saint of that church is of credit and estimation among them. The manner is, on this day which they keep anniversary, for the priest to hire divers of his neighbor priests to help him, as having more dishes to dress for the saint than he can well turn his hand unto. They use besides to visit their parishioners' houses with holy water and perfume commonly once a quarter and so, having sprinkled and becensed the goodman [20] and his wife, with the rest of their household and household stuff, they receive some devotion, more or less, as the man is of ability. This and the rest laid altogether make up for the priest toward his maintenance about thirty or forty rubles a year, whereof he payeth the tenth part to the bishop of the diocese.[21]

The *pop*, or priest, is known by his long tufts of hair hanging

---

[19] Confessions.   [20] Husbandman; man of the house.

[21] While this was probably an accurate estimate of the earning of the priests in the capital, in provincial cities and villages they received substantially less. Cf. Seredonin's discussion, *Sochinenie*, pp. 293–295.

Their Ecclesiastical State

down by his ears, his gown with a broad cope, and a walking staff in his hand. For the rest of his habit he is appareled like the common sort. When he saith the liturgy or service within the church, he hath on him his surplice, and sometimes his cope, if the day be more solemn. They have besides their *popy*, or priests, their *chernye popy*, as they call them, that is, black priests, that may keep their benefices though they be admitted friars withal within some monastery. They seem to be the very same that were called regular priests in the popish church. Under the priest is a deacon in every church that doth nothing but the office of a parish clerk. As for their *protopopy*, or archpriests, and their archdeacons, that are next in election to be their *protopopy*, they serve only in the cathedral churches.

Of friars they have an infinite rabble, far greater than in any other country where popery is professed. Every city and good part of the country swarmeth full of them. For they have wrought, as the popish friars did by their superstition and hypocrisy, that if any part of the realm be better and sweeter than other, there standeth a friary or a monastery dedicated to some saint.

The number of them is so much the greater, not only for that it is augmented by the superstition of the country, but because the friar's life is the safest from the oppressions and exactions that fall upon the commons, which causeth many to put on the friar's weed as the best armor to bear off such blows. Besides such as are voluntary, there are divers that are forced to shear themselves friars upon some displeasure. These are for the most part of the chief nobility. Divers take the monasteries as a place of sanctuary and there become friars to avoid some punishment that they had deserved by the laws of the realm. For if he get a monastery over his head and there put on a cowl before he be attached, it is a protection to him forever against any law for what crime soever, except it be for treason. But this proviso goeth withal, that no man cometh there, except such as are com-

Of the Rus Commonwealth

manded by the Emperor to be received, but he giveth them lands or bringeth his stock with him and putteth it into the common treasury. Some bring 1,000 rubles and some more. None is admitted under three or four hundred.

The manner of their admission is after this sort: first, the abbot strippeth him of all his secular or ordinary apparel; then he putteth upon him next to his skin a white flannel shirt with a long garment over it down to the ground, girded unto him with a broad leather belt. His uppermost garment is a weed of *garus* or say [22] for color and fashion much like to the upper weed of a chimney sweeper. Then is his crown shorn a handbreadth or more close to the very skin and these or like words pronounced by the abbot whiles he clippeth his hair, "As these hairs are clipped off and taken from thy head, so now we take thee and separate thee clean from the world and worldly things," etc. This done he anointeth his crown with oil and putteth on his cowl and so taketh him in among the fraternity. They vow perpetual chastity and abstinence from flesh.

Besides their lands, that are very great, they are the greatest merchants in the whole country and deal for all manner of commodities. Some of their monasteries dispend [23] in lands one thousand or two thousand rubles a year. There is one abbey called Troits [24] that hath in lands and fees the sum of 100,000 rubles or marks a year. It is built in manner of a castle, walled round about, with great ordnance planted on the wall, and containeth within it a large breadth of ground and great variety of building. There are of friars within it, besides their officers and other servants, about seven hundred. The Empress that now is hath many vows to St. Sergius, that is patron there, to entreat him to make her fruitful, as having no children by the Emperor

---

[22] *Garus:* worsted; say: a cloth of fine texture resembling serge; in the sixteenth century it consisted partially of silk.

[23] Have an income from.

[24] Troitskaia-Sergei Monastery in Zagorsk, north of Moscow.

Their Ecclesiastical State

her husband.[25] Lightly every year she goeth on pilgrimage to him from the Moscow on foot, about eighty English miles, with five or six thousand women attending upon her, all in blue liveries, and four thousand soldiers for her guard.[26] But St. Sergius hath not yet heard her prayers, though they say he hath a special gift and faculty that way.

What learning there is among their friars may be known by their bishops, that are the choice men out of all their monasteries. I talked with one of them at the city of Vologda, where to try his skill I offered him a Rus Testament and turned him to the first chapter of St. Matthew's Gospel, where he began to read in very good order. I asked him first what part of Scripture it was that he had read. He answered that he could not well tell. How many Evangelists there were in the New Testament? He said he knew not. How many Apostles there were? He thought there were twelve. How he should be saved? Whereunto he answered me with a piece of Rus doctrine that he knew not whether he should be saved or no; but if God would *pozhalovat* him, or gratify him, so much as to save him, so it was, he would be glad of it; if not, what remedy? I asked him why he sheared himself a friar? He answered because he would eat his bread with peace. This is the learning of the friars of Russia, which though it be not to be measured by one, yet partly it may be guessed by the ignorance of this man what is in the rest.

They have also many nunneries, whereof some may admit none but noblemen's widows and daughters, when the Emperor meaneth to keep them unmarried from continuing the blood or stock which he would have extinguished. To speak of the life of their friars and nuns, it needs not to those that know the hypocrisy and uncleanness of that cloister brood. The Rus himself,

---

[25] St. Sergius (d. 1392) was a great figure in the history of the Moscow church. The reference here is to Irene, wife to Fedor and sister to Boris Godunov.

[26] The distance is but half Fletcher's estimate.

Of the Rus Commonwealth

though otherwise addicted to all superstition, speaketh so foully of it that it must needs gain silence of any modest man.

Besides these, they have certain hermits, whom they call holy men, that are like to those gymnosophists [27] for their life and behavior, though far unlike for their knowledge and learning. They use to go stark naked save a clout about their middle, with their hair hanging long and wildly about their shoulders, and many of them with an iron collar or chain about their necks or midst, even in the very extremity of winter. These they take as prophets and men of great holiness, giving them a liberty to speak what they list without any controlment, though it be of the very highest himself. So that if he reprove any openly, in what sort soever, they answer nothing, but that it is *po graecum,* that is, for their sins. And if any of them take some piece of salesware from any man's shop as he passeth by, to give where he list, he thinketh himself much beloved of God and much beholding to the holy man for taking it in that sort.

Of this kind there are not many, because it is a very hard and cold profession to go naked in Russia, especially in winter. Among other at this time they have one at Moscow that walketh naked about the streets and inveigheth commonly against the state and government, especially against the Godunovs, that are thought at this time to be great oppressors of that commonwealth. Another there was that died not many years ago whom they called Vasilii, that would take upon him to reprove the old Emperor for all his cruelty and oppressions done toward his people. His body they have translated of late into a sumptuous church near the Emperor's house in Moscow and have canonized him for a saint. Many miracles he doth there, for so the friars make the people to believe, and many offerings are made unto him, not only by the people but by the chief nobility and the Emperor and Empress themselves, which visit that church with great devotion. But this last year at my being at Moscow this

[27] A sect of ancient Hindu ascetic philosophers.

Their Ecclesiastical State

saint had ill luck in working his miracles. For a lame man that had his limbs restored, as it was pretended by him, was charged by a woman that was familiar with him, being then fallen out, that he halted but in the daytime and could leap merrily when he came home at night. And that he had intended this matter six years before. Now he is put into a monastery and there raileth upon the friars that hired him to have this counterfeit miracle practiced upon him. Besides this disgrace, a little before my coming from thence there were eight slain within his church by fire in a thunder, which caused his bells, that were tingling before all day and night long, as in triumph of the miracles wrought by Vasilii, their saint, to ring somewhat softlier and hath wrought no little discredit to this miracle worker. There was another of great account at Pskov, called Nikola of Pskov,[28] that did much good when this Emperor's father came to sack the town upon suspicion of their revolting and rebellion against him. The Emperor, after he had saluted the hermit at his lodging, sent him a reward. And the holy man, to requite the Emperor, sent him a piece of raw flesh, being then their Lent time. Which the Emperor seeing, bid one to tell him that he marveled that the holy man would offer him flesh to eat in the Lent, when it was forbidden by order of holy Church. "And doth Ivashka [29] (which is as much to say as Jack) think," quoth Nikola, "that it is unlawful to eat a piece of beast's flesh in Lent and not to eat up so much man's flesh as he hath done already?" So threatening the Emperor with a prophecy of some hard adventure to come upon him except he left murdering of his people and departed the town, he saved a great many men's lives at that time.

This maketh the people to like very well of them, because they are as Pasquils to note their great men's faults that no man

---

[28] Jerome Horsey also noted this hermit and referred to him as Mikula Sweat. Cf. Bond, *Russia*, pp. 159–160.

[29] This is simply a familiar form of Ivan or John. Fletcher had written *Evasko*.

Of the Rus Commonwealth

else dare speak of.[30] Yet it falleth out sometime that for this rude liberty which they take upon them after a counterfeit manner by imitation of prophets they are made away in secret, as was one or two of them in the last Emperor's time for being overbold in speaking against his government.

CHAPTER XXII

Of Their Liturgy, or Form of Church Service, and Their Manner of Administering the Sacraments

THEIR morning service they call *zautrenia*, that is, matins. It is done in this order. The priest entereth into the church with his deacon following him. And when he is come to the middle of the church, he beginneth to say with a loud voice: "*Blagoslovi vladyko*," that is, "Bless us, heavenly Pastor," meaning of Christ. Then he addeth: "In the name of the Father, and of the Son, and of the Holy Ghost, one very God in Trinity," and "*Gospodi pomilui*," or, "Lord have mercy upon us, Lord have mercy upon us, Lord have mercy upon us," repeated three times. This done, he marcheth on toward the chancel, or *sanctum sanctorum*, as they use to call it, and so entereth into the *tsarskaia dver*, or the heavenly door, which no man may enter into but the priest only.[1] Where, standing at the altar or table set near to the upper wall of the chancel, he saith the Lord's Prayer and then again, "*Gospodi pomilui*," or, "Lord have mercy upon us, Lord have mercy upon us," etc., pronounced twelve times. Then, "Praised be the Trinity, the Father, the Son, and Holy Ghost, forever and ever." Whereto the deacons and people say, "Amen." Next after,

---

[30] Fletcher refers to the legendary Pasquin, or Pasquil, from whom the word pasquil, meaning a lampoon, derived.

[1] Fletcher wrote "*gospodi pomilui*" as "Aspody Pomeluy." *Tsarskaia dver* is better translated "royal door."

Of Their Liturgy

the priest addeth the Psalms for that day and beginneth with "Oh, come let us worship and fall down before the Lord," etc. And therewithal himself with the deacons and people all turn themselves toward their idols, or images, that hang on the wall and, crossing themselves, bow down three times, knocking their heads to the very ground. After this he readeth the Ten Commandments and Athanasius' Creed out of the service book.

This being done, the deacon that standeth without the heavenly door, or chancel, readeth a piece of a legend out of a written book, for they have it not in print, of some saint's life, miracles, etc. This is divided into many parts, for every day in the year, and is read by them with a plain, singing note not unlike to the popish tune when they sang their gospels. After all this, which reacheth to an hour and an half or two hours of length, he addeth certain set collects, or prayers, upon that which he hath read out of the legend before and so endeth his service. All this while stand burning before their idols a great many of wax candles, whereof some are of the bigness of a man's waist, vowed or enjoined by penance upon the people of the parish.

About nine of the clock in the morning they have another service called *obednia*, or complin, much after the order of the popish service that bare that name.[2] If it be some high or festival day, they furnish their service beside with "Blessed be the Lord God of Israel," etc., and "We praise thee, O God," etc., sung with a more solemn and curious note.

Their evening service is called *vechernia*,[3] where the priest beginneth with *Blagoslovi vladyko*, as he did in the morning, and the psalms appointed for the *vechernia*, which being read, he singeth, "My soul doth magnify the Lord," etc. And then the priest, deacons, and people all with one voice sing "*Gospodi*

---

[2] *Obednia* may be defined simply as Mass. "Complin" refers to the religious service which closes the day or is said after nightfall. It is the seventh and last of the canonical hours.

[3] Vespers.

125

pomilui," or, "Lord have mercy upon us," thirty times together. Whereunto the boys that are in the church answer all with one voice, rolling it up so fast as their lips can go: "*Verij, Verij, Verij, Verij,*" or, "Praise, praise, praise," etc., thirty times together, with a very strange noise.[4] Then is read by the priest and upon the holidays sung the First Psalm, "Blessed is the man," etc. And in the end of it is added, "Alleluia," repeated ten times. The next in order is some part of the gospel read by the priest, which he endeth with "Alleluia" repeated three times. And so, having said a collect in remembrance of the saint of the day, he endeth his evening service.

All this while the priest standeth above at the altar, or high table, within the chancel, or *sanctum sanctorum,* whence he never moveth all the service time. The deacon or deacons, which are many in their cathedral churches, stand without the chancel by the *tsarskaia dver,* or heavenly door, for within they may not be seen all the service time, though otherwise their office is to sweep and keep it and to set up the wax candles before their idols. The people stand together the whole service time in the body of the church and some in the church porch, for pew or seat they have none within their churches.

The sacrament of baptism they administer after this manner. The child is brought unto the church, and this is done within eight days after it is born; if it be the child of some nobleman, it is brought with great pomp in a rich sled or wagon, with chairs and cushions of cloth of gold and suchlike sumptuous show of their best furniture. When they are come to the church, the priest standeth ready to receive the child within the church porch, with his tub of water by him. And then beginneth to declare unto them that they have brought a little infidel to be

---

[4] Fletcher erred when he said that "*Gospodi pomilui*" was repeated thirty times; it was said either three, twelve, or forty times. I have retained Fletcher's spelling of "*verij,*" because the Slavonic equivalent which he intended is not evident.

Of Their Liturgy

made a Christian, etc. This ended, he teacheth the witnesses, that are two or three, in a certain set form out of his book what their duty is in bringing up the child after he is baptized, viz., that he must be taught to know God and Christ the Savior. And because God is of great majesty and we must not presume to come unto Him without mediators, as the manner is when we make any suit to an emperor or great prince, therefore they must teach him what saints are the best and chief mediators, etc. This done, he commandeth the devil in the name of God after a conjuring manner to come out of the water, and so after certain prayers he plungeth the child thrice over head and ears. For this they hold to be a point necessary, that no part of the child be undipped in the water.

The words that bear with them the form of baptism, uttered by the priest when he dippeth in the child, are the very same that are prescribed in the gospel and used by us, viz., "In the name of the Father, and of the Son, and of the Ghost." For that they should alter the form of the words and say, "by the Holy Ghost," as I have heard that they did, following certain heretics of the Greek Church, I found to be untrue, as well by report of them that have been often at their baptisms as by their book of liturgy itself, wherein the order of baptism is precisely set down.

When the child is baptized, the priest layeth oil and salt tempered together upon the forehead and both sides of his face and then upon his mouth, drawing it along with his fingers over the child's lips, as did the popish priests, saying withal certain prayers to this effect: that God will make him a good Christian, etc. All this is done in the church porch. Then is the child, as being now made a Christian and meet to be received within the church door, carried into the church, the priest going before; and there he is presented to the chief idol of the church, being laid on a cushion before the feet of the image by it, as by the mediator, to be commended unto God. If the child be sick or weak, especially in the winter, they use to make the water luke-

Of the Rus Commonwealth

warm. After baptism the manner is to cut off the hair from the child's head and, having wrapped it within a piece of wax, to lay it up as a relic or monument in a secret place of the church.

This is the manner of their baptism, which they account to be the best and perfectest form, as they do all other parts of their religion, received, as they say, by tradition from the best Church, meaning the Greek. And therefore they will take great pains to make a proselyte or convert either of an infidel or of a foreign Christian, by rebaptizing him after the Rus manner. When they take any Tartar prisoner, commonly they will offer him life with condition to be baptized; and yet they persuade very few of them to redeem their life so, because of the natural hatred the Tartar beareth to the Rus and the opinion he hath of his falsehood and injustice. The year after Moscow was fired by the Crim Tartar there was taken a *divei-murza,* one of the chief in that exploit, with three hundred Tartars more, who had all their lives offered them if they would be baptized after the Rus manner, which they refused all to do, with many reproaches against those that persuaded them. And so, being carried to the river Moscow, that runneth through the city, they were all baptized after a violent manner, being thrust down with a knock on the head into the water through an hole made in the ice for that purpose. Of Lieflanders that are captives there are many that take on them this second Rus baptism to get more liberty and somewhat besides toward their living, which the Emperor ordinarily useth to give them.

Of Englishmen, since they frequented the country, there was never any found that so much forgot God, his faith, and country as that he would be content to be baptized Rus for any respect of fear, preferment, or other means whatsoever save only Richard Relph,[5] that, following before an ungodly trade by keeping a *kabak,* against the order of the country, and being put off

---

[5] Richard Relph, one of those employees of the Muscovy Company who engaged in private trade, in 1584 even disobeyed an order to return to England.

Of Their Liturgy

from that trade and spoiled by the Emperor's officers of that which he had, entered himself this last year into the Rus profession and so was rebaptized, living now as much an idolater as before he was a rioter and unthrifty person.

Such as thus receive the Rus baptism are first carried into some monastery to be instructed there in the doctrine and ceremonies of the Church, where they use these ceremonies. First, they put him into a new and fresh suit of apparel made after the Rus fashion and set a coronet or in summer a garland upon his head; then they anoint his head with oil and put a wax candlelight into his hand and so pray over him four times a day, the space of seven days. All this while he is to abstain from flesh and white meats.[6] The seven days being ended, he is purified and washed in a bathstove, and so the eighth day he is brought into the church, where he is taught by the friars how to behave himself in presence of their idols, by ducking down, knocking of the head, crossing himself, and suchlike gestures, which are the greatest part of the Rus religion.

The sacrament of the Lord's Supper they receive but once a year in their great Lent time, a little before Easter. Three at the most are admitted at one time and never above. The manner of their communicating is thus: first, they confess themselves of all their sins to the priest, whom they call their ghostly father; then they come to the church and are called up to the communion table, that standeth like an altar a little removed from the upper end of the church, after the Dutch manner. Here, first, they are asked of the priest whether they be clean or no, that is, whether they have never a sin behind that they left unconfessed. If they answer no, they are taken to the table, where the priest beginneth with certain usual prayers, the communicants standing in the meanwhile with their arms folded one within another like penitentiaries or mourners. When these prayers are ended, the priest taketh a spoon and filleth it full of claret wine; then he putteth into it a small piece of bread and tempereth them both

[6] Dairy products.

Of the Rus Commonwealth

together and so delivereth them in the spoon to the communicants that stand in order, speaking the usual words of the sacrament, "Eat this," etc.; "Drink this," etc., both at one time without any pause.[7]

After that he delivereth them again bread by itself and then wine carded together with a little warm water to represent blood more rightly, as they think, and the water withal that flowed out of the side of Christ. Whiles this is in doing, the communicants unfold their arms, and then, folding them again, follow the priest thrice round about the communion table and so return to their places again, where, having said certain other prayers, he dismisseth the communicants with charge to be merry and to cheer up themselves for the seven days next following; which being ended, he enjoineth them to fast for it as long time after. Which they use to observe with very great devotion, eating nothing else but bread and salt except a little cabbage and some other herb or root, with water or *kvass*[8] mead for their drink.

This is their manner of administering the sacraments, wherein what they differ from the institution of Christ and what ceremonies they have added of their own, or rather borrowed of the Greeks, may easily be noted.

CHAPTER XXIII

Of the Doctrine of the Rus Church and What Errors It Holdeth

THEIR chiefest errors in matter of faith I find to be these: first, concerning the word of God itself, they will not read publicly cer-

---

[7] Fletcher's rendering here was a bit curt.

[8] A thin sour beer commonly made by pouring warm water on rye or barley and letting it ferment. Cf. below, pp. 150–151.

The Rus Church

tain books of the Canonical Scripture, as the books of Moses, especially the four last, Exodus, Leviticus, Numeri, and Deuteronomy, which they say are all made disauthentic and put out of use by the coming of Christ, as not able to discern the difference betwixt the moral and the ceremonial law. The books of the Prophets they allow of but read them not publicly in their churches for the same reason, because they were but directors unto Christ and proper, as they say, to the nation of the Jews. Only the book of Psalms they have in great estimation and sing and say them daily in their churches. Of the New Testament they allow and read all except the Revelation, which therefore they read not, though they allow it, because they understand it not, neither have the like occasion to know the fulfilling of the prophecies contained within it, concerning especially the apostasy of the Antichristian Church, as have the Western Churches. Notwithstanding they have had their antichrists of the Greek Church and may find their own falling off and the punishments for it by the Turkish invasion in the prophecies of that book.

Secondly, which is the fountain of the rest of all their corruptions both in doctrine and ceremonies, they hold with the papists that their church traditions are of equal authority with the written word of God. Wherein they prefer themselves before other churches, affirming that they have the true and right traditions delivered by the apostles to the Greek Church and so unto them.

3. That the Church, meaning the Greek, and especially the Patriarch and his Synod as the head of the rest, have a sovereign authority to interpret the Scriptures, and that all are bound to hold that interpretation as sound and authentic.

4. Concerning the divine nature and the three persons in the one substance of God, that the Holy Ghost proceedeth from the Father only and not from the Son.

5. About the office of Christ they hold many foul errors and the same almost as doth the popish church, namely, that he is

the sole mediator of redemption but not of intercession. Their chief reason, if they be talked withal, for defense of this error is that unapt and foolish comparison betwixt God and a monarch or prince of this world that must be sued unto by mediators about him, wherein they give special preferment to some above others, as to the blessed Virgin, whom they call *prechistaia*, or undefiled, and St. Nicholas, whom they call *skoryi pomoshchnik*, or the speedy helper, and say that he hath three hundred angels of the chiefest appointed by God to attend upon him. This hath brought them to an horrible excess of idolatry after the grossest and profanest manner, giving unto their images all religious worship of prayer, thanksgiving, offerings, and adoration, with prostrating and knocking their heads to the ground before them as to God Himself, which because they do this to the picture, not to the portraiture of the saint, they say they worship not an idol but the saint in his image and so offend not God, forgetting the commandment of God that forbiddeth to make the image or likeness of anything for any religious worship or use whatsoever. Their church walls are very full of them, richly hanged and set forth with pearl and stone upon the smooth table. Though some also they have embossed that stick from the board almost an inch outward. They call them *chudotvornye*, or their miracle workers; and when they provide them to set up in their churches, in no case they may say that they have bought the image, but exchanged money for it.

6. For the means of justification, they agree with the papists that it is not by faith only apprehending Christ but by their works also, and that *opus operatum*, or the work for the work's sake, must needs please God. And therefore they are all in their numbers of prayers, fasts, vows, and offerings to saints, alms deeds, crossings, and suchlike, and carry their numbering beads about with them continually, as well the Emperor and his nobility as the common people, not only in the church but in all other

The Rus Church

public places, especially at any set or solemn meeting, as in their fasts, law courts, common consultations, entertainment of ambassadors, and suchlike.

7. They say with the papists that no man can be assured of his salvation till the last sentence be passed at the day of judgment.

8. They use auricular confession and think that they are purged by the very action from so many sins as they confess by name and in particular to the priest.

9. They hold three sacraments, of baptism, the Lord's Supper, and the last anoiling, or unction. Yet concerning their sacrament of extreme unction, they hold it not so necessary to salvation as they do baptism, but think it a great curse and punishment of God if any die without it.

10. They think there is a necessity of baptism and that all are condemned that die without it.

11. They rebaptize as many Christians, not being of the Greek Church, as they convert to their Rus profession, because they are divided from the true Church, which is the Greek, as they say.

12. They make a difference of meats and drinks, accounting the use of one to be more holy than of another. And therefore in their set fasts they forbear to eat flesh and white meats, as we call them, after the manner of the popish superstition, which they observe so strictly and with such blind devotion as that they will rather die than eat one bit of flesh, eggs, or suchlike for the health of their bodies in their extreme sickness.

13. They hold marriage to be unlawful for all the clergymen except the priests only and for them also after the first wife, as was said before; neither do they well allow of it in laymen after the second marriage, which is a pretense now used against the Emperor's only brother, a child of six years old, who therefore is not prayed for in their churches, as their manner is otherwise for

Of the Rus Commonwealth

the prince's blood, because he was born of the sixth marriage and so not legitimate.[1] This charge was given to the priests by the Emperor himself by procurement of the Godunovs, who make him believe that it is a good policy to turn away the liking of the people from the next successor.

Many other false opinions they have in matter of religion. But these are the chief, which they hold partly by means of their traditions, which they have received from the Greek Church, but especially by ignorance of the Holy Scriptures, which notwithstanding they have in the Polonian tongue, that is all one with theirs, some few words excepted, yet few of them read them with that godly care which they ought to do.[2] Neither have they, if they would, books sufficient of the Old and New Testament for the common people, but of their liturgy only or book of common service, whereof there are great numbers.

All this mischief cometh from the clergy, who, being ignorant and godless themselves, are very wary to keep the people likewise in their ignorance and blindness for their living and bellies' sake; partly, also from the manner of government settled among them, which the emperors, whom it especially behooveth, list not to have changed by any innovation but to retain that religion that best agreeth with it, which notwithstanding, it is not to be doubted but that, having the word of God in some sort, though without the ordinary means to attain to a true sense and understanding of it, God hath also His number among them. As may partly appear by that which a Rus at Moscow said in secret to one of my servants, speaking against their images and other superstitions—that God had given unto England light today and might give it tomorrow, if He pleased, to them.

As for any inquisitions or proceeding against men for matter of religion, I could hear of none, save a few years since against one man and his wife, who were kept in a close prison the space

---

[1] This, of course, is another reference to Dimitrii, son of Ivan IV.

[2] Probably a reference to the *Biblia Swieta* published in Brest in 1563.

The Manner of Solemnizing Their Marriages

of twenty-eight years till they were overgrown into a deformed fashion for their hair, nails, color of countenance, and suchlike and in the end were burned at Moscow in a small house set on fire. The cause was kept secret, but like[ly] it was for some part of truth in matter of religion, though the people were made to believe by the priests and friars that they held some great and damnable heresy.

CHAPTER XXIV

Of the Manner of Solemnizing Their Marriages

THE manner of making and solemnizing their marriages is different from the manner of other countries. The man, though he never saw the woman before, is not permitted to have any sight of her all the time of his wooing, which he doth not by himself but by his mother or some other ancient woman of his kin or acquaintance. When the liking is taken as well by the parents as by the parties themselves—for without the knowledge and consent of the parents the contract is not lawful—the fathers on both sides, or such as are to them instead of fathers, with their other chief friends, have a meeting and conference about the dowry, which is commonly very large, after the ability of the parents, so that you shall have a market man, as they call them, give 1,000 rubles or more with his daughter.

As for the man, it is never required of him nor standeth with their custom to make any jointure to recompense of the dowry. But in the case he have a child by his wife, she enjoyeth a third deal after his decease. If he have two children by her or more, she is to have a courtesy more, at the discretion of the husband. If the husband depart without issue by his wife, she is returned home to her friends without anything at all save only her dowry, if the husband leave so much behind him in goods. When the agreement is made concerning the dowry, they sign bonds one to the other, as well for the payment of the dowry as the performing of the marriage by a certain day. If the woman were never married before, her father and friends are bound besides to assure her a maiden, which breedeth many brabbles and quarrels at law if the man take any conceit concerning the behavior and honesty of his wife.

Thus, the contract being made, the parties begin to send tokens the one to the other—the woman first, then afterward the man—but yet see not one another till the marriage be solemnized. On the eve before the marriage day, the bride is carried in a *kolymaga*, or coach, or in a sled if it be winter, to the bridegroom's house, with her marriage apparel and bedstead with her, which they are to lie in,[1] for this is ever provided by the bride and is commonly very fair, with much cost bestowed upon it. Here she is accompanied all that night by her mother and other women, but not welcomed nor once seen by the bridegroom himself.

When the time is come to have the marriage solemnized, the bride hath put upon her a kind of hood made of fine knitwork or lawn that covereth her head and all her body down to the middle. And so, accompanied with her friends and the bridegroom with his, they go to church all on horseback, though the church be near-hand and themselves but of very mean degree. The words of contract and other ceremonies in solemnizing the marriage are much after the order and with the same words that are used with us, with a ring also given to the bride. Which being put on and the words of contract pronounced, the bride's hand is delivered into the hand of the bridegroom, which standeth all this while on the one side of the altar, or table, and the bride on the other. So, the marriage knot being knit by the priest, the

---

[1] There is no evidence that this practice existed. Fletcher apparently confused the conveying of the dowry with that of the bride to the home of the bridegroom.

The Manner of Solemnizing Their Marriages

bride cometh to the bridegroom, standing at the end of the altar, or table, and falleth down at his feet, knocking her head upon his shoe in token of her subjection and obedience. And the bridegroom again casteth the lap of his gown or upper garment over the bride in token of his duty to protect and cherish her.

Then, the bridegroom and bride standing both together at the table's end, cometh first the father and the other friends of the bride and bow themselves down low to the bridegroom. And so likewise his friends bow themselves to the bride in token of affinity and love ever after betwixt the two kindreds. And withal, the father of the bridegroom offereth to the priest a loaf of bread, who delivereth it straight again to the father and other friends of the bride with attestation before God and their idols that he deliver the dowry wholly and truly at the day appointed and hold love ever after one kindred with another; whereupon they break the loaf into pieces and eat of it to testify their true and sincere meanings for performing of that charge and thenceforth to become as grains of one loaf or men of one table.

These ceremonies being ended, the bridegroom taketh the bride by the hand and so they go on together with their friends after them toward the church porch, where meet them certain with pots and cups in their hands with mead and Rus wine. Whereof the bridegroom taketh first a *charka*, or little cup, full in his hand and drinketh to the bride, who, opening her hood or veil below and putting the cup to her mouth underneath it, for [2] being seen of the bridegroom, pledgeth him again. Thus, returning together from the church, the bridegroom goeth not home to his own but to his father's house and she likewise to hers, where either entertain their friends apart. At the entering into the house they use to fling corn out of the windows upon the bridegroom and bride in token of plenty and fruitfulness to be with them ever after.

When the evening is come, the bride is brought to the

[2] For fear of.

Of the Rus Commonwealth

bridegroom's father's house and there lodgeth that night with her veil or cover still over her head. All that night she may not speak one word, for that charge she receiveth by tradition from her mother and other matrons her friends, that the bridegroom must neither hear nor see her till the day after the marriage. Neither three days after may she be heard to speak, save certain few words at the table in a set form with great manners and reverence to the bridegoom. If she behave herself otherwise, it is a great prejudice to her credit and life ever after and will highly be disliked of the bridegroom himself.

After the third day they depart to their own and make a feast to both their friends together. The marriage day and the whole time of their festival the bridegroom hath the honor to be called *molodoi kniaz,* or young duke, and the bride, *molodaia kniaginia,* or young duchess.

In living with their wives, they show themselves to be but of a barbarous condition, using them as servants rather than wives —except the noblewomen, which are or seem to be of more estimation with their husbands than the rest of meaner sort. They have this foul abuse, contrary to good order and the word of God itself, that upon dislike of his wife or other cause whatsoever the man may go into a monastery and shear himself a friar by pretense of devotion and so leave his wife to shift for herself so well as she can.

CHAPTER XXV

Of the Other Ceremonies of the Rus Church

THE other ceremonies of their church are many in number, especially the abuse about the sign of the cross, which they set up in their highways, in the tops of their churches, and in every door of their houses, signing themselves continually with it on

The Ceremonies of the Rus Church

their foreheads and breasts with great devotion, as they will seem by their outward gesture, which were less offense if they gave not withal that religious reverence and worship unto it which is due to God only and used the dumb show and signing of it instead of thanksgiving and of all other duties which they owe to God. When they rise in the morning, they go commonly in the sight of some steeple that hath a cross on the top and so, bowing themselves toward the cross, sign themselves withal on their foreheads and breasts. And this is their thanksgiving to God for their night's rest, without any word speaking except peradventure they say, *"Gospodi pomilui,"* or, "Lord have mercy upon us." When they sit down to meat and rise again from it, the thanksgiving to God is the crossing of their foreheads and breasts, except it be some few that add, peradventure, a word or two of some ordinary prayer impertinent to that purpose. When they are to give an oath for the deciding of any controversy at law, they do it by swearing by the cross and kissing the feet of it, making it as God, whose name only is to be used in such trial of justice. When they enter into any house where ever there is an idol hanging on the wall, they sign themselves with the cross and bow themselves to it.[1] When they begin any work, be it little or much, they arm themselves first with the sign of the cross. And this commonly is all their prayer to God for good speed of their business. And thus they serve God with crosses, after a cross and vain manner, not understanding what the cross of Christ is nor the power of it. And yet they think all strangers Christians to be no better than Turks in comparison of themselves, and so they will say, because they bow not themselves when they meet with the cross nor sign themselves with it as the Rus manner is.

They have holy water in like use and estimation as the popish church hath. But herein they exceed them, in that they do not

[1] Fletcher refers to an icon, hardly idolatrous in the Byzantine Christian religion.

only hallow their holy water stocks and tubs full of water but all the rivers of the country once every year. At Moscow it is done with great pomp and solemnity, the Emperor himself being present at it with all his nobility, marching through the streets toward the river of Moscow, in manner of procession, in this order as followeth. First go two deacons with banners in their hands, the one of Prechistaia, or Our Lady, the other of St. Michael fighting with his dragon. Then follow after the rest of the deacons and the priest of Moscow, two and two in a rank, with copes on their backs and their idols at their breasts, carried with girdles or slings made fast about their necks. Next the priests come their bishops in their *pontificalibus;* then the friars, monks, and abbots; and after the patriarchs, in very rich attire with a ball or sphere on the top of his miter to signify his universality over that Church. Last cometh the Emperor with all his nobility. The whole train is of a mile long or more. When they are come to the river, a great hole is made in the ice where the market is kept, of a rod and a half broad, with a stage round about it to keep off the press. Then beginneth the Patriarch to say certain prayers and conjureth the devil to come out of the water, and so, casting in salt and censing it with frankincense, maketh the whole river to become holy water. The morning before, all the people of Moscow use to make crosses of chalk over every door and window of their houses lest the devil, being conjured out of the water, should fly into their houses.

When the ceremonies are ended, you shall see the black guard[2] of the Emperor's house and then the rest of the town with their pails and buckets to take off the hallowed water for drink and other uses. You shall also see the women dip in their children over head and ears and many men and women leap into it—some naked, some with their clothes on—when some man would think his finger would freeze off if he should but dip it into the water. When the men have done, they bring their

[2] Kitchen servants.

The Ceremonies of the Rus Church

horse to the river to drink of the sanctified water and so make them as holy as a horse. Their set day for this solemn action of hallowing their rivers is that we call Twelfth Day. The like is done by other bishops in all parts of the realm.

Their manner is also to give it to their sick in their greatest extremity, thinking that it will either recover them or sanctify them to God. Whereby they kill many through their unreasonable superstition, as did the Lord Boris his only son at my being at the Moscow, whom he killed, as was said by the physicians, by pouring into him cold holy water and presenting him naked into the church to their St. Vasilii in the cold of the winter in an extremity of sickness.

They have an image of Christ which they call *Nerukotvornyi*, which signifieth as much as "made without hands," for so their priests and superstition withal persuadeth them it was. This in their processions they carry about with them on high upon a pole, enclosed within a pix made like a lanthorn, and do reverence to it as to a great mystery.[3]

At every brewing their manner is likewise to bring a dish of their wort[4] to the priest within the church; which, being hallowed by him, is poured into the brewing and so giveth it such a virtue as when they drink of it they are seldom sober. The like they do with the first fruit of their corn in harvest.

They have another ceremony on Palm Sunday of ancient tradition: what time the Patriarch rideth through the Moscow, the Emperor himself holding his horse bridle, and the people crying "Hosanna" and spreading their upper garments under his horse's feet. The Emperor hath of the Patriarch, for his good service of that day, two hundred rubles of standing pension. Another pageant they have much like to this the week before the nativity of

[3] Fletcher wrote *Nerukotvornyi* as *Neruchi*. A pix is a box which in the ecclesiastical sense often serves as the vessel in which the Eucharist is carried.

[4] That sweet infusion of malt which ferments and forms beer, or any similar liquid in incipient fermentation.

Of the Rus Commonwealth

Christ, when every bishop in his cathedral church setteth forth a show of the three children in the oven,[5] where the Angel is made to come flying from the roof of the church with great admiration of the lookers-on, and many terrible flashes of fire are made with resin and gunpowder by the Chaldeans, as they call them that run about the town all the twelve days, disguised in their players' coats, and make much good sport for the honor of the bishop's pageant. At the Moscow the Emperor himself and the Empress never fail to be at it, though it be but the same matter played every year without any new invention at all.

Besides their fasts on Wednesdays and Fridays throughout the whole year—the one because they say Christ was sold on the Wednesday; the other because He suffered on the Friday—they have four great fasts, or Lents, every year. The first, which they call their great Lent, is at the same time with ours; the second, about midsummer; the third, in harvesttime; the fourth about Hallontide,[6] which they keep not of policy but of mere superstition. In their great Lent for the first week they eat nothing but bread and salt and drink nothing but water, neither meddle with any matter of their vocation but intend their shriving and fasting only. They have also three vigils or wakes in their great Lent, which they call *Stoianie*,[7] and the last Friday their great vigil, as they call it. What time the whole parish must be present in the church and watch from nine o'clock in the evening till six in the morning, all the while standing, save when they fall down and knock their heads to their idols, which must be an hundred and seventy times just through the whole night.

About their burials also they have many superstitious and profane ceremonies, as putting within the finger of the corpse a letter to St. Nicholas, whom they make their chief mediator and,

---

[5] Referring to the legend of St. Nicholas, Bishop of Myra. Cf. p. 132.
[6] Hallontide, or, preferably, Hallowtide. The season of All Saints; the first week of November.
[7] In Russian literally "standing."

The Ceremonies of the Rus Church

as it were, the porter of heaven gates, as the papists do their Peter.

In the wintertime, when all is covered with snow and the ground so hard frozen as that no spade nor pickax can enter, their manner is not to bury their dead but to keep the bodies, so many as die all the wintertime, in an house in the suburbs or outparts of the town which they call *Bozhedom,* that is, "God's house," where the dead bodies are piled up together like billets on a woodstack, as hard with frost as a very stone, till the springtide come and resolveth the frost, what time every man taketh his dead friend and committeth him to the ground.

They have, besides, their year's and month's minds [8] for their friends departed. What time they have prayers said over the grave by the priest, who hath a penny ordinary for his pains. When any dieth, they have ordinary women mourners that come to lament for the dead party and stand howling over the body after a profane and heathenish manner—sometimes in the house, sometimes bringing the body into the back side, asking him what he wanted and what he meant to die. They bury their dead as the party used to go, with coat, hose, boots, hat, and the rest of his apparel.

Many other vain and superstitious ceremonies they have which were long and tedious to report. By these it may appear how far they are fallen from the true knowledge and practice of Christian religion, having exchanged the word of God for their vain traditions and brought all to external and ridiculous ceremonies, without any regard of spirit and truth, which God requireth in His true worship.

[8] Repasts of remembrance.

Of the Rus Commonwealth

CHAPTER XXVI

Of the Emperor's Domestic or Private Behavior

THE Emperor's private behavior, so much as may be or is meet to be known, is after this manner. He riseth commonly about four o'clock in the morning. After his appareling and washing, in cometh his ghostly father, or priest of his chamber, which is named in their tongue *otets dukhovnyi,* with his cross in his hand, wherewith he blesseth him, laying it first on his forehead, then upon his cheeks or sides of his face, and then offereth him the end of it to kiss. This done, the clerk of the cross, called *krestnyi diak,* bringeth into his chamber a painted image representing the saint for the day.[1] For every day with them hath his several saint, as it were the patron for that day. This he placeth among the rest of his image gods, wherewithal his chamber is decked as thick almost as the wall can bear, with lamps and wax candles burning before them. They are very costly and gorgeously decked with pearl and precious stone. This image being placed before him, the Emperor beginneth to cross himself after the Rus manner, first on the forehead, then on both sides of his breast, with "*Gospodi pomilui, pomilui menia, gospodi, sakhrani menia greshnika ot zlago deistriia,*" which is as much to say as, "Help me, O Lord my God, Lord comfort me, defend and keep me, a sinner, from doing evil," etc.[2] This he directeth toward the image or saint for that day, whom he nameth in his prayer, together with Our Lady, whom they call Prechistaia, St. Nicholas, or some other to whom he beareth

---

[1] *Otets dukhovnyi* is better translated "spiritual father." Fletcher recorded *krestnyi diak* as *Chresby Deyack Profery.*

[2] Fletcher noted this as *Aspody pomeluy, pomeluy mena hospody, sacroy mena gresnick syhodestva.*

The Emperor's Private Behavior

most devotion, bowing himself prostrate unto them with knocking his head to the very ground. Thus he continueth the space of a quarter of an hour or thereabouts.

Then cometh again the ghostly father, or chamber priest, with a silver bowl full of holy water, which they call in Rus *Sviataia voda*, and a sprinkle of basil, as they call it, in his hand and so all to-besprinkleth, first the image gods and then the Emperor. This holy water is brought fresh every day from the monasteries far and near, sent to the Emperor from the abbot or prior in the name of the saint that is patron of that monastery as a special token of good will from him.

These devotions being ended, he sendeth in to the Empress to ask whether she hath rested in health, etc. And after a little pause goeth himself to salute her in a middle room betwixt both their chambers. The Empress lieth apart from him and keepeth not one chamber nor table with the Emperor ordinarily, save upon the eve of their Lents or common fasts, what time she is his ordinary guest at bed and board. After their meeting in the morning, they go together to their private church or chapel, where is said or sung a morning service called *zautrenia* of an hour long or thereabouts. From the church he returneth home and sitteth him down in a great chamber to be seen and saluted by his nobility such as are in favor about the court. If he have to say to any of them or they to him, then is the time. And this is ordinary, except his health or some other occasion alter the custom.

About nine in the morning he goeth to another church within his castle where is sung by priests and choristers the high service called *obednia*, or complin, which commonly lasteth two hours, the Emperor in the meantime talking commonly with some of his council, nobility, or captains, which have to say to him or he to them. And the council likewise confer together among themselves as if they were in their council house. This ended, he returneth home and recreateth himself until it be dinnertime.

Of the Rus Commonwealth

He is served at his table on this manner. First, every dish as it is delivered at the dresser is tasted by the cook in the presence of the high steward or his deputy. And so is received by the gentlemen waiters, called *zhiltsy,* and by them carried up to the Emperor's table, the high steward or his deputy going before. There it is received by the sewer,[3] called *kraichii,* who giveth a taste of every dish to the taster and so placeth it before the Emperor. The number of his dishes for his ordinary service is about seventy, dressed somewhat grossly with much garlic and salt, much after the Dutch manner. When he exceedeth upon some occasion of the day or entertainment of some ambassador, he hath many more dishes. The service is sent up by two dishes at a time, or three at the most, that he may eat it warm—first the baked, then the roast meats, and last the broths. In his dining chamber is another table where sit the chief of his nobility that are about his court and his ghostly father, or chaplain. On the one side of the chamber standeth a cupboard or table of plate, very fair and rich, with a great cistern of copper by it, full of ice and snow, wherein stand the pots that serve for that meal. The taster holdeth the cup that he drinketh in all dinnertime and delivereth it unto him with a say [4] when he calleth for it. The manner is to make many dishes out of the service after it is set on the table and to send them to such noblemen and officers as the Emperor liketh best, and this is counted a great favor and honor.

After dinner he layeth him down to rest, where commonly he taketh three hours' sleep except he employ one of the hours to bathing or boxing. And this custom for sleeping after dinner is an ordinary matter with him, as with all the Rus. After his sleep he goeth to evensong, called *vechernia,* and, thence returning,

---

[3] In medieval Europe a household officer of rank in charge of serving the dishes at the table. Fletcher called the sewer *erastnoy.*

[4] The aphetic form of "assay," meaning "taste": the taster always took a sip before handing the cup to the Emperor.

The Emperor's Private Behavior

for the most part recreateth himself with the Empress till suppertime with jesters and dwarfs, men and women that tumble before him and sing many songs after the Rus manner. This is his common recreation betwixt meals that he most delights in. One other special recreation is the fight with wild bears, which are caught in pits or nets and are kept in barred cages for that purpose against the Emperor be disposed to see the pastime. The fight with the bear is on this sort: the man is turned into a circle walled round about, where he is to quit[5] himself so well as he can, for there is no way to fly out. When the bear is turned loose, he cometh upon him with open mouth. If at the first push he miss his aim so that the bear come within him, he is in great danger. But the wild bear, being very fierce, hath this quality that giveth advantage to the hunter: his manner is when he assaileth a man to rise up right on his two hinder legs and so to come roaring with open mouth upon him. And if the hunter then can push right into the very breast of him betwixt his forelegs, as commonly he will not miss, resting the other end of their boar-spear at the side of his foot and so keeping the pike still toward the face of the bear, he speedeth him commonly at one blow. But many times these hunters come short and are either slain or miserably torn with the teeth and talons of the fierce beast. If the party quit himself well in this fight with the bear, he is carried to drink at the Emperor's cellar door, where he drinketh himself drunk for the honor of Hospodar; and this is his reward for adventuring his life for the Emperor's pleasure. To maintain this pastime the Emperor hath certain huntsmen that are appointed for that purpose to take the wild bear. This is his recreation commonly on the holy days. Sometimes he spendeth his time in looking upon his goldsmiths and jewelers, tailors, embroiderers, painters, and suchlike, and so goeth to his supper. When it draweth toward bedtime, his priest saith certain prayers; and then the Emperor blesseth and crosseth himself, as in

[5] Archaic for "acquit" or "conduct."

Of the Rus Commonwealth

the morning, for a quarter of an hour or thereabouts, and so goeth to his bed.

The Emperor that now is, called Fedor Ivanovich, is for his person of a mean stature, somewhat low and gross, of a sallow complexion, and inclining to the dropsy, hawk-nosed, unsteady in his pace by reason of some weakness of his limbs, heavy and unactive, yet commonly smiling almost to a laughter. For quality otherwise: simple and slow-witted, but very gentle and of an easy nature, quiet, merciful, of no martial disposition, nor greatly apt for matter of policy, very superstitious and infinite that way. Besides his private devotions at home, he goeth every week commonly on pilgrimage to some monastery or other that is nearest hand. He is of thirty-four years old or thereabouts and hath reigned almost the space of six years.

CHAPTER XXVII

Of the Emperor's Private or Household Officers

THE chief officers of the Emperor's household are these which follow: the first is the office of the *koniushii boiarin,* or master of the horse, which containeth no more than is expressed by the name, that is, to be overseer of the horse, and not *magister equitum,* or master of the horsemen. For he appointeth other for that service as occasion doth require, as before was said. He that beareth that office at this time is Boris Fedorovich Godunov, brother to the Empress. Of horse for service in his wars, besides other for his ordinary uses, he hath to the number of ten thousand, which are kept about Moscow.

The next is the lord steward of his household, at this time one Grigorii Vasilevich Godunov. The third is his treasurer, that keepeth all his money, jewels, plate, etc., now called Stepan Vasilevich Godunov. The fourth, his controller, now Andrei Pe-

The Emperor's Household Officers

trovich Kleshnin. The fifth, his chamberlain. He that attendeth that office at this time is called Istoma Bezobrazov, *postelnichii*. The sixth, his tasters, now Fedor Aleksandrovich and Ivan Vasilevich Godunov. The seventh, his harbingers,[1] which are three noblemen and divers other gentlemen that do the office under them. These are his ordinary officers and offices of the chiefest account.

Of gentlemen besides that wait about his chamber and person, called *zhiltsy striapchie*, there are two hundred, all noblemen's sons.[2] His ordinary guard is two thousand hagbutters, ready with their pieces charged and their match lighted, with other necessary furniture, continually day and night, which come not within the house but wait without in the court or yard where the Emperor is abiding. In the nighttime there lodgeth next to his bedchamber the chief chamberlain, with one or two more of best trust about him; a second chamber off there lodge six other of like account for their trust and faithfulness. In the third chamber lie certain young gentlemen of these two hundred, called *zhiltsy striapchie*, that take their turns by forties every night. There are grooms besides, that watch in their course and lie at every gate and door of the court, called *istopniki*.[3]

The hagbutters, or gunners, whereof there are two thousand, as was said before, watch about the Emperor's lodging or bedchamber by course—two hundred and fifty every night and two hundred and fifty more in the courtyard and about the treasure house. His court or house at the Moscow is made castle-wise, walled about with great store of fair ordnance planted upon the

---

[1] Officials who act as royal messengers or who precede the sovereign when he travels to arrange proper accommodations.

[2] The *zhiltsy* and the *striapchie* were in reality two different types of guards. Seredonin, *Sochinenie*, pp. 154–155, indicates that Fletcher exaggerated their combined numbers.

[3] It is difficult to discern any distinction between these "grooms" and the "hagbutters" (harquebusiers), or *streltsy*.

Of the Rus Commonwealth

wall, and containeth a great breadth of ground within it, with many dwelling houses, which are appointed for such as are known to be sure and trusty to the Emperor.

CHAPTER XXVIII

Of the Private Behavior or Quality of the Rus People

THE private behavior and quality of the Rus people may partly be understood by that which hath been said concerning the public state and usage of the country. As touching the natural habit of their bodies, they are for the most part of a large size and of very fleshly bodies, accounting it a grace to be somewhat gross and burly. And therefore they nourish and spread their beards to have them long and broad. But for the most part they are very unwieldy and unactive withal, which may be thought to come partly of the climate and the numbness which they get by the cold in winter and partly of their diet, that standeth most of roots, onions, garlic, cabbage, and suchlike things that breed gross humors, which they use to eat alone and with their other meats.

Their diet is rather much than curious.[1] At their meals they begin commonly with a *charka*, or small cup, of aquavite, which they call Rus wine, and then drink not till toward the end of their meals, taking it in largely and all together, with kissing one another at every pledge. And therefore after dinner there is no talking with them, but every man goeth to his bench to take his afternoon's sleep, which is as ordinary with them as their night's rest. When they exceed and have variety of dishes, the first are their baked meats (for roast meats they use little) and then their broths or pottage. To drink drunk is an ordinary matter with them every day in the week. Their common drink is mead;

[1] Dainty.

The Private Behavior of the Rus People

the poorer sort use water and thin drink called *kvass*, which is nothing else as we say but water turned out of his wits with a little bran mashed with it.

This diet would breed in them many diseases but that they use bathstoves or hothouses instead of all physic commonly twice or thrice every week. All the wintertime and almost the whole summer they heat their *pechi*, which are made like the German bathstoves, and their *palati*, like ovens, that so warm the house that a stranger at the first shall hardly like of it. These two extremities, especially in the winter, of heat within their houses and of extreme cold without, together with their diet, maketh them of a dark and sallow complexion, their skins being tanned and parched both with cold and with heat, especially the women, that for the greater part are of far worse complexions that the men. Whereof the cause I take to be their keeping within the hothouses and busying themselves about the heating and using of their bathstoves and *pechi*.

The Rus, because that he is used to both these extremities of heat and of cold, can bear them both a great deal more patiently than strangers can do. You shall see them sometimes, to season their bodies, come out of their bathstoves all on a froth and fuming, as hot almost as a pig at a spit, and presently to leap in the river stark naked, or to pour cold water all over their bodies, and that in the coldest of all the wintertime. The women, to mend the bad hue of their skins, use to paint their faces with white and red colors so visibly that every man may perceive it, which is made no matter because it is common and liked well by their husbands, who make their wives and daughters an ordinary allowance to buy them colors to paint their faces withal and delight themselves much to see them of foul women to become such fair images. This parcheth the skin and helpeth to deform them when their painting is off.

They apparel themselves after the Greek manner. The nobleman's attire is on this fashion: first, a *tafia*, or little nightcap, on his head, that covereth little more than his crown, commonly very rich wrought of silk and gold thread and set with pearl and precious stone. His head he keepeth shaven close to the very skin, except he be in some displeasure with the Emperor; then he suffereth his hair to grow and hang down upon his shoulders, covering his face as ugly and deformedly as he can. Over the *tafia* he weareth a wide cap of black fox, which they account for the best fur, with a tiara or long bonnet put within it, standing up like a Persian or Babylonian hat. About his neck, which is seen all bare, is a collar set with pearl and precious stone, about three or four fingers broad. Next over his shirt, which is curiously wrought, because he strippeth himself into it in the summertime while he is within the house, is a *zipun*, or light garment of silk, made down to the knees, buttoned before, and then a *kaftan*, or a close coat, buttoned and girt to him with a Persian girdle, whereat he hangs his knives and spoon. This commonly is of cloth of gold and hangeth down as low as his ankles. Over that he weareth a loose garment of some rich silk, furred and faced about with some gold lace, called a *ferez*. Another over that of camlet [2] or like stuff called an *okhaben*, sleeved and hanging low, and the cape commonly brooched and set all with pearl. When he goeth abroad, he casteth over all these, which are but slight though they seem to be many, another garment called an *onuchek*, like to the *okhaben*, save that it is made without a collar for the neck. And this is commonly of fine cloth or camel's hair. His buskins, which he weareth instead of hose, with linen folds under them instead of boothose, are made of a Persian leather called *safian* embroidered with pearl.[3] His upperstocks commonly are of cloth of gold. When he goeth abroad, he mounteth on horseback, though

---

[2] A beautiful and costly Eastern fabric or its imitations. Originally made of silk and camel's hair; then of wool and silk.

[3] Buskins are a boot-like covering for the foot and leg reaching to the calf or knee. Fletcher presumably meant "folds" when he wrote "folles."

The Private Behavior of the Rus People

it be but to the next door, which is the manner also of the *boiarskie,* or gentlemen.

The *boiarskie,* or gentleman's, attire is of the same fashion but differeth in stuff; and yet he will have his *kaftan,* or undercoat, sometimes of cloth of gold, the rest of cloth or silk.

The noblewoman, called *zhena boiarskaia,* weareth on her head, first a caul [4] of some soft silk, which is commonly red, and over it a frontlet,[5] called *naurusa,* of white color. Over that, her cap, made after the coif fashion, of cloth of gold, called *shapka zemskaia,* edged with some rich fur and set with pearl and stone, though they have of late begun to disdain embroidering with pearl about their caps because the diaks' and some merchants' wives have taken up the fashion. In their ears they wear earrings, which they call *sergi,* of two inches or more compass, the matter of gold set with rubies or sapphires or some like precious stone. In summer they go often with kerchiefs of fine white lawn or cambric fastened under the chin with two long tassels pendent,[6] the kerchief spotted and set thick with rich pearl. When they ride or go abroad in rainy weather, they wear white hats with colored bands, called *shliapa zemskaia.* About their necks they wear collars of three or four fingers broad, set with rich pearl and precious stone. Their upper garment is a loose gown, called *opashen,* commonly of scarlet, with wide loose sleeves hanging down to the ground and buttoned before with great gold buttons or at least silver and gilt, nigh as big as a walnut, which hath hanging over it fastened under the cap a large broad cape of some rich fur that hangeth down almost to the midst of their backs. Next under the *opashen,* or upper garment, they wear another called a *letnik,* that is made close before with great wide sleeves, the cuff or half sleeve up to the

[4] A network covering for a woman's hair.
[5] A frontlet is something worn on the forehead.
[6] Lawn is a kind of fine white linen resembling cambric, which, in turn, is a fine white linen originally from Cambrai in Flanders. The name is also applied to an imitation made of hard-spun cotton yarn.

153

Of the Rus Commonwealth

elbows, commonly of cloth of gold, and under that a *ferez zemskaia*, which hangeth loose, buttoned throughout to the very foot. On the hand wrists they wear very fair bracelets, about two fingers broad, of pearl and precious stone. They go all in buskins of white, yellow, blue, or some other colored leather, embroidered with pearl. This is the attire of the noblewoman of Russia when she maketh the best show of herself. The gentlewoman's apparel may differ in the stuff but is all one for the making of fashion.

As for the *muzhik* and his wife, they go poorly clad. The man with his *odnoriadka*, or loose gown, to the small of the leg, tied together with a lace before of coarse white or blue cloth, with some *shuba*, or long waistcoat, of fur or of sheepskin under it, and his furred cap and buskins. The poorer sort of them have their *odnoriadka*, or upper garment, made of cow's hair. This is their winter habit. In the summertime commonly they wear nothing but their shirts on their backs and buskins on their legs. The woman goeth in a red or blue gown when she maketh the best show and with some warm *shuba* of fur under it in the wintertime; but in the summer, nothing but her two shirts (for so they call them) one over the other, whether they be within doors or without. On their heads they wear caps of some colored stuff, many of velvet or of cloth of gold, but for the most part kerchiefs. Without earrings of silver or some other metal and her cross about her neck, you shall see no Rus woman, be she wife or maid.

As touching their behavior and quality otherwise, they are of reasonable capacities if they had those means that some other nations have to train up their wits in good nurture and learning, which they might borrow of the Polonians and other their neighbors but that they refuse it of a very self-pride, as accounting their own fashions to be far the best. Partly also, as I said before, for that their manner of bringing up—void of all good learning and civil behavior—is thought by their governors most

The Private Behavior of the Rus People

agreeable to that state and their manner of government, which the people would hardly bear if they were once civilled and brought to more understanding of God and good policy. This causeth the emperors to keep out all means of making it better and to be very wary for excluding of all peregrinity [7] that might alter their fashions, which were less to be disliked if it set not a print into the very minds of his people. For as themselves are very hardly and cruelly dealt withal by their chief magistrates and other superiors, so are they as cruel one against another, especially over their inferiors and such as are under them. So that the basest and wretchedest *krestianin,* as they call him, that stoopeth and croucheth like a dog to the gentleman and licketh up the dust that lieth at his feet, is an intolerable tyrant where he hath the advantage. By this means the whole country is filled with rapine and murder. They make no account of the life of a man. You shall have a man robbed sometime in the very streets of their towns, if he go late in the evening, and yet no man to come forth out of his doors to rescue him though he hear him cry out. I will not speak of the strangeness of the murders and other cruelties committed among them, that would scarcely be believed to be done among men, especially such as profess themselves Christians.

The number of their vagrant and begging poor is almost infinite, that are so pinched with famine and extreme need as that they beg after a violent and desperate manner with, "Give me and cut me; give me and kill me," and suchlike phrases. Whereby it may be guessed what they are toward strangers, that are so unnatural and cruel toward their own. And yet it may be doubted whether [8] is the greater, the cruelty or intemperancy that is used in that country. I will not speak of it, because it is so foul and not to be named. The whole country overfloweth with

---

[7] The condition of being foreign or outlandish, or foreign travel producing such a condition.
[8] Which.

Of the Rus Commonwealth

all sin of that kind: and no marvel, as having no law to restrain whoredoms, adulteries, and like uncleanness of life.

As for the truth of his word, the Rus for the most part maketh small regard of it, so he may gain by a lie and breach of his promise. And it may be said truly, as they know best that have traded most with them, that from the great to the small, except some few that will scarcely be found, the Rus neither believeth anything that another man speaketh nor speaketh anything himself worthy to be believed. These qualities make them very odious to all their neighbors, especially to the Tartars, that account themselves to be honest and just in comparison of the Rus. It is supposed by some that do well consider of the state of both countries that the offense they take at the Rus government and their manner of behavior hath been a great cause to keep the Tartar still heathenish and to mislike, as he doth, of the Christian profession.

FINIS

GLOSSARY OF RUSSIAN WORDS
AND INDEX

RUSSIAN WORDS USED BY FLETCHER

CORRECT RUSSIAN	FLETCHER'S SPELLING
altyn	*alteen*
arbuz	*arbouse*
belorybitsa	*riba bela*
beluga	*bellouga*
beluzhina	*bellougina*
bescheste	*bestchest*
Blagoslovi vladyko	*Blas(s)lauey Vladika*
boiare vladychnye	*boiaren vladitskey*
boiarskaia duma	*boarstua dumna*
boiarskie	*boiarskey, boiarskeis*
Bolshoi Prikhod	*Bulsha Prechode, Prec(h)od*
bolshoi voevoda	*voyauodey bulshaia* & *bulsha voiauoda*
Bozhedom	*Bohsedom*
bulat	*bullate*
bulatnyi	*bullatnoy*
charka	*chark, charke*
chernye popy	*churnapapaes*
chetverti	*chetfyrds, chetfirds*
chudotvornye	*chudouodites*

Glossary of Russian Words

CORRECT RUSSIAN	FLETCHER'S SPELLING
denga Novgorodskaia	*dingoe Nouogrodskoy*
dengi	*dingoes*
derevni	*darieunes*
desiatskie	*decetskeis, decetskies, decetskoies*
deti boiarskie	*dyta boiarskey*
diaki (cf. *dumnye diaki* below)	*diacks, dyacks, deiakeis, diakeis, doyack*
Dikie Lopari	*Dikoy Lopary*
divei-murzy	*diuoymorseis, diuoymorsey*
dumnye	*dumnoy*
dumnye boiars	*dumnoy boiaren*
dumnye diaki	*dumnoy dyakey, dumnoy deiakey*
dvoriane	*dworaney*
dvoriane bolshie	*dworaney bulshey* & *bulsha dworaney*
Dvortsovyi Prikaz	*Dwoertsoua*
dynia	*deene*
ferez	*ferris*
ferez zemskaia	*ferris zemskoy*
garus	*garras*
golovy	*gul auoy*
gornostai	*gurnestalles, gurnstales*
Gospodi pomilui, pomilui menia, gospodi, sokhrani menia greshnika ot zlago deistviia	*Aspody Pomeluy, Pomeluy mena hospody sacroy mena gresnick Syhodestua*
gubnye starosty	*gubnoy starets*
gubnyi starosta	*gubnoy starust*
guliai-gorod	*gulay gorod*
hospodar/gospodar	*hospodare*
iamy	*yammes*
ikra	*icary, ickary*
istopniki	*estopnick*
kabak(i)	*caback(s)*

Glossary of Russian Words

CORRECT RUSSIAN	FLETCHER'S SPELLING
kaftan	caftan
Kazanskii Dvorets	Cassanskoy dworets
kholopy/khlopy	cholopey, kolophey
Kniaz	Knez
kniazia	knazey
kolpak	colpack
kolymaga	collimago
koni	cones
koniushennaia sloboda	conaslue sloboday
Koniushii	Connick
koniushii boiarin	boiaren conesheua
kraichii	erastnoy
Kreshchenie	Kreshenea
krestiane	christianeis
krestianin	christianoe
krestnoe tselovanie	creustina chelouania
krestnyi diak	chresby deyack profery
kvass	quasse
letnik	leitnick
letuchie vekschy	letach vechshe
levyi polk	leuoy polskoy
logovoi	lugauoy
los	losh
luchiny	luchineos
molitva	molitua
molodaia kniaginia	moloday knezay
molodoi kniaz	moloday knez
morzh	morse
murzy	morseys, morseis
muzhik(i)	mousick(s)
nagie	naga
nagornyi	nagornay
naleika	naloi
nariadnyi voevoda	naradna voiauoda
naurusa	obrosa

161

Glossary of Russian Words

CORRECT RUSSIAN	FLETCHER'S SPELLING
nemtsy	nimschoy
nerukoyvornyi	neruchi
Novremanskie Lopari	Nowremanskoy Lapary
obednia	obeidna, obeadna
obrok	obrokey
odnoriadka	odnoratkey
okhaben	alkaben
olen	olen, ollen
Olla Billa, Olla Billa	Olla Billa, Olla Billa
onuchek	honoratkey
opashen	oposhen, oposken
Oprichnina	Oppressini
osetrina	ositrina
otets dukhovnyi	otetz duhouna
ozera	ozeraes
palachi	polachies
palati	potlads
pechi	peaches
piatidesiatskie	petyde setskoy
podat	podat
polki	polskeis, polskey
pomeste	pomestnoy
Pomestnaia Chetvert	Chetfird of Pomestnoy
pop	papa
popy	papes, papaes
Posolskaia	Chetfirds of Posolskoy, Pososkoy Chetfird
postelnichii	pastelnischay
pozhalovat	poshallouate
pravezh	praueush
pravyi polk	praua polskoy
prechistaia	precheste
Prikaz Shishevoi Nemskii	Prechase, Shisiuoy Nemshoy
pristav	praestaue
protopopy	protopapaes, protopapas, protopapes

162

Glossary of Russian Words

CORRECT RUSSIAN	FLETCHER'S SPELLING
Pusharskii	Pusharskoy
pytka	pudkey
Razboinyi Prikaz	Roisbonia
razpop	rospapa
riasa	reis
Rozriadnaia Chetvert	Roseradney Chetfird
Rozriadnyi	Roserad(e)
rusnyi polk	rusnoy polskoy
rybii zub	ribazuba
serednie dvoriane	seredney dworaney
sergi	sargee
sevriuga	sueriga
shapka zemskaia	shapka zempska
shestoper	shestapera
shliapa zemskaia	stapa zemskoy
shuba	shube
skoryi pomoshchnik	scora pomosnick
sliuda	slude
sobor	zabore
Sobornoe voskresene	Saburney voscreshenca
sotskie	sotskey
sotskie starosty	sotskoy starets
sotskii starosta	sotskoy starust
starosty	starusts
sterliad	sterledey
stoianie	stoiania
stoly	stollie
storozhevoi polk	storeshouoy polskoy
strelets	strelsey
streletskii	strelletskoy
streltsy	strelsey
stremiannye streltsy	stremaney strelsey
sudi	soudia
sukhar	sucharie
sviataia voda	sweta voda
syn boiarskii	sinaboiarskey

Glossary of Russian Words

CORRECT RUSSIAN	FLETCHER'S SPELLING
synovia boiarskie	sina boiarskey, sinaboiarskey
tafia	taffia
tiaglo	tagla
tolokno	tollockno
tsarskaia dver	scharsuey dwere
udelnye kniazyia	vdelney knazey
vechernia	vecherna, vechurna
vezha	beza
–vich [ending]	–wich
vladychnye	vladitskey
vladyki	vladikey, vladikeis
voevoda	voiauodey, voyauodey
voevoda gulevoi	voiauoda gulauoy
votchina	vochin
vypis	wepis
vyt	wite
zautrenia	zautrana
Zemskie	Zempskey, Zemskey
Zemskii House	Zempskey house
zhalovanie	schalouaney
zhena boiarskaia	chyna boiarshena
zhiltsy	shilshey
zhiltsy striapchie	shilsey strapsey
zipun	shepon
Zolotaia Baba	Slata Baba

INDEX

Abramov, Sapun [Abramoue, Zapon], *diak*, 44, 51
Aleksandrovskaia Sloboda [Alexandrisca], 52
Alexander I of Lithuania, 86
Alexander II, Tsar, xxix
Alexander the Great, 102
Alferev, Roman Vasilevich [Alferioue, Romain Vasilowich], 51
Anderson, M. S., cited, xiii n., xxxi
Andrew I of Hungary, 23
Andronicus II, Palaeologus, 99
Apparel, 114-115, 151-154
Archangel, xx
Architecture, xiv, 20, 22-23
Armenia, 12, 58, 62
Asia Minor, 100
Assyria, 102
Astrakhan [Astracan], xlii, 5, 6, 7, 16, 19, 22, 29, 30, 39, 44, 87, 88, 92, 102
Athanasius' Creed, 125
Aylmer, John, Bishop of London, xvi
Azov [Azou], 10, 95

Baltic [Baltick] Sea, xiii, xv, xlii, 10
Basel, xxix
Bathory, Stephen [Batore, Stepan], King of Poland, xxxvii, 40, 85, 86

Bear fight, 147
Beaumont, Francis, xliii n.
Bekbulatovich, Kniaz Simeon [Velica Knez Simeon], Tsar, 61
Bela, house of (Hungarian), 23-24
Bela [Beala], house of (Russian), 23-26, 36, 44
Bela I of Hungary, 23
Bela II of Hungary, 23
Bela IV of Hungary, 93-94
Belgorod, 86
Beloozero [Bealozera], 5, 19, 29
Belskii, Ivan Dimitrievich [Belschey, Iuan Demetrowich], 92
Belyi Gorod, 20 n.
Berossus (Berosus), source for *Rus Commonwealth*, xxxvi, 19
Berry, Lloyd, editor of *Rus Commonwealth*, cited, xvi n., xvii n., xxiii n., xxvi n., xxvii n., xxx n., xliii n.
Bezan, *see* Riazan
Bezobrazov, Istoma Osipovich [Bisabroza, Estoma], 149
Biblia Sweta, 134 n.
Birds, 18
Black Sea, called Euxine [Euxin], 4
Blum, Jerome, cited, xxxi n.
Bodianskii, O. M., xxix-xxx
Bolshoi Dvorets, *see Dvortsovyi Prikaz*

Index

Bolshoi Prikhod [*Bulsha prechode*], xli, 52-58
Bombasey (Umba), 16 n.
"Bonaventure, Edward," xii
Bond, Edward A., editor of *Rus Commonwealth*, cited, xii-xiii n., xviii n., xxi n., xxv n., xxvii, xxix, xxx, xxxvi n., xxxvii n., 17 n., 38 n., 123 n.
Bonfinius, source for *Rus Commonwealth*, xxiii n., xxxvi, 23
Borísthenes (Dnieper) River, 4, 9
Borough, Christopher, xx n.
Bouzet, Charles du, editor of *Rus Commonwealth*, xxvii, xxx
Brest, 134 n.
Bukhara [Bougharia], xxi, xxxiii, 12, 17, 58, 62
Bulgakov [Bulgaloy], 40
Bulgaria [Boulghoria, Bulghouria], 5, 29
Burghley, William Cecil, Lord, xxiv, xxv, xxvii
Bushevoi (Bushev), Dorofei [Bushew, Dorofey], 52
Buturlin, Ivan Mikhailovich [Buterlyney, Iuan], 51
Byzantine Church, 139 n.

Camden, William, Elizabethan antiquarian and historian, xxxvi
Cape Grace, 105
Caspian Sea, xiv, 4, 9, 98, 102
Cathedral of St. Vasilii (St. Basil the Blessed) in Moscow, 87 n.
Catholic League, xxxvii, 109-112
Cawley, Robert R., cited, xxvi n., xliii n.
Cecil, William, *see* Burghley, William Cecil, Lord
Chalcondyles, Laonikos [Chalcacondylas, Laonicus], historian and source for *Rus Commonwealth*, xxxvi, 98, 100, 108
Chancellor, Richard, Elizabethan discoverer of Muscovy, xii, xxvi
Charde, Thomas, Elizabethan printer of *Rus Commonwealth*, xxiii
Cheremisian Tartar, *see* Tartars, other
Cheremisinov, Dementii Ivanovich [Cheremissen, Demenshoy Iuanowich], 51
Cherkasskii [Cherechaskoy], 79
Cherkasy, *see* Tartars, other
Cherkizovo [Chara], 52
Chernigov [Chernigo], 5, 29, 86
Chetvert:
    jurisdictions, Russia divided into, 6, 43-48, 51, 58, 70-73, 80
    measure, 11, 12, 53, 54
    office of income, 52-54, 57
China, xii
Church, Russian, xxxii, xxxvii
    archbishops, 107, 113, 115
    attire, 114-115
    bishops, 113-115
    clergy, lesser, 107, 119
    conspiracy to place under Pope, 110
    criticism by Fletcher, xxix
    doctrine, 130-135
        confession, 133
        errors, 131-132, 134
        fasts, 133, 142
        intercession, 131-132
        justification, 132-133
        salvation, 133
        Scripture, 130-131
        Trinity, 131
    friars, 107, 119-121
    hermits, 107, 122-123
    idolatry, 132
    jurisdiction, 113-114
    liturgy, 124-126
    marriage, 133-134, 135-138
    metropolitans, 107, 113, 115
    nunneries, 121-122
    offices, 107-124
    patriarch, 107, 110-114
    persecution, 134-135
    practices, 133, 138-143

Index

Church, Russian (*cont.*)
  abstinence, 133
  confession, 133
  dead, 142-143
  hallowing of rivers, 139-140
  holy water, 139-140
  Palm Sunday, 141-142
  sign of cross, 138-139
  preaching, 115-116
  priests, 107, 116-119
  revenues, 114
  sacraments, 126-130, 133
  service, 124-130, 144-145
  Troitskaia-Sergei Monastery, 120
Cities, 19-23 and *passim*
Climate, 7-9
Colonies:
  administration, 88-90
  fortifications, 88
  history, 85-90
Commons, *see* Russian people
Constantinople, 10, 110, 111
Cook, John Q., cited, xii
Coote, C. H., cited, xv n., xx n.
Coronation, 27-30
Council, Emperor's, *see Duma*
Council of Nicaea, 111
Councilors (*Duma*) of state, names of, 50-51
Cross, S. H., cited, 3 n.
Cyrillic alphabet, 69
Cyrus the Great, 98

Daniel Aleksandrovich, 20 n.
Daniel Romanovich of Galich, 20 n.
Danilovo [Danielska], 52
Darius Hystaspes, 98
Dekker, Thomas, xliii n.
Demitrio [Demetrio], Archbishop of Larissa, 112
Denmark, 78, 105, 106
Derbent, 102
Deti boiarskie, see Nobility, *synovia boiarskie*
Diaki, xxxix, 32, 34, 35, 43, 45, 46, 47, 48, 51, 59, 69, 70, 80, 114, 144
Dimitrii, son of Ivan IV, xlii, 25, 26 n.

Dnieper River, called Boristhenes, 4, 9
Don River, called Tanais, 4, 10
Dorogobuzh [Dorogobose], 13, 16, 41
Dorpat [Dorp], Livonia, 5
Drake, Sir Francis, xi, xxxvii n.
Duma, xxxix-xl, 47-48, 50-52
Dutch, xiii, xv, xvii, xx, 57, 67, 78
Dvina [Duyna], river, xii, xiv, 10, 17, 19; province, 4, 5, 16, 54
Dvortsovyi Prikaz [*Dwoertsoua*], 52
Dynasty, Russian, 23-27

Efimov, A. V., cited, 5 n.
Elizabeth I of England, xv, xix, xxi, xxiii, xxiv, xxv, xxxiv-xxxv, 1, 109
Elizabethan travel literature, xi
Ellis, Henry, xviii n., xxv n.
Emperor, *see* Tsar
English, xii, xiii, xiv, xix, 15, 62, 102, 128, 134
Essex, Robert Devereux, Earl of, xvi, xvii
Eton, xvi
Euxine [Euxin], or Black Sea, 4, 9, 100
Expansion of Muscovy, 85-90

Fedor [Theodore Iuanowich], Tsar, xv, xviii, xxv, 25, 27, 28, 29, 40, 60, 86, 109, 144-150. *See also* Tsar
Fedorov, Ivan, printer, 116 n.
Fine, John H., xxx n.
Finland Gulf, 10, 15
Finns, 103 n.
Fire of Moscow (1571), 91-92
Fisher, R. H., cited, 5 n.
"Fletcher affair" (1848-1864) at Moscow University, xxvii-xxx
Fletcher, Giles, the Elder:
  early life, xvi-xviii
  education, xvi
  embassies, xvii

167

Index

Fletcher, Giles, the Elder (*cont.*)
  embassy to Moscow, xv-xxii, 39, 109
  interrogator of papists, xvii
  marriage, xvii-xviii
  master of requests, xvii
  member of Parliament, xvii
  Of Rus Commonwealth, composes, xxiii-xxiv
  patrons, xvi-xvii
  political alignment, xvii
  Protestantism, xvi
  Remembrancer of London, xvii
  scholarship, xvi-xvii
Fletcher, Giles, the Younger, xviii
Fletcher, John, xviii, xliii
Fletcher, Phineas, xviii, xliii n.
Fletcher, Richard, the Elder, xvi
Fletcher, Richard, the Younger, Bishop of London, xvi, xvii
Florinsky, Michael, cited, xxxi
Foxe, John, xvi
Foxnose, 14
Frederick II of Denmark, 26, 40
Freeman, John, xxiii n.
Fuller, Thomas, xxiii

Galich [Ghaletsa, Gallets], 5, 13, 20 n.
Geneva, xxix
Georgia, 12, 58, 109
Germans, 91 n.
Gippius, D. I., translator of *Rus Commonwealth*, xxviii, xxx
Glinskii, Ivan Mikhailovich [Glinskoy, Iuan Michailowich], 41-42, 50, 79
Godunov, Boris Fedorovich [Godonoe, Borris(e) Federowich], xviii, xix, xxii, xxv, xlii, 26 n., 32, 39, 41, 42, 44, 51, 53, 57-58, 141, 148
Godunov, Dimitrii [Godonoe, Demetrie Iuanowich], 51
Godunov, Fedor Aleksandrovich [Godonoe, Theodore Alexandrowich], 149
Godunov, Grigorii [Godonoe, Gregorie Vasilowich], 51, 53, 148

Godunov, Ivan Vasilevich [Godonoe, Iuan Vasilowich], 51, 149
Godunov, Stepan Vasilevich [Godonoe, Step(h)an Vasilowich], 51, 57, 148
Godunovs [Godonoes], 39, 47, 122, 134
Golitsyn [Guletchey], family of, 40
Golitsyn, Vasilii Iurevich [Golloohen, Vasilie Vrywich], 39
Golovin, Petr [Gollauni, Peeter], 39
Golovnin, Minister of Public Instruction to Tsar Alexander II, xxix
Gorodets [Gorodetskey], 13
Gote, Iu., cited, xiii n.
Government, xxxix-xli
  duma, 50-52. *See also Duma*
  forms of, 30-33
  justice, 70-75. *See also* Justice
  local, 43-49
  military, 75-85. *See also* Military
  Parliament, 33-35
  revenues, 52-64. *See also* Revenue and customs of Emperor
Greeks, 78
Gregorian calendar, 112
Gregory XIII, Pope, 110 n., 112 n.
Grey, Ian, cited, xiii n.
Grigorovich, Professor, xxix
Gyda of England, 22 n.

Habsburgs, xxxvii, 109-110
Hakluyt, Richard, editor of *Rus Commonwealth*, xi, xxv-xxvi
Hamburg, xvii
Hanse, xvii
Harcave, Sidney, cited, xxxi n.
Harold of England, 22
Harris, John, editor of *Rus Commonwealth*, xxvii
Herberstein, Sigismund von, source for *Rus Commonwealth*, xxxvi, xli, 8 n., 20 n., 21 n., 23 n., 103 n.

Index

Herodotus, 22 n.
Hieronimo (Jeremiah), Patriarch of Constantinople, 107, 109-113
Holy Nose, see Sviatoi Nos
Horsey, Jerome, source for *Rus Commonwealth,* xix, xxi, xxvii, xxxvi, 26 n., 41 n., 61 n., 123 n.
Hotson, Leslie, cited, xliii n.
Household officers, 148-150
  chamberlain, 149
  comptroller, 148-149
  gentlemen of chamber, 149
  grooms, 149
  guard, 149
  harbinger, 149
  master of horse, 148
  steward, 148
  tasters, 149
  treasurer, 148

Iam [Yama], 10
Iaroslav the Wise, Grand Prince of Kiev, 22 n.
Iaroslavl [Yaruslaue, Yaruslaueley], xxxviii, 5, 9, 13, 16 n., 17, 19, 22, 29, 55, 66
Imperial house of Russia, see Dynasty, Russian
Imperial Society of History and Russian Antiquities, xxvii
Innocent IV, Pope, 20
Irene, wife to Tsar Fedor, 25, 32 n., 120-121
Italian architects, xii
Iugorsk [Youghoria], 5, 12 n., 29
Iurev, Nikita Romanovich [Micheta Romanowich], 40
Ivan I, Kalita, 20
Ivan III, the Great, 24, 25 n., 86
Ivan IV [Iuan Vasilowich], xii-xv, xxv, xxxi, xxxiv, xxxix, xlii, 24-26, 32, 33, 36, 39, 53, 59, 60, 61, 63, 64, 86, 87, 91, 92, 110, 112, 116, 123, 124, 134 n., 149
Ivan Ozero, or lake, 10 n.
Ivangorod, 87

Janus, 96
Jenkinson, Anthony, Elizabethan in Russia, xiv-xv, xix, xxvi, 5 n.
Jesuits, xxxvii
Job, Patriarch of Moscow, 110-111
John VIII, Byzantine emperor, 108
Jonson, Ben, possible use of *Rus Commonwealth,* xliii n.
Josephus, source for *Rus Commonwealth,* xxxvi, 4
Justice, 32, 45-46, 70-75
  capital punishment, 73-75
  courts of civil law, 70-73
  criminal law procedures, 73-75
  cross kissing, 71-72
  judgments, 72

Kabak, 56, 63
Kadom, 12, 13
Kaffa, 95
Kalachev, N. V., translator of *Rus Commonwealth,* xxviii
Kama River, 11 n., 88 n.
Kandalaksha [Candelox], 105
Karamzin, N. M., xxxi, 116 n.
Karelia [Corelia, Corelska], xiv, 17, 52, 105, 106, 113 n.
Kargopol [Cargapolia], 4, 5, 10 17, 19
Kazan [Cazan], xlii, 5, 7, 12, 13, 14, 19, 22, 29, 39, 44, 47, 54, 55, 61, 87, 88, 92, 99, 113
Kazan University, xxix
Kazanskii Dvorets, 44
Kholmogory [Golmigroe], xiv, xviii, xix, 19, 54
Khoriv [Cheranus], legendary founder of Moscow, 3
Khvorostinin, Dimitrii Ivanovich [Forestine, Demetrie Iuanowich], 50, 79
Khvorostinin, Fedor Ivanovich [Forestine, Feoder Iuanowich], 50
Kiev, 3 n., 108 n.
Kildin [Kilden], 106
Kineshma [Kenitsma], 16

169

Index

King's College, Cambridge, xvi
Kiriak Murza, Tartar, 97
Kitai Gorod, commercial center of Moscow, 20 n.
Kiy [Kio], legendary founder of Moscow, 3
Kleshnin, Andrei Petrovich [Cleshenina, Andriew Petrowich, and Clesinine, Andreas Petrowich], 51, 148-149
Kliuchevskii, Vasilii, cited, xii n., xxxi, xxxix-xl
Knatchbulls, related to Fletcher, xviii
Koger [Kegor], 106
Kola [Cola], xiii, 6, 7, 13, 19, 105 n., 106
Kolomenskoe [Collomenska], 113
Kolomna [Columna], 19, 113 n.
Kondiinsk [Condora, Condensa], 5, 29
Kormlentshiki, xli
Kostroma, 54, 55
Kremlin of Moscow, 27 n., 111
Kromer, Martin, source for *Rus Commonwealth*, xxiii n., xxxvi, 69 n., 90 n., 108
Krutitsk [Crutitska], 113
Kukonos, 14
Kurakin, Andrei Grigorievich [Curakine, Andriew Gregoriwich], 50
Kurakin, Andrei Petrovich [Guraken Bulgatkoue, Andreas], 39

Land tenure:
  pomeste [*pomest, pomestnoy*], xxxviii, 38, 41
  votchina [*vochin*], xxxviii, 43 n., 44, 52
Langdale, A. B., cited, xvi n.
Lappia (Lapps), xiv, xxxvi, 4, 105, 106
Law, *see* Justice
Lee, Sidney, cited, xvii n.
Liefland (Latvia), 4, 29, 87, 128
Lindsay, Robert O., cited, xxiv n.

Lithuania [Lituania], xiii, xxxix, 4, 5, 7, 9, 86, 91 n., 101
Liubimenko, Inna, cited, xii n., xxxi
Livonia [Liuonia], xii, xv, 4, 5, 13 n., 86, 91 n.
London, xxix, 21
Lybed [Libeda], legendary founder of Russia, 3

Maeotis, 10
Magnus, Duke of Holstein, 26, 40
Mangazeia [Momgosorskoy], 12
Maria, niece of Ivan IV, 26, 40
Marian martyrs, xvi
Marriage in Russian Church, 133-134, 135-138
Marsh, Anthony, agent of Russia Company, xxxvi-xxxviii, 41 n.
Mary Tudor, Queen of England, xvi
Matislavets, Petr, early Russian printer, 116 n.
Matthias Corvinus, King of Hungary, 23 n.
Maximilian II of Habsburg, Emperor (1564-1576), 109
Media, xxii, 102
Merchants, foreign in Russia, xiii, 13, 15, 58, 62, 68
Meschera [Meschora], 5
Mestnichestvo, xl, 37 n.
Metropolitanate of Moscow, 20, 113
Metropolitanate of Novgorod, 114
Michael VIII, Palaeologus, 99
Military, 49, 75-85
  armor, 81-82
  captains [*voevody*], 78-80
  cavalry (*dvoriane, deti boiarskie*), 76-77, 83
  foot soldiers (*streltsy*), 57, 78, 82-84
  formations (*polki*) and organization, 79, 80-81
  mercenaries, 57, 78
  mustering, 80-81

Index

Military (cont.)
   Rozriad, office of, 44, 52, 56–57, 75, 81
   salaries, 75-78
   tactics, 83-85
   victuals, 82-83
Miller, Edwin, cited, xxv
Milton, John, use of *Rus Commonwealth*, xxvi, xxx, xliii n.
Molyneux, patrons, xviii
Monarchomachus, xxxv
Monasteries, 60-61, 120
Mongol Russia, xxxviii
Mordvinians, *see* Tartars, other
Morgan, E. D., cited, xv n., xx n.
Morton, Graham, cited, xv n.
Mosalsk [Moisalskoy], 52
Moscow, xiv, 4, 5, 7, 10, 11, 19, 20, 21, 28, 29, 38, 41, 45, 47, 52, 54, 55, 57, 64, 66, 67, 76, 85, 91, 92, 97, 109, 110, 111, 112, 113, 116, 122, 140, 141, 142, 149
Moscow River, 10, 41, 140
Moscow University, xxvii, xxviii, xxix
Moses, xxxvi, 4
Mstislavskii, Fedor Ivanovich [Methisloskey, Feoder Iowanowich, Iuanowich], 50, 79
Mstislavskii [Metheloskey], Ivan, 40
Murad II, Ottoman, 100
Murmansk [Murmonskey], 13
Murom [Morum], 12, 13, 14, 54
Muscovy (or Russia) Company, xii-xv, xxxiv

Nagoi [Nagaies], house of, 26
Narva [Narue], xiii, xx, xxi, 5, 6, 15, 87
Nashe, Thomas, cited, xxv
Natural resources, 11-19, 66, 67
   animals, fur-bearing, 11-13, 17, 58
   caviar, 15
   fish, 18
   flax, 15
   hemp, 15
   hides, 13
   honey, 13
   iron, 17
   salt, 16
   saltpeter, 17
   sliuda [*slude*], 17
   sulphur, 17
   tallow, 13
   tar, 16
   train oil, 14
   walrus tusk, 16-17
   wax, 13, 62
Nenoksa [Nonocks], 16
Netherlands, *see* Dutch
Nevilles, patrons, xviii
Nicephorus Gregoras, xxxvi, 108
Nicholas I, Tsar, xxviii, xxix
Nikola, the hermit of Pskov, 123
Nizhnii Novgorod, 5, 19, 29, 55
Nobility, xxxviii-xli, 36-43
   attire, 151-154
   boiars, 40-42, 50-51
   extortion of, 48-49, 64
   local government, 45, 46, 48
   names, 39-41, 50-51, 79, 148-149
   oppression of, 36-42, 121
   political role, 30-31, 45-46, 48
   synovia boiarskie [*Sina Boiarskey, Sinaboiarskey*], or *deti boiarskie* [*Dyta Boiarskey*], xxxviii, 42-43, 66, 74, 76, 77, 80-81
   udelnye kniazia [*Vdelney Knazey*], or appanage nobility, 36, 38-40, 42
   voevody [*voiauod, voiauoda, voiaudey, voyaudey*], 42, 78-80
Nogai, *see* Tartars, other
North Cape, 104, 105
North Sea, 17
Norwegians, 106
Novgorod [Nouograd, Nouograde, Nouogradia, Nouogrod velica], 4, 5, 7, 13, 14, 16 n., 19, 21, 29, 47, 54, 55, 85, 113

171

Index

Ob [Obba] River, 88, 104
Obdorsk [Obdoria, Obdorskoy], 5, 12, 29, 104
Obolenskii, M. A., attempts to edit *Rus Commonwealth*, xxviii, xxix, xxx
Obrok [Obrokey], 53
Odoevskii [Odgoskey], family of, 40
Oguzalpes, 100
Oka [Ocka] River, 10
Okona [Ocona], *see* Una River and town
Onega River, 10
Oprichnina [*Oppressini*], xxxiv, xxxviii-xxxix, 37-38
Ortelius, 5 n.
Ottoman, or Osman, 100

Pachymeres, Georgius, source for *Rus Commonwealth*, xxxvi, 99
Palaeologi, 99, 108
Pannonia, 24
Papacy, xxxvii, 107-112
Parliaments, 33-35
Pechenga [Pechinga], 6, 105 n.
Pechora, xxi, 12, 17, 58, 88
Pereiaslavl [Perislaue], xix, 19
Perm [Permia], 5, 11, 12, 13, 14, 16, 29, 58, 68, 88, 103
Persia, xiv, xxii, xxxii, xxxiii, 12, 17, 58, 102, 109
Petelin, Druzhina [Penteleoue, Drezheen/Druzhine], *diak*, 44, 51
Philip II of Spain, 109
Pipes, Richard, xxx n.
Pivov, Roman Mikhailovich [Peua, Romain Michailowich], 51
Platonov, Sergei, cited, xxxi
Podat, tax, 54
Poland [Polonia], xiii, xxi, xxxvii, 4, 15, 38, 40, 47, 57, 62, 78, 79, 80, 85, 86, 87, 89, 90, 109, 111, 116, 134, 154
Polotsk [Plotsko, Polotskoy], 15, 29
Pomeste, *see* Land tenure

Pomestnaia Chetvert [*Chetfird* of *Pomestnoy*], 44
Portugal, xiii
Posolskaia Chetvert [*Chetfird* of *Posolskoy, Pososkoy Chetfird*], 41, 43
Possevino, Antonio, papal legate, 110
Prikazy, xli, 41, 43-44, 52-58, 75, 81
Primary Chronicle, 3 n.
Principal Navigations of Hakluyt, xxiv-xxvi
Printing, 116
Pskov [Plesko, Vobsko], 5, 7, 16, 19, 22, 29, 47, 54, 55, 86, 88, 113, 123; siege of, 39-40, 85
Punishment, 46, 47, 73, 74, 75
Purchas, Samuel, editor of *Rus Commonwealth*, cited, xxvi
Pusharskii [*Pusharskoy*] *Prikaz*, 57

Raleigh, Sir Walter, xliii n.
Randolph, Sir Thomas, patron of Fletcher, xvi, xxvi
Razboinyi Prikaz [*Roisbonia*], 56
Red Square, Moscow, 87 n.
Religion, 107-143. *See also* Church, Russian
Relph, Ralph, English renegade in Russia, 128-129
Renaissance, xi
Revenue and customs of Emperor, 52-64
  confiscations, 58
  extortion, 59-62, 64
  forestalling and engrossing, 62
  furs, 58
  kabak, 63
  monopolies, 62-63
  offices of receipt (*prikazy*), 52-58
Riazan [Bezan, Rezan], xxxviii, 4, 5, 7, 13, 29, 41, 54, 113
Riazan Ozero [Rezan Ozera], 10
Ridley, Nicholas, xvi
Riga, xx, xxi, 10

Index

Rivers, 9-11
Robarts, related to Fletcher, xviii
Rome, *see* Papacy
Rose Island, xiv
Rostov [Rostoue], 5, 14, 19, 29, 54, 113
Roxellani, 4
Rozriadnyi Prikaz [*Roserad, Roserade, Roseradney*], xii, 44, 52, 56-57, 75, 81
Ruffmann, Karl H., cited, xliii n., 33 n.
Rurik [Rurico], legendary founder of Russia, 3
Rus Commonwealth, Of the:
  controversial work, xi
  criticisms of, xxx-xxxvi
    Seredonin, xxxi-xxxiii
    Soviet historians, xxxiii-xxxv
  dedication, xxiii
  evaluation, xxxvii-xliv
  issues of, xxiii, xxv-xxx
  sources for, xxxvi-xxxvii
  suppression by Burghley, xxiv-xxv, xxvii
  suppression in tsarist Russia, xxvii-xxx
Russia, xi-xv
  expansion of, xi, xlii, 85-106
  founders of, 3
  size of, 6
Russia Company, *see* Muscovy Company
Russian language, 69
Russian people (commonalty), called *muzhiki* [*mousicks*], 43
  behavior, 150-156
    apparel, 154
    diet, 150-151
    hardiness, 151
    immorality, 155-156
    intemperancy, 67, 155
    poverty, 155
    untruthfulness, 156
    violence, 155
  education denied, 68-69
  law, inequalities of, 74
  oppression, 30-31, 49, 64-69
  possessions, 65-66
  vocations, 66

Saburov, Bogdan Iurevich [Sabaroue, Bodan Iuanowich], 50
Sadukov, cited, xxxiv
St. Nicholas, Bishop of Myra, 132, 142
St. Nicholas, town and bay, xx, xxii, 7, 10, 11, 14
St. Paul's, xxiii
St. Sergius, 120
St. Stephen, King of Hungary, 24 n.
Samoyeds [Samoits, Samoites, Samoyts], xiv, 103-105
Sarmatia, 3, 4
Saxo Grammaticus, possible source for *Rus Commonwealth*, 22 n.
Schinick, Nicholas, 93
Scotland, xvii, 57, 78
Scythians, 21
Seal hunting, 14
Semchinskoe [Sametska], 52
Seredonin, Sergei Mikhailovich, cited for critique of *Rus Commonwealth*, xxxi-xxxiii, xxxvi, xliii, 6 n., 11 n., 16 n., 19 n., 22 n., 33 n., 41 n., 44 n., 52 n., 61 n., 65 n., 67 n., 72 n., 74 n., 77 n., 78 n., 82 n., 91 n., 114 n., 118 n., 149 n.
Serfdom, xl-xli
Seversk [Seuer, Seuerskoy], 13, 41
Shchelkalov, Andrei [Shalcaloue, Andreas, Andrew], xv, xviii, xix, xxii, 43, 51
Shchelkalov, Vasilii [Shalcaloue, Vasilie, Basilie], 44, 51
Shchelkaly, *see* Tartars, other
Shchok [Ścieko], legendary founder of Russia, 3
Sheaffe, Joan, wife to Fletcher, xvii
Shemakha [Zamachie], 102
Sherbowitz-Wetzor, O. P., 3 n.
Sheremetev, Fedor Vasilievich [Sheremitoue, Feoder], 51

173

Index

Shestunov, Fedor Dimitrievich [Shestinoue, Feoder Demetriwich], 50-51
Shishevoi Nemskii, Prikaz [*Prechase, Shisiuoy Nemshoy*] (military mercenaries), 57
Shuiskii, Andrei Ivanovich [Suskoy, Andrieu Iuanowich], 39
Shuiskii [Suskoy], family of, 40
Shuiskii, Ivan Petrovich [Suskoy, Iuan Petrowich], 39-40
Shuiskii, Vasilii Ivanovich [Suskoy, Vasilie Iuanowich], 50
Shuiskii Skopin, Vasilii Fedorovich, *see* Skopin-Shuiskii
Siberia, xlii, 5, 6, 7, 12, 29, 39, 54, 58, 67, 68, 78, 87, 88, 89
Sidney, Sir Philip, used *Rus Commonwealth*, xliii n.
Sigismund III, Vasa, of Poland, xxxvii, 109
Silk trade, 102
Sineus [Sinees], legendary founder of Russia, 3
Sitskii, Ivan Vasilevich [Iuan Vasilowich], 50
Skopin-Shuiskii, Vasilii Fedorovich [Suskoy Scopin, Vasilie Iuanowich], 50
Slavs, 69
Smolensk [Smolensko], 5, 7, 13, 15, 16, 19, 22, 29, 47, 55, 86, 88, 113
Sobor, public assembly, 33-35
Soil, 7
Solovetskii [Solouetskey, Solouetsko], 10, 16
Sophy of Persia, xvi
Spain, xiii, xxxvii, 109
Stalin, xxxv
Staraia Rusa [Stararouse], 16, 52, 55
Steward, office of [*Dvortsovyi Prikaz*), 52
Strabo, source of *Rus Commonwealth*, xxxvi, 4
Stroganov, S. G., "Fletcher affair" at Moscow University, xxviii
Stroganovs in Siberia, 16 n., 67, 68

Sukhona [Suchana] River, 10
Suzdal [Susdalla], xxxviii, 113
Sveno the Dane, 22
Sviatoi Nos [Sweetnesse], 105
Sweden, xxi, xxxvii, 15, 47, 57, 78, 80, 87, 90, 105

Tamerlane [Tamerlan], 98
Tanais (Don) River, 4, 10, 99
Tartars:
  reference usually to Crims, or Crimean, xli-xlii, 4, 7, 10, 13, 20, 21, 38, 47, 77, 78, 79, 80, 84, 87, 90-103
  apparel, 93
  booty, quest for, 95
  conquests, 98-99
  courage, 93-95
  cruelty, 93-94
  diet, 97
  exchange, 98
  firing Moscow, 91
  Hungary of Bela IV, 93
  marriage customs, 96
  military tactics, 92, 93
  Moscow relations, 91-92
  nomadic life, 97-98
  physical characteristics, 99
  religion, 95-96, 128
  Scythae Nomads, called, 99
  speech, 99
  subtlety, 93
  Turkish relations, 95-96, 99-100
  other:
    Cheremisian [Cheremissen], 13, 101
    Cherkasy [Chircasses], 78, 101, 103
    Mordvinian [Morduite, Mordwites], 13, 101
    Nogai [Nagaian, Nagaies, Nagay], 4, 101
    Shchelkaly [Shalcan(s)], 98, 101, 102
Tatev [Taytoue], family of, 40
Tatishchev, Ignatii Petrovich [Tatisloue, Ignatie Petrowich], 51

Index

Tauride, 100 n.
Teliatevskii [Tellerskoy], family of, 40
Thames River, 11
Tiaglo [*tagla*], tax, 54
Tiberius, 59
Time of Troubles, xxxi, xlii, 38 n.
Titov, A. A., cited, xxx
Tolstoi, George, cited, xix n.
Torture, 46, 47, 73-75
Torzhok [Torshock(e), Turiock], 41, 54, 55, 113
Totma, 16
Trade, xii-xv, xix-xxii. See also Merchants, foreign in Russia
Trinity College, Cambridge, xxiii
Troekurov, Fedor Mikhailovich [Troyconioue, Feoder Michailowich], 51
Troitskaia-Sergei Monastery, 120
Tromschua River, 6
Trubetskoi [Hubetskoy, Trowbetskoy], family of, 40, 79
Trubetskoi, Fedor Mikhailovich [Feoder Michailowich], 50
Trubetskoi, Nikita Romanovich [Trowbetskoy, Micheta Romanowich], 50
Trubetskoi, Timofei Romanovich [Trowbetskoy, Timophey Romanowich], 50
Truvor [Trubor], legendary founder of Russia, 3
Tsar:
   coronation, 27-30
   daily life, 144-148
      amusement, 146-147
      devotions, 144-145
      Fedor, an appraisal, 148
      greeting of Empress, 145
      meals, 146
   duma, 50-52
   dynasty, 23-27
   household, 148-150
   revenues, 52-64
Turberville, George, xxvi
Turks, xxi, xxxii, xxxvii, 12, 58, 62, 78, 95, 96, 99, 100, 109, 111, 131

Tver [Otfer, Twerra, Twerria], xxxviii, 5, 13, 29, 41, 52, 54, 55, 113

Udorsk [Oudoria], 5, 29
Uglich [Ouglites], 13, 17
Umba [Bombasey] River and town, 16
Una [Ocona] River and town, 16
Urtoghrul, 100
Uspenskii Cathedral, 27 n., 111 n.
Ustiug [Vstick, Vstiuck, Vstug, Vstuga], 4, 5, 17, 19, 54
Ustiug Zhelezna [Vstug Thelesna], 17
Uvarov, Sergei S., Minister of Public Instruction under Tsar Nicholas I, xxviii

Vaga [Vagha] province, 4, 5, 41, 44
Vardguz, see Wardhouse
Varivus [Variuus], legendary founder of Russia, 3
Varzuga [Versega], 105
Vasilii II [Basileus], of Moscow, 86
Vasilii III, of Moscow, 20, 24, 25, 86, 92
Vasilii the hermit [Basileo], 122-123
Velokurov, S. A., cited, xxvii n.
Vernadsky, George, cited, 3 n.
Viatka [Vadska], 5, 29
Viazma [Vasma], 13, 16, 41
Vilenskaia, E. S., cited, xx n.
Vitebsk, 86
Vitia-Guba [Vedagoba] Bay, 106
Vladimir [Volodemer, Volodomer], province and town, 4, 5, 19, 24, 28, 29, 85, 113
Vladimir Monomakh, Grand Prince of Kiev, 22 n.
Vladimir [Vlodomirus, Volodemer] the Saint, Grand Prince of Kiev, 40, 108
Volga [Volgha] River, 4, 7, 9, 10, 11, 17, 18, 44, 102
Vologda, xiv, xix, 4, 7, 13, 16 n., 19, 54, 55, 66, 113, 121

175

Index

Volok [Volock] River, 10
Vorontsovo [Bransoue], 52
Vorotynskii [Vorallinskoy], family of, 40
Votchina, see Land tenure
Vsevolod, Grand Prince of Kiev, 22 n.
Vychegda [Wichida] River, 11, 14, 16, 67, 68, 88
Vyluzgin, Elizar [Wellusgin(e), Eleazar], *diak,* 44, 51

Waliszewski, K., cited, xxx
Walsingham, Sir Francis, patron of Fletcher, xvi
Wardhouse, or Vardguz [Wardhouse, Wardhuyse], 6, 106
Wayland, Henry, friend of Fletcher, xxiii

Webster, John, use of *Rus Commonwealth,* xliii n.
White Sea, xii, xiii, xx, 10, 15 n.
Willan, T. S., cited, xii n., xliii n.
Willoughbys, patrons, xviii
Wipper, Robert, critic of Fletcher, xxxiv-xxxv
Women, costume of, 153-154
Wretts-Smith, M., cited, xiii n.

Yakobson, Sergei, cited, xiii n.

Zagorsk, 120 n.
Zemlianoi Gorod, section of Moscow, 20 n.
Zemshchina [*Zemskey, Zempskey* (house)], xxxix, 37, 38, 47, 61 n.
Zemskii Sobor, 33 n.
Zolotaia Baba [Slata Baba], myth of, 104

Fletcher, Giles, LL.D, d. 1610, uncle of John Fletcher, the dramatic poet, was educated at King Coll., Camb. In 1588 he was Eng. Ambassador to Russia, and on his return wrote a curious account of the Russe Common Wealth pub. 1590, 8vo. It was promptly suppressed for fear of giving offense to the Russian court. It was reprinted in 1643, 12mo. and is inserted, somewhat abridged, ...

Page 605
Allibone's Dictionary of authors
R/ 928/ A43

WITHDRAWN